# The Cinema of Satyajit Ray

CHIDANANDA DAS GUPTA

NATIONAL BOOK TRUST, INDIA

For
Supriya

*Cover photograph:* Shri Nemai Ghosh. Courtesy: *Desh* 28 March 1992.

*End papers:* Apu (Subir Banerjee), Sarbajoya (Karuna Banerjee) and Durga (Uma Das Gupta) in *Pather Panchali*, 1955. The guest (Utpal Dutt) and children in *Agantuk*, 1991. Courtesy: Technica, Nemai Ghosh.

*Photographs: Pather Panchali to Chidiakhana,* courtesy: Technica; *Goopi Gyne Bagha Byne to Agantuk.* Courtesy: Nemai Ghosh.

*Ray's illustrations:* Courtesy: *Desh* 28 March 1992.

ISBN 81-237-0753-3

First NBT Edition, 1994
Second Revised and Enlarged Edition 2001 (*Saka* 1922)

© Chidananda Das Gupta, 1994

**Rs 130.00**

Published by the Director, National Book Trust, India
A-5 Green Park, New Delhi-110016

# Contents

## *Foreword*

This, the third edition is a considerably revised and enlarged version of the book originally published in 1981 and updated in 1994. Nonetheless, I remain grateful to Shri Raghunath Raina and Ms Bindu Batra of the Directorate of Film Festivals for having urged me to undertake the first edition of this book at very short notice and for arranging for me to see many of Ray's films again. And now I am indebted to Shri Arvind Kumar, and Shri Nirmal Kanti Bhattacharjee, successive Directors of the National Book Trust, without whose support and interest this new edition would not have been activated. And without Shri Binny Kurian's rigorous application to its editing and its progress, the successive publication of the two increasingly revised and enlarged editions would not have been possible. Shri Nemai Ghosh has earned my gratitude by making prints of his own and others' stills especially for this book. The original edition had been out of print for several years despite the continued interest in Satyajit Ray's work in India and abroad. Although highly condensed, it was the first book written on Ray's cinema by an Indian and remains of interest to scholars and cinephiles. Ray's death in April 1992 only enhanced the world wide admiration for his work and the desire to understand it more fully in its social context and its aesthetic traits. Years have now passed since his demise; yet with his work acquiring a permanant place in the cinema's hall of fame, interest in it remains unabated. As such the National Book Trust's enterprise in presenting an extensively revised and enlarged edition is of significance.

CHIDANANDA DAS GUPTA

# Introduction

To see *Pather Panchali* again today, close to half-a-century after it was made, is still (in Lindsay Anderson's phrase) to go down on one's knees in the dust, into the heart of Indian reality, and the human condition.

In the grinding poverty of the Indian village, *Pather Panchali* sees, not the anonymous antheaps of Louis Malle, but the individual human being, unique as much in his joy in love and nature and childhood, as in the wrenching sorrow of death and in the endless daily struggle to live. It is the human face of rural poverty, and not its statistical horrors, that makes us see Apu or Durga, Sarbajaya or Harihar, as one of us. We recognize that Harihar is a poet, an intellectual; Sarbajaya, a woman of great strength and dignity; Apu is a boy of fine sensitivity; and Durga a beautiful, innocent child of nature. They become a part of us, and change something in us and our view of humanity.

A purely "aesthetic" appreciation of Satyajit Ray's work can hardly be a complete one. Ray was a classicist, an inheritor of a traditional Indian approach to art in which beauty is inseparable from truth and goodness. Despite his fine understanding of a very wide range of Western culture—which Jean Renoir in 1949 used to find "fantastic"—it is his Indianness which gives him his value for India, and for the medium imported from the West in which he worked. Thirty-seven years of his work is a chronicle of more than a century of social change in India. From the final eclipse of Mughal glory in *Shatranj Ke Khilari* to the decay of the feudal zamindar in *Jalsaghar*, the impoverished Brahmin's movement from traditional to modern India in the Apu trilogy, the Indian elite's awakening to rationalist ideas in *Devi*, *Charulata*, the beginning of the liberation of woman in *Mahanagar*, to the anguish of the unemployed after decades of the country's Independence in *Pratidwandi*, the inexorable death of conscience in a corrupt society in *Jana Aranya* and *Shakha*

*Proshakha*, and finally the glimmer of hope in a new agenda of a simplification of human needs and a reassertion of basic values in *Agantuk*—Ray's work first traces the essential outline of social evolution of the middle class in modern India and then begins to go beyond it.

The films of Ray's first ten years (1955-65) are buoyed up by an affirmation of faith in the human being. As so many critics have remarked, there are hardly any villains in Ray's films. The oppressor and the oppressed are both victims. Even in his worst aspect, the human being bears on him some mark of the ultimate possibility of goodness. Hence, no matter what his role, he needs compassion, not anger. Ray's work has more than a trace of traditional Indian "fatalism". It has a sense of detachment, a distance from the event. It is imbued with the sense that no man chooses the time or place of his birth or the circumstances that surround it. It is within the circle predetermined by these that he struggles to exist, to make something of his opportunities. The nobility of man lies in the effort itself. This knowledge does not take away from man's effort, but gives it a serenity denied to those who think they have the power to change the world, and hence hold the end to be above the means that finally corrupt them. The philosophical outlook underlying Ray's work is Indian and traditional in the best sense of that overused word. It finds joy in birth and in life; it accepts death with grace. It arises from a knowledge that brings detachment, freedom from fear, and from restlessness. The detachment or distance, combined with compassion, makes it possible for the artist to see a wider arc of reality and to combine largeness of canvas with fineness of detail. In the earlier decades after Independence, the faith was not merely in the hereafter; but in the here and now. Despite all the disappointments in the lack of sufficient progress for all, there was a basic belief that sooner or later, the country would turn the corner; that the regeneration of India was inevitable. It is a vision born in the Nehru era which has been pulled, sometimes violently, in contradictory directions but persists in a diluted form even today, though perhaps in an increasingly materialist sense.

Conversely, the affluence of a few breeds a sense of guilt in the intellectual who, by virtue of his education, belongs to the privileged minority. Perhaps nowhere in the world is poverty discussed so much (and so little done about it, some would add). Behind all the talk, there is some genuine concern, more so in the case of an artist with a conscience, working in a mass medium. The need to achieve material prosperity for all creates a spiritual condition. Indeed, the artist is presented with the conditions of religious art. The framework already exists; all he has to do is to fill in his part. Not to do so, or to stray away from it in pursuit of personal artistic visions, is somehow sacrilegious.

To ignore the poverty and the superstition, the oppression and the injustice, in order to explore the psychology of alienation in sexual love, is immoral, almost obscene. *Charulata's* exquisiteness would be hollow without the "Bengal Renaissance" reformism which makes up more than its background, the foreground itself hinting at the emergence of woman in an individual identity.

Ray's lack of anger, his distance from the event, his avoidance of overt, direct action, did not always endear him to the younger generation. Some grew progressively disenchanted with him and sought alternative models, in Ritwik Ghatak—in his films almost as much a Tagorean syncretist as Ray—and Mrinal Sen, a more avowedly political film-maker. Ray's own work entered an indeterminate watershed after the peak of *Charulata*. The pressure of those who would have him abandon Chekhov for Marx may have had some effect on him. Combined with the changed conditions of the country, the waning of the euphoric visions of the Nehru era, the mounting evidence of the privileged classes running away with the fruits of development, brought about a subtle change in the temper of Ray's work. In his treatment of contemporary life, there was a distinct departure from the traditional attitudes that marked his earlier work. The Calcutta of the vast political meetings and the lengthening queues, notably absent from his films of the first decade, began to make its presence felt, bringing a new nervous edge to his classicism. *Pratidwandi* abounds in the negative image, abrupt cuts to medical diagrams, and shots of the unemployed exploding in anger; *Jana Aranya*, for the first time in Ray, gets down to the seamy side of Calcutta, its grimy alleys leading to the brittle "shiny fronts of call-girl haunts".

But even in Ray's second decade where the recognition of decay is increasingly marked, the pessimism recognises the compulsions under which compromises with evil are made. The face of evil is somewhat averted and we do not make a direct confrontation with it. The ambitious executive of *Seemabaddha* continues to need the esteem of his critical sister-in-law. The PRO of *Jana Aranya*, who procures a girl the young businessman needs for his client, is redeemed like the madam of the brothel, by his good humour, and a certain clinical detachment from the evil goings-on. *Shatranj Ke Khilari* clearly sees the picture of decadence in Wajed Ali and his Lucknow and the historical inevitability of its collapse before the vigour of the British, yet it also recognises the exquisiteness, the pride, and the hint of noble tragedy that envelopes the fall.

It is from *Ghare-Baire*, during the making of which Ray suffered his first heart attack, that we begin to see a new and increasing inclination in him to point a finger at the villain and to allow his statements to become wordy and explicit.

For a comprehensive understanding of Ray it is necessary to see the contradiction between his overt statements about his relationship with the west and his intuitive links with the Indian spiritual tradition. In terms of aesthetics, Ray derived from western musical forms and western narrative traditions in the cinema, in which Hollywood had the largest share. Apparently his meticulous story telling with its beginning, middle and end, its sequence of exposition, conflict and resolution is an Aristotelian, cathartic form as opposed to the more open, discursive, circular tendencies in classical Sanskrit literature. But behind this one finds an umbilical cord connecting him directly with the Vedantic world view, which supplied the spiritual content of his films. Although he described himself as an atheist or agnostic, there was in him a sense of the mystery of the cosmos and its vast movements across space and time in which his scientific background merged with his background in early Brahmo spirituality, at the hub of which was an Upanishadic awareness of the infinite. For instance, the *Kathopanishad* speaks about the invisible force behind creation as *Brahma* which (who) is beyond the reach of the senses and of the mind. The sage says he does not know the nature of this force and cannot therefore explain it (him). All he can say is that, it (he) is what (the one who) enables us to hear, see, think, speak. Some of the descriptions clearly suggest a high consciousness of the vastness of time and space; *Brahma* is "where the sun does not shine nor the stars or the moon; all of these shine in the light of *Brahma*." The spirit of enquiry into the nature of the universe and the mystery of death expressed in innumerable such statements in the *Upanishads* lend themselves to a synthesis with modern scientific thinking. It is a spirit so constantly expressed in many of Rabindranath Tagore's songs and poems and cultivated in Santiniketan in his time that Ray, brought up in this ambience, could not have bypassed. The way it permeated his films behind their western exterior is discussed later in the book, particularly in the last chapter.

A foreign critic who intuitively understood this without knowing the background is Pauline Kael. She found Ray's work full of "The sense of immanence—the suspension of images in a larger context." "Ray's images", she said (speaking of *Days And Nights In the Forest*)" are so emotionally saturated that they become suspended in time, and in some cases fixed forever—"we are caught up in a blend of the fully accessible and the inexplicable, the redolent, the mysterious—.Two young men sprawled on a porch after a hot journey, a drunken group doing the twist in the dark on a country road, Sharmila Tagore's face lit by a cigarette lighter—the images are suffused with feeling and become overwhelmingly, sometimes unbearably, beautiful. The emotions that are immanent may never develop, but we're left with the sense of a limitless yet perhaps harmonious natural drama that the characters are part of. There are always larger, deeper associations impending; we recognize the presence of the mythic in the ordinary. And it's the mythic we're left with after the ordinary has been (temporarily) resolved—as if the viewer could see the present as a part of the past and could already reflect on what is going on". She could have said the same thing for all of his masterworks.

Although the period he spent in Santiniketan was only two and a half years, it must have served to consolidate in him the spiritual heritage derived from his Brahmo-Vedantic background. The kind of education of sensibility he received there can be guessed from a quotation from what Nandlal Bose, the painter under whom Ray studied, told a student while instructing him on how to paint a tree.

> Observe the tree for a while first, sit near it in the morning, the afternoon, the evening and again in the dead of night. It will not be easy. After some time, you will get fed up. It will be as if the tree is saying: 'What are you doing here? Leave me alone.' Then you must plead with the tree. You have to say: 'It's my guru's order; I cannot disregard it. Please don't be angry with me. Be kind, reveal yourself to me'. After you have silently studied it for a few days, if you feel that you have now *seen* the tree, lock yourself up in your room, and draw a picture of it.
>
> This tree that you are contemplating and painting—if you really come to live it, it will become a treasure for all your life. Some day you will come across sorrow, lose those whom you love, find the world empty of everything. It is then, that from the roadside, this tree will comfort you; it will say 'Look, here I am'.

The compassion that Ray's guru reveals here arises from the depths of Indian thought. It comes from a constant awareness of the impermanence of life, and yet also of its immanence in all things.

Satyajit Ray never saddled himself with the baggage of Marxist guilt for being born a bourgeois. He never put his faith in a "system". *Pather Panchali* bore some superficial resemblance to the Indian Peoples Theatre Association (IPTA)'s tradition in so far as it pictured the poverty-ridden circumstances prevailing in rural Bengal. But the family whose fortunes he followed belonged to the privileged class of a previous era, the village Brahmin priest-poet, now fallen on evil times because of the shift of accent to western education and urbanisation to which his son is eventually drawn. Although *Pather Panchali* did to Bengali cinema what IPTA's stage production *Nabanna* had done to Bengali theatre a decade ago, the comparison cannot be pushed far. Ray was a believer in the uniqueness of the individual right from the beginning and did not have to struggle with the pressures of socialist collectivity. From Apu to *Agantuk*, he saw the ethical development of the individual, the importance of good means to achieve good ends, as the key to social regeneration. This was most clearly defined in *Ghare Baire*. His mentor was not Marx but Tagore. Throughout a period of Marxism-dominated ideological ambience and state power, he worked steadfastly in opposition to one of its basic, and to him most evil, tenets—that the end justifies the means. He repeatedly stressed this in films like *Jana Aranya* and *Shakha Proshakha*, leaving one in no doubt about where his sympathies lay. Thus the heritage he upheld was of the Bengal renaissance and the Brahmo movement beginning with Rammohun Roy and culminating in Rabindranath Tagore. It is the ideology of this reformist movement anxious to make religion compatible with modern science and western democracy on the basis of an upanishadic, monotheistic rationalism that Ray internalised and expressed in his cinema. Today his faith in the individual and the importance of his development and his personal ethics, can be seen as the main agenda of the post-Marxist world.

Sometimes, the Western response to Ray is truer for seeing the wood where the Indian sees only the trees. In Ray's work, drawn more from literary rather than personal experience, the local truth is at times in doubt; the universal, almost never. There is a warmth and grace in his treatment of people in his films which makes an instant appeal in the West but which we in India often take for granted or do not see in our search for social significance. In *Ashani Sanket*, for instance, most Indians looked for a stronger indictment; Pauline Kael found in this very element the film's weakness: "In Ray's work what remains inarticulate is what we remember; what is articulated seems reduced, ordinary." Similarly, *Aranyer Din Ratri* was dismissed by many in India as a well-constructed yet inconsequential work but was seen by most Western critics as a complex exploration of human relationships. Perhaps we fail to recognize the "presence of the mythic in the ordinary" in his work, and are unable to accept that "the resolutions he effects not merely as resolutions of the stories but as truths of human experience" (Pauline Kael).

The fact is that Ray's material happens to be Indian but his statements are about humanity. As Ananda Coomaraswamy said at India's Independence day celebrations in Boston (1947): "Indian culture is important to us not because it is Indian, but because it is culture." Ray sees the oneness of all human beings. He observes them and feels about them not as Indians but as people, caught in the meshes of specific time and place. Perhaps, it is in this that the rest of the world feels an affinity with him and finds in the serenity of his faith a uniqueness that distinguishes it from the restless search of a Bergman or a Fellini. It is important that we recognize the element in Ray's work that transcends national boundaries and takes away from us the right to be his final judges merely because we are his countrymen.

Yet the films are made primarily for the region; *Charulata* abounds in carefully chosen literary readings in Bengali; *Jana Aranya* features a particularly significant song at a critical moment. In both, understanding of the words, impossible to convey in subtitles, enrich the impact enormously. Many foriegn critics (for example Robin Wood in *The Apu Trilogy*) did not quite understand why Apurba in *Apur Sansar* should marry Aparna when her husband-to-be is found insane, or why, brought up in affluence, she should so readily accept the penury of life with her husband. In both cases, the lack of understanding proceeds from a lack of knowledge of the social and religious tradition. Decades ago, Eric Rhode, writing in *Sight and Sound*, wondered whether the trilogy showed Ray to be a communist—a suggestion which provoked amusement for many in Calcutta.

Particularly in a tradition that equates the beautiful with the good and the true, the relationship of the sociological to the artistic plays a vital role. This saddles Indian critics with a duty that they have so far done little to perform. The present book, originally a product of urgings to produce a review of Ray's work to mark the passage of twenty-five years since *Pather Panchali*, was surprisingly, the first by an Indian. This revised, enlarged edition updates the account of his work and seeks to add new dimensions to the discussion of the films and their background.

CHIDANANDA DAS GUPTA

২২
৩
৮৪

# The Bengal Renaissance and the Tagorean Synthesis

Seldom has a film director's work chronicled the process of social change in a country over a long span of time as Satyajit Ray's. The subjects of his films range over the shifting social scene in India for over one hundred and fifty years. *Devi* (*The Goddess*, 1960) is placed in the 1830s. *Shatranj Ke Khilari* (*The Chess Players*, 1977) in the 1850's. *Charulata* (1964)'s story is laid in 1879, *Jalsaghar* (*The Music Room*, 1958)'s at the turn of the century, the Apu trilogy in the early years of this century. *Sadgati* (*The Deliverance*, 1981) was written by Premchand in the 1930's about an unspecified, as it were timeless, period; *Ashani Sanket* (*Distant Thunder*, 1973) deals with the British-made wartime famine of 1943; besides, he of course made host of contemporary films. Even within the contemporary subjects it is possible to identify minute divisions of periods marked by particular tendencies. There was, needless to say, no planned exercise going over the years grid by grids; Ray picked the subjects at will at different times according to what he felt concerned with, what he happened to read and what met the exigencies of filmmaking at a given time. Yet it is possible to rearrange the films to set up a chronological sequence of insights into the changing Indian social order. Of course there would be plenty of gaps in such a sequential arrangement since there was no conscious or consistent desire in the filmmaker to address every layer of the palimpsest of Indian history.

At a time when Japan had closed its doors on the west in order to protect its integrity, India lay open to the political and cultural invasion of the European powers, allowed them to stage a war of domination which was eventually won by the British. This led to the transition from the mediaeval to the modern that forms the core of the social content of most of the films of Satyajit Ray. For this reason it is essential (particularly for the non-Indian reader) to go over a very broad outline of the major trends in Indian social history in order to understand the full import of Ray's social as well as stylistic statements in his films and the attitudes the filmmaker brings to bear upon his subjects.

The movement of ideas that determined India's course towards political independence from two hundred years of British rule in 1947, had begun in the early nineteenth century. Little more than fifty years had passed after the first British victory in Bengal before there were stirrings of discontent over traditional education, traditional religious practices and the layers of superstitious ritualism that had encrusted over them, firmly blocking the way for new modes of thinking to emerge from within.

At the time the British began their conquest in 1757, the major part of the country had been under the occupation of Islamic rulers for well over five hundred years. The last of these, the Mughal descendants of Timur or Tamerlaine, spread their kingdom over almost the whole country but in the process adopted India as their own, with none other to go back to. Although their religion, Islam, was radically different from Hinduism, which is the dominant faith in the country, the social and political relationship between the two took the form of a workable detente. In matters of religious ritual and intimate social intercourse (such as marriage, eating together, etc.) Hindus remained a xenophobic, closed society, but arrived at a *modus vivendi* with the rulers in other matters. Patterns of peaceful co-existence with a mutuality of cultural borrowings at certain levels emerged. In music, dance and painting— all forbidden under orthodox Islam—there was an efflorescence of amazing vitality. Conversion to Islam remained confined to the poorer sections of Hindu society whereas at the upper levels there was a certain degree of mutual respect and sharing of power.

But the decadence of the Mughal empire and its inability to climb out of the ghetto of mediaevalism made it vulnerable to the scientific and technological upthrust in Europe. There was instead a degree of resurgence of Muslim orthodoxy within the settled patterns of co-existence. One result of this was a hardening of Hindu arteries. A vigorous maritime trade with South-East Asia came to an abrupt halt with the prohibition of sea voyages. There was an increase in the defensiveness of Hindu religiosity and a renewed inability to question the premises of its own orthodoxy which continued into the British period marked by the incursion of another alien faith, Christianity. A new hardening agent was added to the Hindu mind, making it even more rigidly xenophobic in terms of the fears of ritual pollution by the aliens. More than ever before, the Hindu began to treat his home as his fort and set up a wall between it and the outside world. Like the Muslims, the British ate beef, which is forbidden meat to the Hindus. The impossibility of inter-religious marriage was another monumental obstacle to any degree of social fusion. Indeed there were strict and complex rules of exogamy within Hindu society and each of its innumerable sects in any case. The very thought of inter-religious marriage was complete anathema. Any form of familial relationship with the aliens was unthinkable. Furthermore, the slightest lack of faith or deviation from religious tenets and rituals and myths caused grave social ostracism. It is this mindset on which Satyajit Ray turned the searchlight in *Devi (The Goddess)*, a film that can be used as the exemplar of many aspects of his creativity.

But contact with the European Enlightenment through the British soon began to herald a sea change. Besides, the superiority of British power became unquestionable. Their sea power based on a highly mobile navy, shipbuilding and artillery skills plus their ruthless fighting techniques shorn of all mediaeval notions of chivalry, bravery, as also their adoption of bribery and treachery as major means of achieving bloodless coups, soon threw the elephantine grace and grandeur of Mughal might into the dustheaps of history. It became necessary for India to trace and dip into the intellectual-cultural resources of British power. Some Indian leaders persuaded the British to introduce modern education in the sciences and the humanities and sought to fuse the best in ancient (as opposed to the late classical and the mediaeval) Hindu tenets with a modern, scientific worldview. They seized upon the values of the European Renaissance, developed by the Enlightenment and the expansion of science leading to higher levels of technology on the one hand and a more liberal-democratic worldview on the other. From Rammohun Roy (1777-1833) to Mahatma Gandhi (1869-1948) these leaders subtly attacked the weakest spot in the British mind—the contradiction between democracy at home and imperialism abroad. Shades of this are seen in Satyajit Ray's *The Chess Players* in the scene of conversation between General Outram and the Queen Mother of Oudh discussed later in this book.

The major transition witnessed in Satyajit Ray's films ranging across a hundred and fifty years is the change from the extended mediaeval worldview of the Mughal period to the modern brought about under British rule and during the period of India's political independence. The sheer scale of the change is heralded in both the literary story and the film, *The Chess Players*. The original story by Premchand, translated by the actor Saeed Jaffrey (who played one of the two chess players in the film) gives an exquisite picture of Mughal decadence.

An important aspect of this transition was the reform of religion from within and an effort to turn Hinduism's ritualistic xenophobia to an openness to impulses from the west. Furthermore, the transition contained within it the beginnings of an important change from misogyny to the liberation if not the actual empowerment of woman. The control of female sexuality and the reproductive process have always been among the first concerns of virtually all major religions. To this Hinduism is no exception; in fact it can be shown to be one of the prime examples of this trait of religions.

For a hundred and fifty years, first journalism, poetry, fiction and drama, then painting, and finally cinema, trained their guns on this nexus between religion and the oppression of woman. And this has formed one of the important undercurrents in Ray's work.

Despite their many differences, Gandhi was a close friend and soulmate, as it were, of Rabindranath Tagore (1861-1941), the national poet of India and the central figure, the dominant cultural ideologue, of the "renaissance" spanning both centuries. Nehru was similarly close to Tagore and attempted to translate many aspects of his cultural tenets into the realities of politics. Among these were religious freedom, democracy, human rights, the liberation of women and the tenet of unity in the diversity of India's many races, cultures and religions, physiognomies, food and dress habits. These are ideas taken for granted by many today but their slow and gradual acceptance as formal national goals was the result of a bitter struggle with Indian orthodoxy on the one hand and British imperialism on the other in which every inch of ground had to be fought for. One might even say that Gandhi (and Tagore)'s non-violence translated itself into Nehruvian Non-alignment and Gandhi's doctrine of self-reliance into Nehru's effort to develop India's economic self sufficiency in a bipolar world of cold war which attempted to annex every country into the belligerence of one side or the other.

Nehru sent his daughter Indira Gandhi, later to be prime minister of India, to Tagore's Visva-Bharati or "World University" at Santiniketan near Calcutta. It was to this university that Ray too went later, at Tagore's own behest, to study painting. Although he spent only two and a half years there, it left a deep impression on him. It was during this period that he went on a tour of India to see the art treasures and came to understand something of the spirit of Indian art and the traditions that provide its background.

Satyajit Ray was the last great representative of this movement for the regeneration of India—a movement triggered by the coming of the British through whom modernist Indians found a point of contact with the western civilization. This window to the west inspired calls for rationalism, for the reform of religions, especially of the religion of the majority, by peeling off the layers of superstition accumulated during centuries of defensiveness against alien rule resulting in decadence. The movement searched out ways of reforming Indian religions, particularly the dominant religion of Hinduism, from a morass of superstition accumulated through ages of a religion-cultural defensiveness against Islamic rule and a consequent decadence. The movement was marked by an effort by the middle class Indian to establish the primacy of rationalism without severing its umbilical cord with ancient tradition.

## II

Ray has often been termed a humanist, mostly by Marxist critics and in a very western and rather pejorative sense of the word. Historically, the concept has been understood in the west as the credo of an anthrocentric universe. Descartes' Man is in the centre of things and is designated the master of all: *Maitre et proprietaire de la nature*. Baconian inductive logic supplied the first scientific base to this belief. The Enlightenment, followed by the industrial revolution, strengthened this doctrine of the supremacy of man who, having conquered nature, has now set out to conquer space.

"Humanism", in the Indian context, has always meant the exact opposite. The *Rgveda* and particularly the *Upanishads* (early 1st millennium BC), view man as an infinitesimal speck on the cosmic vastnesses of time and space. It is only by perceiving oneself as a minute fragment in the universal consciousness which envelops all that the individual begins to realise his/her destiny. In the *Devisukta (Ode to the Mother Goddess)*, man begs the earth's forgiveness for treading upon her. The sense of infinite time and space is reflected in innumerable verses like this one (in rough English translation): *There, neither the sun shines nor the moon; nor is there fire or lightening,; it is by reflecting the light of that universal being that all these shine.* It is not a personalised God that the Upanishads discover; through step by step enquiry, they try to understand the order of the universe and the power that regulates it. Michaelangelo's bearded, muscular, Caucasian God stretching his muscular arm towards Man across the ceiling of the Sistine chapel is anathema to vedantic (late vedic) thought. What this philosophy finds from its contemplation is a universal, invisible, nameless, formless consciousness permeating existence and non-existence in and out of time and space. Even in later, *Puranic* (mythological) Hinduism, the universe exists within the supreme God

Vishnu's dream. All this represents a cosmocentric way of thinking as far removed as anything could be from the anthropocentricity of the European Renaissance or the Enlightenment. Indeed Indian humanism arises from the sense of the unimportance of man and the evanescence of life. Among the philosophic currents that flow from it are the accent on *Karuna* or compassion and the doctrine of *ahimsa* or non-violence dominantly articulated in Buddhism, both of which have had an abiding influence on the arts in India, despite the eventual virtual disappearance of Buddhism as such from the land. The Indian sense of the sadness of evanescence is untouched by mediaeval Christianity's dark shadow of The Original Sin; its particular value in art comes from the enchantment with which the present is invested. Because the moment will vanish, it invokes compassion for those who are shining in its light. This trend of feeling is central to Tagore and generations of writers (such as Bibhutibhusan Bandyopadhya, the author of the novels on which Ray's Apu trilogy is based) influenced by him. One could recall here the scene in *Apur Sansar*. The World of Apu, in which Apu's young wife Aparna, sitting in the moving hackney coach as they come back from the cinema, lights up a matchstick which bathes her face in an ethereal light. This is the last time we, like Apu, see Aparna in the film, for after this she will go away to her parents in order to bear her child and die in the course of it.

That will perhaps help to show how Satyajit Ray evolved out of what is called the "Bengal Renaissance" originating in the early nineteenth century and going on to the early years of India's Independence till, to find a landmark, the death of Jawaharlal Nehru, India's idealistic, first prime minister, nominated by Mahatma Gandhi. Like the main protagonists of this Renaissance, Ray did not give up his link with tradition in his pursuit of a rationalist-humanist worldview. Indeed he was so taken with the modernist-western aspects of his medium that he hardly realised how far his innate sensibility and his mindset had been moulded by his cultural predecessors. To understand this leavening to his modernism, it is necessary to examine the Bengal Renaissance more closely.

### III

For the major part of British rule in India, Calcutta was the capital of the Indian Empire. The Regulating Act of 1773 and Pitt's India Act of 1784 served to subordinate Madras and Bombay to Bengal and to establish the rule of British India by a Governor-General in Calcutta although its "factory" had been founded in 1690, fifty years after Madras and sixteen years after Bombay.

This closeness to the seat of power gave the Bengalis, besides other advantages, a front seat before the window to the West. A civilization that had always excluded the foreigner from its soul despite dealings with him in material affairs, woke up to find his philosophical ideas challenging its own inward-looking spirituality. Ideas of equality, secular nationalism, political democracy, the liberation of women, in a caste-bound and rigidly hierarchical society, found an inlet through the English language. The language of the ruler had to be studied for material success, just as Persian and Arabic had to be studied under the Mughals; even the orthodox adopted English, little suspecting the effect it would have on the future of Hindu society. A basic question had to be answered: "What is the secret of the success of the British?" The answer had to be found in the study of English literature, history and western science. The search for a synthesis which would give Indian society some of the qualities that made the British great, became inevitable.

The leader of this search was Raja Ram Mohun Roy (1772-1833), often described as the "Father of Modern India". A scholar in Sanskrit, Persian, Greek and Latin, the Raja became the outstanding spokesman of the time for the reformation of Hindu society. His contact with the West was so close and his concern for ideas of equality so great that he held a public dinner in celebration of the French revolution of 1830; he also founded the first newspaper in India in order to champion the cause of civil rights for his people. His movement for the liberation of women—the abolition of superstitious customs like the burning of widows, of female infanticide and slavery—were perhaps less far-reaching than his successful advocacy of Western, in place of traditional education for Indians.

Ram Mohun Roy protested strongly to Lord Amherst, the then Governor-General, against the government's proposal to establish a Sanskrit school under Hindu pundits. Referring to the writings of Francis Bacon and their impact in Europe, he criticized the traditional teacher's concern with empty subtleties, "grammatical niceties and metaphysical distinctions of little or no practical use." His advocacy of Western education had been instrumental in the founding of Hindu College in 1817, and through that the systematic study of Western literature, history and science. Under the firebrand radical Henry Derozio, a half-Portuguese who, unlike other "Eurasians", proudly claimed to be an Indian, the college became a potent force in the promotion of rationalism and in the reformation of Indian society. "An Indian bookseller got 100 copies of Tom Paine's *Age of Reason* and advertised them for sale at Re 1 per copy, but the demand for the book among the Hindu College students was so great that it was sold at Rs 5 per copy. Soon after, a part of this book was translated into Bengali and published in a Bengali paper."

Macaulay's object in recommending the adoption of English education in India was, in his own words, "to form a class of persons, Indian in blood and in colour, but English in tastes, in opinions, and in morals and in intellect." His recommendation was accepted and formalised in Lord Hardinge's Educational Despatch of 10 October 1844. Little did Macaulay and Hardinge realize that they were laying the foundation stone of Indian nationalism.

One of the archetypal products of Hindu College was Michael Madhusudan Dutt (1824-73), whose turbulent life set the model for a discovery of India through the West for more than a hundred years. Michael, "the brightest star" of Hindu College, went all out to embrace the West. He drank, ate beef, turned Christian, married two European women in succession, went to England, and sought to make his name there as a poet in the English language. Much of what he did was typical of the times, although few went as far as him in the absoluteness of passion. In innumerable poems he longed for "Albion's distant shore—for glory, or a nameless death." In his second *Sonnet to Futurity*:

Oft like a sad imprisoned bird I sigh
To leave this land, though mine own land it be;
Its green-robed meads—gay flowers and cloudless sky
Though passing fair, have but few charms for me.
For I have dreamed of climes more bright and free
Where virtue dwells and heaven-born liberty
Makes even the lowest happy;—Where the eye
Doth sicken not to see man bend the knee
To sordid interest:—climes where, science thrives,
And genius doth receive her guerdon meet;
Where man in all his truest glory lives,
And Nature's face is exquisitely sweet:
For those fair climes I heave the impatient sigh
There let me live and there let me die

—Kidderpore, 1842

He very nearly died in the fair clime for which he sighed. When he was in dire straits abroad for lack of money, the man who rescued him was the Sanskrit pundit Ishwar Chandra Vidyasagar. Touched to the quick, Michael wrote sonnets in Bengali, and on his return home, wrote great Bengali poetry in blank verse which, like the sonnet, he introduced into his language for the first time. Some of his early sonnets celebrate, with great poignancy, his joy in rediscovering his language and his country, which he never forsook again.

At the opposite end to Michael was Pundit Ishwar Chandra

Vidyasagar. An unassuming Sanskrit scholar, forever clad in *dhoti* and *chadar*, Vidyasagar's mind was imbued with a great western love of freedom, individuality and rationality. His life-long campaign of widow remarriage became the red rag of the rationalists before the bull of Hindu orthodoxy; so much so that it obscured, in the popular mind, his important contributions to Bengali literature and to the development of a realistic synthesis between Indian and western culture.

It was a product of Hindu College, a contemporary of Michael Madhusudan, Raj Narayan Bose, who, after going through the "young Bengal" phase, concluded that,

> "The Hindus had forgotten their past to such an extent that they had no recollection of the fact that rational thinking and ideas of social and personal freedom were not wanting in the history of their own culture."

It is doubtful if he would have reached this conclusion without going through the excesses of the pro-western upsurge.

In 1795, Gerasim Lebedeff, a Russin, founded the "Bengali Theatre" and made a heroic attempt to introduce western theatre in India. Although it was not a success in Lebedeff's time, it led to flourishing professional theatre in Calcutta, modelled on the western and not on Indian classical or folk drama, within a few decades. When in 1854 Ram Narayan Tarkaratna wrote the first Bengali play, it was a satire on the marital practices of high caste Brahmins.

Thus the rise of a new middle class in nineteenth century Bengal in response to the western stimulus, occasioned by linguistic necessity but going far beyond it in the event, blossomed forth in what is called the Bengal Renaissance.

Elsewhere in India, the same pattern developed. Like Vidyasagar, Behram Malabari, Narmad and others fought for widow remarriage; D K Karve, Dayananda, Eknath Ranade and others for providing equal access to education for women. The Arya Samaj, although more contained within the framework of Hindu orthodoxy and less willing to admit the influence of western ideas, nevertheless realised the need for revitalising the faith and adapting it to the times. Founded by the Gujarati Brahmin, Swami Dayananda in 1875, it rejected caste, idolatry, polygamy, child marriage and the seclusion of widows. Its aggressive fundamentalism, somewhat intolerant of other religions, nonetheless provided the motive force for progress especially in Punjab. In Maharashtra, the difference between the Brahmo and Arya Samaj movements was reflected in the polarity of Gopal Krishna Gokhale's liberalism and the Hindu militancy of Bal Gangadhar Tilak. Like many Bengali leaders, Gokhale was a liberal of the Gladstone mould, rationalist in outlook, reformist in action, deeply imbued with western ideas blended with Indian tradition.

The formidable Tagore clan had a strong international awareness. At the turn of the century, the Tagores invited Count Okakura to visit Calcutta; Gaganendranath Tagore maintained contact with Taikan and Hishida, well-known exponents of Okakura's Bijuitsen School of Japanese painting. Gagendranath's work carries distinct reflections of this contact; Jyotirindranath translated Molière's plays from French into Bengali, practised portrait painting which evoked the admiration of William Rothenstein, besides founding India's earliest shipbuilding company. Two years after the Bauhaus group was formed in Germany, the Tagores organised a Bauhaus exhibition in Calcutta in 1921. Rabindranath (1861-1941) travelled all over the world and remained in personal contact with a vast number of writers, artists and scholars in many countries throughout his long life. Despite the restrictions of foreign rule and the slowness of late nineteenth and early twentieth century communications, the Tagores treated the world as their very own oyster. Little happened in international culture that they were not aware of, and were not in contact with. To this was added an all-India awareness. Rabindranath attracted a number of painters, musicians and writers from various parts of the country; for his own songs, he freely borrowed melodies and stylistic elements from Carnatic music. Jyotirindranath translated from Marathi as much as he did from French. The Tagore University had a Hindi Bhavan just as it had a China Bhavan, and the poet's travels took him all over India as all over the world.

The Indian and the Bengali were deeply rooted in the Tagores and the winds from abroad never swept them off their feet. Perhaps Michael Madhusudan had impressed his example too strongly on them for that. Indeed, some of Rabindranath's songs are so imbued with the Vaishnava spirit that they are hard to understand in English translation; his poetry is so overladen with Sanskrit imagery that it cannot be fully enjoyed without a base in the classics. Gaganendranath was the moving spirit behind the Indian Society of Oriental Art founded in 1907, and it was on his advocacy that Lord Carmichael lent government aid to the Bengal Home Industries Association to save the crafts of Bengal from extinction. Whether it was in opera or painting or handicrafts, theatre or agricultural practices, in interior decoration, music or book production or style of dress, children's literature or educational reform or social behaviour, the Tagores, in particular Rabindranath, tried to create models in many facets of an integrated culture—the product of a fusion of East and West.

Marxist critics have always airily dismissed the word "Renaissance" in respect of the change that began in nineteenth century India because it was confined to the middle class and did not change the class structure of society as the European renaissance did in the transition from feudalism to capitalism. Satyajit Ray, however, saw the landlord of *Jalsaghar* in exactly those terms of transition. It can be argued today that the Marxists stuck a little too closely to orthodoxy in distinguishing the two uses of the word renaissance which need not be exclusively interpreted in western terms. Another reason for deprecating the Bengal (Indian) renaissance is said to be the fact that such things as the superstitions of Hinduism did not affect the common man who did not practise *Sati* or ban widow remarriage and so on. Apart from the fact that the statement itself is challengeable, Ray's film *Sadgati* made in 1981 and based on Premchand's story showed how strongly even the outcaste at the lowest rung of Hindu society was bound by the social laws of Hinduism. The reformist movement's challenge of superstitious Hindu traditions was thus meaningful in beginning a process of removal of the slavery spelt by the rigours of the caste system. The Indian renaissance threw up a forward-looking middle class, including the Marxist leadership which initiated a movement for the liberation of the masses. *Kanchenjungha*'s low British titleholder is a perfect example of the section of the upper middle class that stood against change as opposed to the young man pitted against him who distanced himself from the conformist adherents to British overlordship.

In the classic polarity between Tilak and Gokhale, eventually it was Gokhale's rationalist liberalism which won out; Independent India's tenets of adult franchise, religious tolerance, equality for women and accent on science and industry are largely the outcome of an East-West synthesis. Mahatma Gandhi turned into a half-naked political saint from a cane-swishing man about town in London whose sole regret was his inability to learn ballroom dancing. Nehru came nearest to Macaulay's image of the brown Englishman, but only in a certain obvious way; he translated the cultural definitions of Tagore into the outlines of an integrated political outlook overlaid with a Gandhian concern for the common man.

From a "microscopic minority", Lord Dufferin's Indian middle class, partly a *nouveau riche* creation of the British, partly transformed from traditional professions, had burgeoned, by the time of Independence, into a large all-India community with a basic commonality of outlook and behaviour. The most influential section of it, the section that has provided the highest leadership in India before and after Independence, has been the most westernized; not in attire but deeply in the mind, in its resolution of the conflict of tradition and modernity, and in its success in making one enrich the other. For more than a hundred and fifty years, progress in India has been the outcome of a conscious blend of East and West. But the synthesis was not made for everybody once and for all; everybody had to find his own particular mix. Caught in the cross-currents of the two the middle class, especially the artist and the intellectual, has had to embark on an agonizing search for identity. After more than three decades of Independence, the problem of identity still haunts the middle class and the rising new classes. Nowhere is the crisis more clear than in the arts; in no art is it more clear than in the *nouveau riche* importation from the West—the cinema.

আম আঁটির ভেঁপু
বিভূতিভূষণ বন্দ্যোপাধ্যায়

# Problems of Identity

## I

In one of the cries that rang from his noble heart, Swami Vivekananda (1863-1902) had called upon the rising class of newly educated, privileged Indians to stand up and declare that every illiterate, poor and unfortunate Indian was his brother.

This powerful behest was uttered not so long after Bhudeb Mukherjee (a contemporary of Michael Madhusudan Dutt)'s dictum: "Speak in English, think in English, dream in English." As discussed earlier, the "young Bengal" of the nineteenth century went well beyond the English language in its wild embrace of the West. It rejected tradition and sought a new identity. Inevitably, most of the outstanding men of that generation realized their mistake and rediscovered their roots, made great contributions to the transformation of their country, took steps towards what each thought would be a successful synthesis, a new identity born of an awareness both of tradition and of modernity. It was not as easy as it might at first seem. The individual decision on the nature of the transformation required, and the means of achieving it, were agonizing.

In Rabindranath Tagore's novel *Gora*, the eponymous hero fights the Brahmo reformist movement for its superficiality. Gora finds the Brahmo stance arrogant, lacking identity with the country, and close to the attitude of the brown Sahib in western attire preaching against superstition. The Brahmo, to Gora, is not one of the people; he is the outsider. In reaction to the arrogance of his reformism, Gora defends orthodoxy. He wants to be one with the superstitious first, before beginning to reform them. His Brahmin pride finds joy in the oneness with tradition despite the modernity of his own education. Perhaps his pride is perverse in its extremism; but it is patriotic, its identity unquestionable. Disaster strikes Gora when he discovers that he is actually of English parentage, a *mlechcha*, an outsider whose very shadow brings impurity to the Brahmin.

Tagore was a Brahmo; his father had been the founder of the Brahmo community, and practically the entire family had embraced the new faith. It was against idolatry and superstition, and believed in democracy and in women's liberation. Rabindranath himself took an active part in the Brahmo movement and its religious practices. Of his 2000 or so songs, at least 500 or more are in praise of one *nirakara* (formless) God. These songs, like those of his father Devendranath as well as of his many uncles and brothers, are still sung as hymns in the Brahmo Samaj. Often they are sung to the music of a Victorian cottage organ or its Indian variant,the harmonium, before a congregation sitting in pews in aid of its Sunday "divine service." Yet it was Rabindranath who acutely understood, and deeply expressed, the problem of identity of the new Indian, in *Gora*. It was probably the first powerful statement of a problem that still plagues modern India.

Tagore's contemporary, Vivekananda was, like himself, tall and fair; with his high forehead and aquiline nose, he could well have inspired the character of Gora. He had flirted with Brahmoism for a while but, dissatisfied with what it had to offer, he had become a disciple of the mystic Ramakrishna. He subsequently founded the Ramakrishna Mission for serving the poor, and preached the glories of Vedantic philosophy in the West. Tagore, like Brahmoism itself, shaped, but was also shaped by, the rise of the new middle class in India. Perhaps Vivekananda refused to be contained within this outline, and sought identification with the people at large, even if he did not have the breadth of precision of Tagore's cultural synthesis. It is always the dynamic minority that changes the course of a nation; yet it is possible for such a revolution to remain incomplete if its vital force is not carried to all the limbs and nervous extremities of the body of the nation. This is probably what happened to Tagorean culture, and defined its limits for a period stretching well into, and beyond, the Nehru era.

With Mahatma Gandhi (1869-1948) came a wider, more secular move for bringing the nation as a whole into the orbit of the Indian renaissance. The Mahatma did this by identifying himself with the poorest by means of his simple life and the visible symbols of identity which he developed. It was freer from religion and intellect than Vivekananda's movement, and from the largely middle-class thinking of Tagore. It became a touchstone for framing policies and principles and along with Tagore's cultural model, underlies the ideals, if not all the realities, of Independent India. Perhaps the Tagore strand in modern Indian culture is less readily perceived by intellectuals today; but the Gandhian strand continues to retain something of its significance, even when the realities seem to belie it.

## II

For the artist in modern India, the need soon arose to translate this cultural mix in terms of identity. During the pioneering days of the Bengal School of painting, E B Havell, the English principal of the School of Art in Calcutta, urged his students to stop imitating the West and to continue the country's own traditions. The same urgings came from Vivekananda's western disciple, Sister Nivedita. Abanindranath Tagore gave momentum to this new tendency by nostalgic exercises in the Mughal style; Nandalal Bose's fine draughtsmanship drew much from Ajanta; Gagnendranath's found inspiration in the West and in the Far East. Rabindranath himself, not a trained painter, travelled outside traditional paths, championed the cause of freedom from tradition, but retained an Indian sensibility. Ananda Coomaraswamy (1877-1947), the great philosopher of Indian art born of a Ceylonese Indian father and an English mother, and brought up in England, regarded the revivalism of the Bengal School with misgiving. To him, revivalism was fundamentally a process of creative introspection readying the sensibility for new expression. He was one of the few to see the vital link between national regeneration and its expression in art, and considered the two to be inseparable. There was no doubt that in rediscovering its past and groping to develop a new mode of expression in art, India, in the early decades of the twentieth century, was finding its identity and its self-confidence as a nation. Art functioned as an essential element in the renaissance.

The word "revivalism" has nevertheless got stuck to Bengali painting of this period and even been extended to all arts, indeed the Bengal Renaissance itself. As a matter of fact, Coomaraswamy's analysis proved itself right in no time, for side by side with the traditional approaches and idioms in the work of Rabindranath Tagore himself, Gaganendranath, Binodebehari Mukhopadhyay (to whom Satyajit Ray was to pay homage in his documentary, *The Inner Eye*), and Ramkinkar Baij, all four of whom had in fact a greater influence on later generations than Abanindranath, Nandalal Bose, and others. The extension of the revivalist label to the reform movement is a contradiction in terms, seeing that it challenged and tried to revolutionise a thoroughly moribund tradition.

Modern Indian painting was really launched by Amrita Sher-Gil (1913-41). Born of an Hungarian mother and an Indian father, she was trained in painting at Budapest. Sher-Gil sought identity in a discovery of India which produced its own technical correlative, charged by the depth and sincerity of her search.

Critics are quick to point out that Sher-Gil was half European, and her relationship with reality had an "inside-outside" quality which became her strength as well as her weakness. But the search for identity, if less self-conscious, is no less real in a fully Indian artist. When she said:

> Modern art has led me to the comprehension and appreciation of Indian painting and sculpture—had we not come away to Europe, I should perhaps never have realised that a fresco from Ajanta or a small piece of sculpture in the Museé Guimet is *worth more than a whole Renaissance.*

She was speaking for many a creative artist who discovered India after, or through, a long spiritual sojourn in European culture. Only where this contact acquired no cultural depth, as in the case of Ravi Verma, did the passage to India not become significant. Jamini Roy, trained in Western academic portraiture, turned to folk-painting and evolved his own serene idiom in it, defied West-oriented egocentric and stock-exchange valuations in art by freely duplicating his works, like traditional folk paintings, and selling them at a price suitable for a poor country. Stylistically dissimilar as they are, the works of both Amrita Sher-Gil and Jamini Roy are in their own different ways, informed by a sense of identity with the average Indian, the common man. The melancholy faces of Sher-Gil with a silent forbearance printed upon them, are not without an affinity with the characters in the early work of Satyajit Ray. Kalighat paintings of the eighteenth and nineteenth centuries represent, perhaps, more than the so-called "company" paintings, the most interesting product of Indo-British contact in this sphere. They are, as W.G. Archer puts it in *Kalighat Paintings*, a "byproduct of the British connection and can only be understood against that background." Archer finds them, "with their bounding lines and bold rhythms," obviously close to the Ajanta and Bagh cave murals, and yet displaying a striking affinity to modern art particularly reminiscent of Fernand Leger's work with its bold simplifications, robust and tubular forms. At the folk level of anonymity, there is no better example of the fusion of Indian and British strands as in the bold lines and the vigorous social content of Kalighat "Bazar" paintings.

### III

The trend was not confined to painting. Uday Shankar, the dancer, was trained in Europe and for some years partnered Pavlova in Paris. When the partnership broke up he was at his wit's end until he had what seems today the rather obvious idea of reviving Indian dancing which languished in the darkness of the temples for lack of encouragement from modern India. His abridged presentations, adapted to stage techniques with a fine sense of the dramatic, created a stir in India and abroad and helped the revival of traditional dancing, freeing it from the disrepute into which it had fallen. Indian classical music, for a long time confined to princely courts, made a fairly smooth transfer to governmental and public sponsorship in which the radio and the gramophone played an important part. Yehudi Menuhin's admiration for Indian music and his introduction of the music of Ravi Shankar and Ali Akbar in Europe and America also helped to give it a new respectability for the western-oriented Indian.

The Indian theatre today has a largely western proscenium form and has drawn relatively little from folk drama. Sisir Kumar Bhaduri, perhaps the most brilliant actor-director in Bengali theatre history, had been a famed teacher of English poetry and drama. Apart from the rich knowledge of western drama he brought into it, Bengali theatre had always been quick to assimilate western models and ideas. Yet, as a result, it produced a wealth of plays critical of the British and of the mores of Indian society. Large areas of it have retained something of the passion for identity with the masses which was initiated in the forties by the Indian Peoples Theatre Association. There is also, in English-educated Indian society today, a conscious effort to keep folk drama and folk theatre alive alongside adaptations from the West.

IV

Naturally in social life, the problem is as complex as in the arts. English is a link in communication within the all-India middle class, a barrier for comm     unciation outside it. The economic interests of the upper classes draw them away from the common man; cultural interests tend to draw them towards him through the troubled conscience of the artist and the intellectual culture represents both a lure and a danger wherever it is not soporific. Social customs are ill-defined; few norms are easily recognizable and commonly accepted.

Confusion in social norms is extremely common.* Bridegrooms in

---

\*     I can cite an amusing example of this which happened to me. Sometime in 1948, the Calcutta Film Society was showing a mediocre French film, *Le Cage aux Rossignol* (Jean Delannoy), and had invited the governor of West Bengal. As Dr Katju stepped on to the red carpet we had hired, I stepped out to meet him.

northern India ride a horse in dark lounge-suit and traditional head dress; in the older generation there were people who would wear western dress for the upper half of the body and Indian for the lower. No one ever knows which particular combination of Indian and Western dress, behaviour or attitude a person will sport. That was not so in Tagore's Shantiniketan or Gandhi's Sabarmati Ashram; they had set up clear, unconfused models.

In the country's rather inchoate mixture of revivalism, modernism, nostalgia for forms shaped in the social conditions of bygone eras, there is perhaps more of a search, than a finding, of identity. The urban middle class has so insulated itself from both the industrial working class and the rural people that poetry and drama celebrating the common man is today understood only by the citybred, and much folk art is nurtured in the hothouse of museums. The revival of classical music, perhaps on a wider scale than those times in which it originally existed in various parts of the country, suggests a search for roots in a historical relationship with a cultural product of the past whose relevance and expressive growth in the present-day context can be questioned. It is as if Japanese *Gagaku* were to have a great following in the business world of Tokyo or the Gregorian chant to be sung by numerous performers to hundreds of thousands of people in European cities today. It is a kind of vertical search for identity and continuity with past times, instead of the horizontal identity in the spaces of the country today, inhabited by its vast millions.

The search in independent India is therefore many-sided, but ill-defined, compared to the earlier surges of cultural nationalism. Caught between East and West and unable to accept either completely, the English-educated intellectual in his quest of the roots of emotional security is too often a spiritual refugee. The definitions of culture that leaders like Tagore, Gandhi and Nehru outlined and commentators like Ananda Coomaraswamy crystallised, were clearer in their contours and gave the pre-Independence nationalist generation a more concrete and complete framework than is available today.

## V

In this context, the Indian cinema never succeeded in emerging into the area of national resurgence in the way painting, dance, drama, or music

I can't remember who held out his hand first, but what happened was that every time he folded his hands in a *namaskar*, I found myself going for a handshake, and every time he tried to shake my hand, I did a *namaskar*. After several unsuccessful attempts to coincide our gestures, we both laughed, and gave it up.

did. Although in terms of subject matter, films like K Subramanyam's *Balyogini* or Himanshu Rai's *Achchut Kanya* were against superstition, the language of cinema had not, in their time, become articulate enough to be effective or to participate in the world language to the extent that Japan for instance did. It was held back by the very fact that it is a modern industrial-technological medium imported from the West imposed on an agricultural, pre-industrial society. Not being a traditional medium, there was no ready base for an understanding of it as a new language. The absorption of the cinema into Indian culture was made more difficult by the absence of an industrial-technological culture. Grafted on to an agricultural country, it failed to develop a valid artistic form, a cultural contact-point with tradition or with reality; it subsisted on an imitation of the West, mainly Hollywood, without producing the fusion of art and box office that Hollywood often represented. Except with Phalke and later Himanshu Rai, contact with world cinema was almost nonexistent. The cinema lived in partly enforced isolation in British India, enclosed comfortably within the coccoon of its own standards. The absence of a film culture was as marked as the physical spread of commercial formula-bound cinema. In Europe and America, discussion of film as art, film society and art theatre movements had begun in earnest in the early twenties; at the time of Independence in India, they had practically not been heard of.

In 1929, writing in reply to Sisir Kumar Bhaduri (famous actor on the professional Bengali Stage)'s brother Murari, Rabindranath Tagore made certain very significant statements on the cinema a free translation of which would run as follows:

> Form in art changes according to the means it uses. I believe that the new art that could be expected to develop out of the motion picture has not yet made its appearance. In politics we are looking for independence; in art we must do the same. Every art seeks to find its own independent manner of expression within the world it creates; otherwise its self-expression is undermined for lack of confidence in itself. The cinema is so far acting as a slave to literature—because no creative genius has yet arrived to deliver it from its bondage. This act of rescue will not be easy, because in poetry, painting or music the means are not expensive, whereas in the cinema, one needs not only creativity, but financial capital as well.

> The important thing in the cinema is the flow of images. Its visual movement should be so rich as to be able to fulfil itself without the use of words. Where the meaning of one language is constantly pointed out by another, it only shows how infirm the exercise of the first language is. Music fulfils itself in its autonomous flow of notes, without the help of words; why should not the cinema, with its flow of images? If this does not happen, it is because of the lack of creativity—and the insensibility of a lazy audience

seeking cheap thrills because it has not earned the right to joy.*

The search for identity which brought a new life to literature and the other arts in India had not begun in the cinema. Nor had the understanding of the medium. Film-makers themselves had no respect for their own work, and did little to preserve them for posterity. The film-making community was culturally underdeveloped and there was a special lack of creativity that could cut across cultural barriers and represented the high level of East-West synthesis seen in the other arts.

Jean Renoir used to say, during his stay in Calcutta, first to plan and then to shoot his film *The River* in Calcutta in 1948-49, that he found Satyajit Ray's understanding of Western art and civilization "fantastic". Indeed Ray's cultural inheritance was made up of a rich blend of Indian and Western tradition, heightened by the closeness to the Tagores and the creative genius of his grandfather and father. To this he added an important strand with his lifelong passion for westen classical music. Perhaps it was the main determinant in his sense of structure, form and rhythm. In line with theatre of social and artistic development in India in the British and the Independent period, it was his understanding of western, modern values that gave him an insight into the medium of cinema, and their blend with an equally rich appreciation of Indian tradition that led him to his urge to discover his people, for himself and the medium he chose. Asked how he learnt film-making he would always say: by watching films from the West.

When Lindsay Anderson spoke of Ray going down on his knees in the dust, he understood a universal truth reflected in *Pather Panchali*'s encounter with a regional reality. Ray had little direct experience of the Bengali village at the time. He knew it through the typology and the archetypal relationships celebrated in literature. It was not his knowledge of it but his urge to know it that made it real on the screen. Bibhuti Bhushan Bandyopadhyay drew upon his own experience to create an extraordinary first novel by a then unknown author. Ray made his first film as an unknown film director who knew, compared to the writer, very

---

* It is no less interesting to note that while he was in Germany in 1930, Tagore wrote a film script commissioned by UFA Studios in Germany, entitled *The Child*, inspired by a passion play he saw in a village near Munich. In 1931, Allen and Unwin published the script in London, but no copy of it is traceable in India, nor has it been included in the poet's collected works. No one appears to know if the script was ever filmed. Tagore's letter and information on his film script given here has been taken from Rajat Roy's book in Bengali, *Chalachchitrer Sandhanay* (Sahityasri, Calcutta 1977).

little about either village life or poverty. What he did became significant for re-discovering, on behalf of his somewhat westernized generation of the educated urban middle class, how the other half lives—with infinite compassion and in a cinematic language hitherto unknown in India.

*Pather Panchali* marked the baptism of Indian cinema in both its cinematic language and its Indianness more completely and emphatically than ever before. It brought to bear upon the cinema, for the first time, the outlook of East-West synthesis which had revitalised the traditional arts. The modern educated Indian needs to find the umbilical cord linking him with his own tradition and with the common man and thus save himself from being a refugee. Ray's first film showed the way for an exorcism of his guilt of being privileged. Many of these traits have become a part of the new Indian cinema, and its protest against the commercial formula film's continued lack of identity. The all-India film still avoids surnames, regional costumes and the geography of locations, holding up a superficial commonality which has no roots. It still lives on imitation. It has no conscious understanding of either myth or melodrama. It merely mixes its imitation of folk forms, resulting in the nondescript variety show of Parsi theatre and of the paintings of Ravi Verma—two major factors in causing a break in the continuity of Indian visual and performing tradition. It is only after Ravi Verma that the question of Indianness arose in our painting. He was the *bête noir* of the Bengali school which rejected this bowdlerised form of a dull academic British painting as vigorously as the nostalgic revivalism of its own early practitioners. In the work of Gaganendranath, Rabindranath, Binode Bihari and Ram Kinkar there was a new freedom from traditionalism as well as westernisation.

In cinema, the aftermath of Phalke moved towards social films and away from mythology which Phalke himself continued to hug. Shantaram and Vinayak made films with a notably modernist swing in tune with the country's urge towards the contemporisation of its culture. Nonetheless, their apprehension of the particular genius of cinema as a medium was inadequate; the realistic fragment of life as the basic building block of cinema of many different kinds had not come into its own. Myth still dominated, overwhelmed fact.* A fusion of cinema's realistic vocabulary with the Indianness of style and statement had to await the arrival of Satyajit Ray.

---

* For a fuller discussion of myth and fact and their interaction in the Indian Cinema, see the author's *The Painted Face: Studies in India's Popular Cinema* (Roli Books, Delhi, 1991).

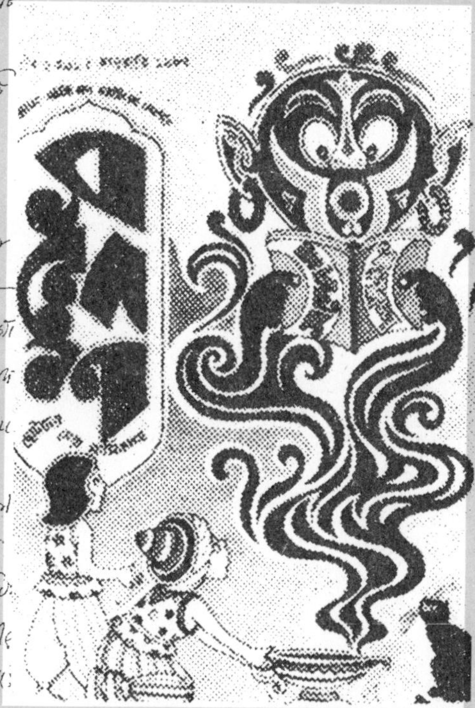

# Before Pather Panchali

## I

Satyajit Ray's family traces its ancestry back up to the mid-sixteenth century in Ramsunder Deb, in a district in West Bengal which is considered the centre of pure Bengali diction and a focal point of Bengali culture. The title Ray (for some time the more grandiose Roy Choudhury), a familiar one for landowners, must have been conferred around the eighteenth century. It was in the nineteenth, with Ray's grandfather, Upendrakishore, that the family emerged in modern Bengal as a distinguished cultural entity, probably next only to the formidable tribe of the Tagores.

Like the Tagores, the Rays joined the Brahmo Samaj, a community of ardent social reformers who blended an ancient Vedantic Hindu content with a Christian form in their religion, and developed the driving force of a puritan ethic in their urge to change traditional Hindu society towards modern times.

Upendrakishore pioneered half-tone block-making, printing and book publishing in Bengal under the name U Ray (later U Ray and Sons) around the turn of the century. He wrote articles for the *Penrose Annual* journal of the British printing industry, improved printing processes with his own inventions, wrote books for children, illustrated, printed, published and sold them. He also wrote songs still sung in the Brahmo Samaj and played the flute and the violin. His elder brother Saradaranjan pioneered the game of cricket; of the other brothers one was a professor, others writers. Kuldaranjan and Pramadaranjan Ray translated Jules Verne and Arthur Conan Doyle to the delight of children and adolescents.

The entire family had a passion for children's literature, but none more than Satyajit's father Sukumar, whose nonsense verses are still memorised by Bengali children and delight their parents with a very high quality of imaginative verse and inventive illustration. He edited and published a children's magazine called *Sandesh* (meaning both news and sweetmeat) which became enormously popular and was revived some years ago by his only offspring, Satyajit Ray.

Sukumar Ray died in 1923, when Satyajit was barely two years old. He was brought up by his mother at her brother's house in the midst of a large extended family full of cousins, uncles and aunts. His mother, tall and stately, was an accomplished singer of Rabindra Sangeet with a powerful voice; her clay Buddha and Bodhisattva figures drew admiration. The family was close to the Tagores; almost inevitably, after graduation from Presidency College, Calcutta, Ray went to Rabindranath Tagore's university at Santiniketan to study painting, having already shown ability at an early age. Here he learnt from the master Nandalal Bose, and Binode Bihari Mukhopadhyay, on whom he was later to make a film, *The Inner Eye*. Santiniketan was, in those days, the centre of a new Indian awareness in literature and the arts, not only the country's own, but the world's. Tagore attracted students and teachers from all over India and many countries abroad, creating conditions for the growth of a new Indian culture based on her own traditions but enriched by the world to which his own presence and his writing contributed.

In 1942, after a tour of Central India's art monuments, Ray left Santiniketan. Soon enough, he found employment in a British advertising agency, D J Keymer and Co., as a commercial artist. While here, he did a good deal of book-jacket designing and illustration work for Signet Press, a pioneering publishing firm which established new standards in Indian book production. Among the books he illustrated was an abbreviated version of Bibhutibhushan Bandyopadhyay's *Pather Panchali*.

By this time, his interest in flim was already pronounced; in 1947 he founded, along with others (including myself), the Calcutta Film Society, and wrote articles on the problems of Indian cinema and on what it should be like. The Calcutta Film Society gathered together a number of cinephiles some of whom later turned into noted film-makers. Ray's initiative brought film education to himself as much as to others, for the Calcutta Film Society showed a large number of outstanding products of world cinema never seen in India before. These included films by Eisenstein and Pudovkin, Robert Flaherty, John Grierson, Marcel Carne, Julien Duvivier, and so on. Until his first trip abroad, the society was Ray's sole means of exposure to world cinema and later remained, for a long time, the major means of continuing that exposure. He was already a voracious reader of film magazines and books and was able to recognize many famous French films hiding under English title on Hollywood distributors' shelves, for instance Duvivier's *Carnet du Bal* which was called *Dance of Life* in the English dubbed version. Among the people he met at the society were Jean Renoir, Pudovkin, Nikolai Cherkassov, John Huston and others. During 1948-49 he came to know Jean Renoir, who was in Calcutta in order to make *The River* on the banks of the Ganga. In 1950, his employers sent him to London for further training. Here he became friends with Lindsay Anderson and Gavin Lambert, and saw nearly a hundred films in a stay of four and a half months, including *Bicycle Thieves* and other Italian neo-realist works, which made a profound impression on him. It was on the way back to India by ship that he began writing the script of *Pather Panchali*. In 1952 came the First International Film Festival of India, which gave him renewed exposure to Italian neo-realism and films from other countries, including Japan.

For all the sensation *Pather Panchali* caused at the time, it had apparently done no more than transfer the values of India's other contemporary arts to the cinema. Realist narrative, social awareness, compassion for the Indian human being, trueness to the medium had been present in plenty in many short stories of Rabindranath Tagore, in Saratchandra Chatterjee's longer stories such as *Mahesh, Ramer Sumati*, in the fiction of Rampada Mukhopadhyay, Bibhuti Bandopadhyay, Bibhuti Mukhopadhyay, Premendra Mitra, and had achieved a new raucous force in Manik Bandopadhyay. The novels of Sita and Shanta Devi, Ashapurna Devi, and Gajendranath Mitra were remarkable for their portrayal of the daily life of the middle class.

By World War II, many of the values of this rich literature had begun to find its way into the other arts. Around 1940, the Youth Cultural Society and Benoy Roy's 'song squad' had begun to give an activist shape to this consciousness. The 1943 British-made famine, with its mind-boggling toll of lives, sharpened the consciousness further and gave birth to Bijan Bhattacharya's play *Nabanna* and the Indian Peoples Theatre Association (IPTA). The drawings of Chittaprasad, the poems of Jyotirindra Moitra, Bishnu Dey, Subhas Mukhopadhyay and others, the formation of the Anti-Facist writers and Artists Association (later styled the Progressive Writers' & Artists' Association) led to a new awareness of the role of the arts in understanding society and in changing its course. The IPTA, in particular, left an indelible mark on the performing arts in Bengal. It led to the creation of a whole new movement in theatre, liberating it from the cobwebs of Victorian decadence. By the mid-fifties, avant-garde theatre in Bengal had already made its mark. Bohuroopee's plays like *Chhenra Taar* had reached unscaled heights in dramatic realism and social awareness. Uday Shankar had created new forms in Indian dancing and moved from the woes of Radha to unheard of subjects like 'Labour and Machinery'. In fact in *Kalpana* (1948) he tried, with some success, to express his new dance forms in the medium of cinema. Before World war II, Amrita Sher-Gil had already made her spiritual transition from Europe to Indian and in her best paintings brought out a deep sense of the tranquility, dignity, fatalism and suffering of the Indian people, often of the poorest classes. Jamini Roy, similarly, had turned away from Western academic art to folk forms. The revival of classical music through all-India "conferences" was in full swing. In other words, Indian writers and artists had, long before *Pather Panchali*, set out on their quest for a sense of identity with the common man and with tradition, in all forms of artistic expression—except the cinema.

In the thirties, the Bengali cinema did display some signs of reformist patriotism but its main anchor was in traditionalism. Its social-reformist zeals were not based on a pervasive world view. As a result, its style never developed the independent view of cinema as an art free of the baggage of literature that Rabindranath Tagore had urged upon it. Its links with world cinema were indeed limited by the violation imposed by British rule and by the problem of language in the talkies; but apart from these outward difficulties, there was no movement within it to break out of its confines which were basically self-imposed. Thus neither in content nor in style did Ray's films own anyting at all to Bengali, indeed Indian cinema traditions. That is why he was able to cut its Gordian knot with the one stroke of *Pather Panchali* and thereafter to follow his own thoroughly independent course.

The prominent name before Ray's in the Bengali film scene was that of P.C. Barua, the maker of *Debdas*, that undying archetype of Indian cinema. Barua and New Theatres had an all-India impact with their double-version productions. In *Debdas*, Barua espoused the cause of marriage by personal choice as against family arrangement, in *Mukti*, he voiced the right of divorce in a marriage that did not work. As such he may be dubbed progressive in his social outlook. Yet Ray had no affinity with him and derived nothing from him.

Ray said he had learnt the methods of narrative cinema from Hollywood. So had Bengali cinema before him, including Barua's. Yet there is no visible link between Ray's work and earlier Bengali cinema. In fact *Pather Panchali* shook Bengali cinema as no other film before or after it had done. This can be significantly ascribed to the Italian neo-realist element which had been virtually unknown to Bengali film makers. One can also add the catalytic effect of Jean Renoir's constant urgings that

Indian cinema must free itself from Hollywood and become itself by concentrating on Indian reality. Actually the Bengali cinema establishment rejected Renoir altogether and was contemptuous of the "documentary" realism of *Pather Panchali* during the long period of its search for funds. Indeed, underneath a show of respect for his world stature, it continues to be so to this day.

II

Not that no effort had been made in India to extend this new proletarian consciousness to the new medium. Khwaja Ahmed Abbas had, as early as 1941, in *Naya Sansar* (New World), his maiden screen play, for Bombay Talkies, about a journalist pressurised by a business tycoon. In 1949, he made *Dharti-Ke-Lal* based on IPTA's Hindi version of *Nabanna* with Shambhu and Tripti Mitra from the original cast of the Bengali play. Earlier there had been a plethora of nationalistic and socially progressive films denouncing caste prejudices and the dowry system and so on; but this was the first time there was film directly inspired by the radical left, and distinctly proletarian in its sympathies. Unfortunately, Abbas' feeling for cinema did not match Shambhu Mitra's for the theatre as in *Nabanna* or *Chhenra Taar*. Although the film was shown in Paris, London and Moscow and came to be regarded as a landmark, it was basically filmed theatre. Abbas' progressive content had always tended to be marred by the schematism of his style, which later grew very close to the commercial cinema. At the end of *Saat Hindustani*, seven Indians from seven parts of the country drive up in seven yellow-black taxi cabs, their doors opening identically, to produce a highly operatic effect distinctly derived form IPTA's dance and drama productions, themselves stylistically allied to Uday Shankar's. This IPTA-operatic streak ran so strong in the cultural bloodstream of many who later left it to turn independent that it is visible even in the ending scenes of Mrinal Sen's *Mrigaya* made in 1976, with tribals silhouetted on hilltops at the end.

In 1952 Ritwik Ghatak made *Nagarik*, his first film. It had occasional sparks of talent but generally followed the conventions of traditional Bengali film without being able to forge the new cinematic language which sparkled in *Ajaantrik*, made three years after *Pather Panchali* and obviously activated by it, even though it bore no resemblance to the style of Ray's first film. (It only took over some of the material innovations of Ray such as extensive outdoor shooting, realistic *mise-en-scène*, the elimination of excessive use of filters and similar features).

Ray's early apprenticeship in the cinema was spent in the study of Hollywood films—virtually the only kind he could see before Independence. As he himself had repeatedly said, he learnt film-making by seeing mainly American films again and again. The logical and (at least on the surface) realistic narrative style of Hollywood made a deep impression on him. (I still remember his excitement when he had an opportunity to meet Paulette Goddard soon after World War II.) Yet the average Hollywood product's superficiality and its studio stamp overpowering the individuality of the artists also left him dissatisfied. At a speech at Asia Society, New York in 1981, he made it clear that he had learnt from Hollywood "not only what to do, but what not to do."

The need to see films from other countries that we had read about in Roger Manvell's *Film* (Penguin 1944) became a pressing one. This was what prompted Ray to say to me one day around the middle of 1947: "Why don't we start a film society?" It was at the Calcutta Film society that he saw Eisenstein's *Battleship Potemkin*, *Strike*, *General Line* and *Alexander Nevsky*, Flaherty's *Nanook of The North* and *Louisiana Story*, saw Pudovkin's *Storm over Asia* and met him, together with Nikolai Cherkassov who had played Nevsky in *Alexander Nevsky*, Ivan in *Ivan The Terrible*, and later John Houston. But perhaps no meeting was more significant than the one with Jean Renoir who was in India in 1948-49 to make *The River*. Thanks to Roger Manvell, a handful of us, led by Ray, knew what the name Jean Renoir meant in film history. Ray wrote about him in *Sequence*, then edited by Lindsay Anderson, met him frequently all through Renoir's stay in Calcutta, and watched him work. Two remarks of Renoir are probably the most significant pointers to the character of Ray's future works. The first was a humanist statement about characterisation in Renoir's films, that he loved all his characters and could not condemn any: "The trouble is that everybody has his reasons (for doing as he does)". Of no film maker other than Renoir himself has this been more true than of the early Ray. The second statement of Renoir acted as a catalyst on all of us: "When Indian cinema gives up its imitation of Hollywood and tries to express the reality around itself, it will discover a national style". I have come across many versions of this statement, couched in different words, and doubt if anyone has it exact, but the meaning is clear. Its significance manifested itself in *Pather Panchali*'s total dedication to regional reality and refusal to imitate any model whatsoever. But apart from Renoir's words, there was his film, *The River*, with its warmth, its brilliant improvisations and its remarkable use of Indian music, as in the sequence of the kite flying in the sky to a Carnatic *taal*. Although its philosophy lacked in depth of knowledge of India and its ancient history and literature, its effect at the time was electrifying for us.

Close on the heels of his return home from London came India's first international film festival, loaded with neo-realism and a first glimpse of

Kurosawa's *Rasho Mon*. Had he not been exposed to these influences, his first film may have been an adaptation of *Prison of Zenda* (which he had scripted sometime in the early forties, or Tagore's *Ghare-Baire* (The Home And The World). Although he was already thinking of casting non professionals (proof, as Marie Seaton points out, that in *Pather Panchali* he was not imitating the Italians), one doubts if the Tagore story, not to speak of *Prisoner of Zenda* would have made as good a first film as *Pather Panchali*.

It was only after the unqualified success of *Pather Panchali* that Ray, who had been given some months of leave with pay during its making, finally left his job at D J Keymer and Co. He never completely lost his interest in advertising; besides designing his own publicity for his early films he remained for many years a Director of Clarion Advertising Services (successors to D J Keymer, and owned by the employees) where many of his old colleagues still work. *Seemabadha*, made in 1971, has a whole ad-film in it which Ray must have enjoyed making.

২২/
৩/
৮৪

শ্রীমান দন্যুত্বাইট সমীপে —

সাদর সম্ভাষন,

[হস্তাক্ষরে লেখা বাংলা পত্র — অধিকাংশ দুষ্পাঠ্য]

...

Science Fiction ও Fantasy ...

Staples ...

# The Apu Trilogy

## I

The Apu trilogy, nationally and internationally Ray's most famous work, is perhaps structurally his most Indian film, free-flowing in its form, less pre-composed, more spontaneous. Much of this probably comes not directly from Ray but from his writer, Bibhuti Bandyopadhyay's idealistic, meditative and spiritual quality which marginalises evil and brings the good, the "eternal", in human nature to the fore. Thus Sarbajaya's selfishness is in this view a manifestation of the mother's concern for her children's good, not for her own well-being or self-aggrandisement. Ray is moved by Bandyopadhyay's treatment and is led by it not in a slavish manner but in the manner of a devoted disciple, merging his own identity in his mentor's—something he could not have done if he had not been able to identify himself as completely with the author's vision as he has done. Indeed, in the spirit of the works, the two identities are hard to distinguish. Ray only updates the writer's work in the sense of making it believable to his present audience's susceptibilities, reducing the degree of romanticism and idealisation and introducing a modicum of present-day realism. The consideration he has in mind is the requirements of his own medium and the more mundane need for an acceptable length for his film. Despite these orientations, such is the fusion of outlooks that the two works, the two related novels and the film trilogy, have become indivisible to the Bengali mind. Both are equally respected and there is little sleep lost over the changes—which are many—made by the film maker from the literary work. Ray's departures from the text merely seem to update the literary work to our times and to fashion a latter-day version of Bandyopadhyay's sense of wonder, his philosophic calm and detachment, his faith in the innate goodness of the human being, his spirit of tolerance and non-violence and his quiet refusal to create villains and other objects of hatred. The cantankerous neighbour in *Pather Panchali*, the lustful man who eyes the widowed Sarbajaya in *Aparajito*, the landlord desperately trying to get his monthly rent from Apu in *Apur Sansar*, are all as much a part of a pattern of inevitability in the cycle of life as the monkeys tolling the bells of the temple in Benares in *Aparajito*. In a deeply Indian sense of the world, both the novelist and the film maker are "humanists" who believe in certain undying "eternal" traits of human nature everywhere and in every age. Such a proposition should have seemed trite and devoid of meaning in the modern, not to speak of the post-modern world. Curiously, it does not. It seems to grip people of all ideologies practically everywhere in the world. It seems to do the impossible by capturing something elemental in human society and behaviour in a manner that cannot but recall millennia-old traditions in Indian art and literature. Ray's own words may be of interest here:

> The novel, *Pather Panchali* was a sprawling saga whose leisurely, episodic unfolding perfectly caught the rhythm and pace of life in a Bengal village. In this it had wholly departed from the terseness of the earliest 19th century Bengali novel inspired by European models. In adapting it I tried to combine the relaxed quality of the original with a tightness called for by the exigencies of the conventional feature film.

## II

Two things were remarkable about the making of *Pather Panchali*. One was the concept itself: the way it set itself up in total opposition to all the norms of film-making in India at the time. The other was the uncompromising persistence in realising the concept.

All day scenes in the film were shot on location; only the night scenes were shot in the studio, and that too by duplicating the location setting in exact photographic detail. Its budget of Rs. 2,00,000 was low, even for those days; it had no stars and many of the performers were non-professionals appearing completely without make-up. Even the ones with acting experience were generally unknown to the public. Whoever had heard of a bent eighty-year-old woman acting in a film? It used Indian music as background music (considered in those days to be unsuitable for films, because it had no "body"). It had no songs, dances, romance in it; it was uncompromisingly realistic (condemned as "documentary"). It was completely regional, taking place at a specific time and place. It was also intensely personal, and all the aspects of film-making were firmly in the hands of the Director. Both he and his unit were completely without experience. Each one of them broke the rule of film-making obtaining at that time.

After *Pather Panchali*, Ray often said he learnt film-making by seeing films. Some of them he saw dozen of times. What they did not tell him he learnt them on the job.

From the first draft of its script to its release, *Pather Panchali* was on the anvil for five years of apprenticeship to an ideal. Throughout this period, Ray was working for D J Keymer and Co. as its Art Director. A good part of the film was shot on weekends, some of them spent in experimentations to master the mechanical technique. Throughout the period, Ray was able to keep his vision intact, and his unit of devoted followers never wavered in their faith in that vision. The story of how he pawned his insurance policy and his wife's ornaments to make about forty per cent of the film and how he was able to complete it with the help of a somewhat uncomprehending Government of West Bengal, is too well-known to need repetition. The period of waiting was fraught with the danger of the children suddenly growing up, and Chunibala Devi, the aged once-actress from the red-light district dying before shooting could be resumed. At times, it was touch and go; Satyajit was at the end of his tether and ready to sell what he had shot to get his money back— but the commercially successful director whose word would have done it did not have time to take up the film before the Government of West Bengal came to its rescue.

The film had its world premiere at the Museum of Modern Art in New York, where it appeared alongside Ali Akbar Khan's sarod recital and Shanta Rao's Bharatanatyam dancing, as a representation of Indian culture. It received excellent reviews from the few critics who had seen it, but hardly anything of this kind appeared in the Indian Press. In India, the first show was held on the annual day of the Advertising Club of Calcutta in the ballroom of the Ordnance Club before an audience more interested in drinking whisky than in seeing stark reality on the screen. Only a handful of those present that evening knew the worth of what they had seen. Shortly thereafter, when *Pather Panchali* was released commercially, it ran to half-empty houses for the first two weeks; then word began to spread, and people started to come. The film had a very successful fourth week in houses filled by ordinary Calcuttans. It was their enthusiasm over the film that made it an unqualified success in later revivals. They were moved by it, and shocked that such things were possible in cinema. In coarse language, some were overheard saying: "The bastards had been cheating us all this time—this is the real stuff!" Contrary to popular impressions outside Bengal, *Pather Panchali*'s initial success had nothing to do with its reputation abroad; that reputation was yet to be made. Although *Pather Panchali* was awarded a prize at Cannes in 1956, it was really the award of the Grand Prize of the Venice Festival in 1957 to *Aparajito* that brought *Pather Panchali* into the international limelight. It was not until September 1958 that *Pather Panchali* was released in New York.

## III

In one of India's more than five hundred thousand villages, a Brahmin boy is born, emerging into the nineteen twenties from the depths of two millennia of tradition. The event brings much joy to his impoverished poet-priest father, his toiling mother, and a sister greedy for all that life may have to offer. He goes to a traditional village school, where his natural curiosity is kept in check. He learns from life; his old aunt dies, then his sister. They leave the village. He wanders around ancient Benares, learning through sight and sound and smell. Then his father dies too, amidst a flight of pigeons and a muscleman doing his push-ups by the river. For a while he goes back to village life, but finds a school and a teacher that beckon him to the wider world outside. Vainly he tries to explain the intense mystery of the globe to his uncomprehending mother. More and more, he feels drawn to the world and is estranged from his mother who would keep him under her wing without a thought for the changes that are taking place in him. She spends her time sitting under a tree near a tank pining for her son. On an evening full of fireflies, she dies. He is sad, but he is free. He is alone. He acquires a friend in Pulu. He lives in an attic near a railway track, cooks his own, plays his flute, and studies in college. By a traditional accident, he marries, to save his friend's sister from social ostracism. Equally traditionally, she leaves her father's affluence to live her life with the one that providence has decreed for her. He loves her deeply, inevitably, not as one he has found by his prowess, but as an outcome of the good actions of many former lives, with a love ordained by some superior will. Suddenly she is dead. All meaning is drained out of life; death becomes preferable. But mysteriously, he cannot die. He roams the forests, renouncing the world like a *sanyasi*. He gives up his beloved first novel and lets the pages float down to the bottom of the hill. He refuses to see his son; he is the cause of the death of the mother. But the time comes when he has to go and find his son and reclaim him and go back to the business of living. The story of the trilogy has a noble, classical simplicity.

Bibhutibhushan's two-volume novel on which the Ray trilogy is based has a rambling form, a romantic, wandering-wondering philosophy of love without attachment in a life that constantly moves beyond joy and sorrow. It has an irresistible charm, no matter how clear-eyed you may be. It always flies a few feet above earthly reality, seeing it close enough and yet remaining untouched by it. Over all he sees, there is stretched a magic film, turning it into something seen in moonlight. Bibhutibhushan had an enormous love for nature, and a knowledge of it in fine detail; it is an expression of some invisible divinity, and helps man to rise above pain. Every parting is sorrow, and yet it is also a new freedom from attachment. At the end of the vast second volume (*Aparajito*), Apu, after living awhile with his son Kajal, leaves him in the care of friends, and resumes his wanderings, going off across the seas, perhaps to Tahiti....

Apu is the archetypal character in Bibhutibhushan's mirror image of the world, so real and yet so abstracted. His philosophy of wonder and detachment soars higher and higher through many novels. In *Drishtipradip* his boy-hero is angelic in his purity and detachment, in *Debajan* he actually *becomes* an angel. Bibhutibhushan's fine observation of reality always, tends to take us away from it, or perhaps, one might say, above it.

Ray subtly manages to remove the *Sonar Bangla* (golden Bengal) sheen from Bibhutibhushan's closely observed reality, making it grimmer, more contemporary, yet retaining something of the purity of vision of the original. Ray's Apu grows to maturity; when he reclaims his son there is no hint of the possibility of his resuming his romantic wanderings. Ray also plays down Bibhutibhushan's emphasis on detachment and release. Apu's progression from his village to Benares and to Calcutta becomes more of a chronicle of social change in the films than in the novel, brought about by the railways and the globe. Poet-priest Harihar would have had more respect and easier circumstances a century, or even decades ago; today he has neither; the world-view that his son will obtain from his studies and his movement to the city is vastly different from his own. It is not "progress"; the commitment to humanity is too deep to take sides with progress, with one age pitted against another. It is the inevitable movement of one era into another, like many others before it and many others to come. Hence, there are no heroes and villains; only human beings, every one with his reason for being what he is.

At the same time, the trilogy is a paean to love. Not love between man and woman which has been so overblown in literature and the cinema at the expense of love in the all-embracing sense in which it exists here. Love between mother and son, brother and sister; between unrelated people, between man and nature, between being and becoming. Indira Thakrun is called "auntie" by the children; but she is only some kind of distant cousin of Harihar who floated into their lives in some dim past, and found refuge among them. The children love her not so much because she is their aunt, as because she represents a mysterious force of life and death that fascinates them. It is only when her own children's survival is at stake that Sarbajaya turns her face against the old woman, and she dies like an animal. In *Apur Sansar*, it is as if Apu and Aparna's romantic love for each other is only another aspect of Sarbajaya's love for her children or theirs for their aunt or their father—a comprehensive, all-pervasive, non-sexual love which has seldom been celebrated in the cinema with such purity.

In turning the novels into film, Ray gives them a harsher reality; at the same time, he shares Bibhutibhushan's Hindu view of life as a continuum, a flow in which loss and gain are two sides of the same coin, and the befitting goal of the human being is to love and yet to remain detached, unshaken by sorrow and unelated by happiness.

The chorus of praise (sometimes blame) for the elemental quality of poverty brought into focus in *Pather Panchali* often obscures the fact that its protagonists were not born poor. Harihar is a Brahmin member of a traditionally privileged and powerful caste (class). We know by implication that his present state represents a fall from the status the family once enjoyed. He had *yajamanas* now lost, used to be paid in cash and in kind for his priestly services. He is not only literate but a village poet and is not without some command of Sanskrit. In British times, with the rise of the salaried middle class and of a different set of values brought in by the beginning of the industrial revolution, his occupation has lost its earlier relevance. Indeed this is why, when he is pushed to the point of no return, he decides to go to Varanasi which is the home of traditional Hinduism and where his occupation still has a clear-cut place in society yet unaffected by the erosion of religious faith caused by the pressures of increasing materialism. The story, and the film, are not thus about India's poverty as such, but of the fall of a class and a deep-seated change in the heart of Indian society.

IV

Yet poverty in the trilogy, especially *Pather Panchali*, is grim, unadorned, real; and we know that it is not only something that this family suffers from, but that it also symbolizes a vast mass of humanity in India. Yet how different it is from the antheaps of Louis Malle! The poor are no statistic here; indeed, as a mass lumped together they are inconceivable in relation to the trilogy, where they are, before all else, individual human beings. *Pather Panchali*'s picture of poverty is heartbreaking because of the mother's innate sense of decency, and her desperate striving to save her children, because of the children's laughter and their fascination with the train clattering past the field of white flax; in other words, because of their individuality. The film represents the conscience of modern India. Many decades after it was made, *Pather Panchali* is still a cleansing experience.

It still conveys the purity and the directness of a first film, its structure holds up perfectly, and its technique betrays no lack of experience. It is only in Durga's death scene that there is a slightly theatrical over-concentration on the business at hand which sets it apart from the interrelated style of the rest. Something of the rambling nature of Bibhutibhushan's narrative is retained; yet the script organizes the events in a thoroughly convincing structure, and manages to carry the interest from one apparently inconsequential thing to another until it acquires meaning and substance. The scene of Harihar's return and the breaking of the news of Durga's death has a powerful directness in the depiction of sorrow that Ray was never to achieve, even to attempt, in his later films, where such fullness of statement is replaced more and more by an evocative obliqueness. When he needs it in *Apur Sansar*, the answer does not have the same inevitability; Apu's reaction to the news of Aparna's death is simply not comparable—it tries to be direct, but does not quite succeed.

*Pather Panchali* presents archetypal characters at a basic level of existence—the father, the mother, the decrepit old woman vaguely related to the family, the young daughter, the son, the crude school teacher cum grocer, and presents them with such freshness, warmth and authenticity that they become an inseparable part of our experience. Almost every scene is memorable—Sarbajaya's first verbal duel with the old woman, the introduction of Apu, the children's sighting of the railway train followed by their first encounter with death as the old woman unexpectedly falls over with a thud, the village school, the sweetmeat vendor, the coming of rain, the wind ruffling the lotus leaves on the pond, the long, stormy night of Durga's death, the morning of the father's return to find the house ravaged by storm and his daughter dead, the family's departure from the village. Not one scene seems *déjà vu*; there is a constant sense of discovery that the audience shares with the director in a warm intimacy of feeling.

The script sees the presentation of every event and character as a problem which it solves by finding a way to make it fresh, unique, free of conventions.

The main musical theme, played on a bamboo flute and taken from a song the old woman sings to herself in her long wait for death and struggle to live, tugs at the heartstrings with an openness and freshness rare in the history of cinema. The song itself refers to the crossing of the river at the end of the day by one who has no money to pay the boatman—in an obvious evocation of the crossing over from life to death. Birth and death, affection and anguish, pettiness and joy in the midst of grinding poverty leave indelible images in the mind. The ordinary is turned into the extraordinary by a highly deceptive simplicity backed up not just by inspiration but constant invention. An invisible chain of tiny links of suspense and surprise is made up with detail after detail.

The deaths in the trilogy are each marked by brilliant innovation calculated to give them the depth of new personal experience, and the process begins with *Pather Panchali*, with the remarkable scene of Indira Thakrun's death. She dies just when the children are full of the excitement over their viewing of the train, that magical, monumental force and reality beyond their comprehension. In the oppressive heat, she sits by the side of a pond. Durga calls out to her and, not getting an answer, pushes her and her frail body falls over. The water pot flies from her hand and falls into the water. She has disappeared from life; it has fallen from her body like a dried leaf. The children have suddenly seen death as mysterious to them as that giant of a train shaking up the countryside. They don't understand its significance. It is one more thing in the process of their growth. No Indian film had ever shown death with such stark reality nor with such a profound sense of the cycle of birth and death, evocative of a cosmic view of mortality, embedded in Indian traditon. Durga's death is long, painful as we behold it on the screen, perhaps even a shade too dramatic for Ray's style; it really hits us later, on Harihar's return with presents for the family. The recollection is more powerful than the event. Notable too is the fact that in their grief over the girl's death, there is no gender-bred negligence, perhaps because of their education and their innate goodness.

In *Aparajito*, we have the death of Harihar, again awesome in the event itself as his eyes burst out of their sockets when he tries to swallow a drop of holy water from the Ganga. A large flock of birds suddenly fly out into a wide sky, evoking the traditional Indian idea of the soul leaving the body. Later Sarbajaya's death comes slowly, like the fall of evening; she sits under a huge tree and watches the reflection of Orion in the shadowy pond. Apu arrives on hearing of her illness and sees his uncle standing in grim silence. Nothing more needs to be said.

*Apur Sansar* presents us with the death of its most delicate creature, Aparna. Apu's youg wife, named after Lord Shiva's wife at a time when she did not even eat a leaf (*parna*) in penance for the humiliation suffered by Shiva at the hand of her father, Daksha, the Mountain God. Aparna's death takes place off-screen, but it had been heralded in the pale light of .

the matchstick that illuminated Aparna's face in the hackney coach on the way back from a film show. Apu hits Aparna's brother who brings the news of her death. Some have debated the aptness of the reaction. Others see in it the desperation in Apu, driven out of his mind by the unbelievability of the news. All these deaths have a forceful impact; they come with suddenness and a sense of inevitability that visits them either at the moment (Indira Thakrun, Harihar) or afterwards (Durga, Sarbajaya Aparna)—dramatic, but imbued with a sense of the inexorable cycle of birth, life and death. Apu begins a process of self-rehabilitation by going to the city and graduating to a new kind of society. As such he is more than an individual; he is willy nilly the representative of a certain class growing up into a new India.

The trilogy powerfully reminded the middle class intellectual, the leading agents of change in independent India of how the other half lives. It made it just a little more difficult to forget. For the English-educated, city-centric people destined to rule the country, it was a reflection of the rediscovery of India by Macaulay's brown Englishmen, heeding, as it were, Vivekananda's behest not to forget the illiterate millions, and Gora's contention that the reformers must first of all identify themselves with those whom they wish to reform. Obviously this was also close to Mahatma Gandhi's identification with his people. The film thus struck some important chords in the heart of those times and developed a great potential that many recognised without being entirely conscious of it.

Apart from the concept itself, what was remarkable about the making of *Pather Panchali* was Ray's ability to keep his vision intact over the long gaps between the concept and its realization. His uncompromising persistence paid off at the end because he was able to protect his mental image in the film, like a tiny flame, from all the winds that buffetted it through the years of waiting and the intermittent nature of the work, shooting on weekends and holidays from his advertising job, and later waiting for money to come.

One of the most significant departures from the literary original is in Apu and Durga's experience of the railway train that goes past them spreading a fade of smoke. In the novel, they never see a train. Much has been said about the train's suggestions of a world beyond his village which Apu is later to discover. The change Ray makes from the novel seems to justify this reading. Most of the other changes from the novel to the film are structural, they fulfil the need to create a tightly knit narrative from the ramblings of the novel—without losing the sense of meandering flow.

Every viewing of *Pather Panchali* has such an overwhelming impact that some of its shortcomings tend to escape us. The first half of the film which was shot in continuous narrative sequences in order to raise money for the rest—have traces of somewhat static art in compositions. In the second half, as Ray himself pointed out, his camera placements are better designed and there is hardly any evidence of straining after pictorial effect. The other is the use of classical music on the Sitar (played by cameraman Subrata Mitra) which was added on later to avoid awkward silences and fails to mesh with the mainly folk based melodies developed by Ravishankar. Durga's death sequence also seems to be built up a shade too deliberately and predictably, separating itself stylistically from the rest of the film. But these pale into insignificance beside the memorability of its great scenes, the perfect timing of the shots and that sense of the authentic and the inevitable which can, in the cinema, give the feeling of something actually happening before our eyes. It is all the more remarkable because the events that take place are simple, cyclical, "eternal." They are familiar and inevitable elements of existence which would surface in the lives of other families and their mother and father and aunt and children if only we were to look at them closely.

## V

*Aparajito* (1956) does not have quite the elemental quality of its predecessor, nor does its structure build into a similarly satisfying whole. It falls into rather separate parts; Benares, the village, Calcutta. Yet it has a still finer perception of individual beings and moments. Its less passionate observation reflects the protective cover that Apu must acquire in order to grow. Sarbajaya's sorrow is as inevitable as her son's indifference. She must obey life's inexorable laws and go, like a leaf dropping from the tree in autumn. The loss of his parents and the agony of Apu's survival in body and in spirit, is all that *Aparajito* holds by way of action. Yet the sheer palpability of Apu's emotional growth overwhelms us. The cyclical repetition of the Benares *ghats*, Harihar's readings at the riverside and his walk up the steep steps, Apu's trips to the monkey temple and the wild pealing of the bells by the unthinking animals worshipped as manifestations of God, brings a traditional religion to life in India's most ancient city as perhaps no film has ever done.

A fine economy of expression makes an epic out of a two-hour film. After Harihar's death, Sarbajaya is working as a servant and so is Apu, for kind employers. She has the offer of going to live with a relative, but does not take it. Coming down the staircase in her employer's house, Sarbajaya sees her son, at a distance, lighting the bowl of the boss's waterpipe. She stops, shocked by her vision of her son's future. The sound of a train overlaps her face. Cut to the train entering the bridge over the river. They are going away to the village of Mansapota where Apu can study and make a better life at his uncle's house. Music: the *Pather Panchali* theme.

Structurally *Aparajito* is meaningful mainly as a bridge between *Pather Panchali* and *Apur Sansar*. Within itself, it is not sufficiently balanced; Benares comes to life but Calcutta does not. There is a great promise at the beginning of this section that is not fulfilled. The most significant chapter is the relationship between an adolescent son drawn to the outside world and a mother seeing him unchanged from his boyhood, full of resonances of a complex, unspoken, Oedipal tension that all men must, in their growth, overcome. Apu's release is perhaps more important than the poignancy of his mother's death.

*Aparajito*, in a way, is the closest in spirit to Bibhutibhushan; its rambling and repetitive charm will never be found in Ray's work again. It is the only film in which Ray repeats both elements within the film itself and elements from the previous film, *Pather Panchali*. It is the repetitions which build the rhythm of life in Benares and register Harihar's death as a part of its flux, like thousands of deaths before it, important to those who lose, but insignificant in the cosmic cycle. As Harihar nears his dying moment, Apu goes to fetch water down the familiar steps, sees the same lane into the house. Again, when the train enters Bengal at dawn, there is an instant change in the landscape, and the theme tune of *Pather Panchali* plays on the sound track. There are many evocations of the earlier film in life at Mansapota. The film also juxtaposes the main event with an unnecessary detail which makes it a part of larger flow. As Harihar nears his end, Nandababu's polished black shoes come down the steps in close-up, and he tries to seduce Sarbajaya. She turns on him with her kitchen knife; cut back to Harihar breathing hard. His imminent death is a part of an inexorable process which the priests in the temple are celebrating with the circling lights, the deafening bells, and the chanting. Sarbajaya's face is taut with misgiving; cut to a wide-angle evening view of Benares, with dark clouds massed above it, a rim of light picking out the horizon. Such juxtapositions never again appear in Ray's work. In its philosophical depth and emotional directness. *Aparajito* is unique among Ray's films, especially in its Benares sequences.

What Stanley Kaufman had found "discursive, novelistic material" is its most Indian element. In "Indian music" Ray was to observe later, "the duration is flexible and depends on the mood of the musician. But the (Western) composition is bound by time."

The fact is that Ray's later films are more attuned to the inexorable timing of western musical compositions in their "fixed form", such as *Days and Nights in the Forest*. *Aparajito*'s flow, as of the trilogy itself, is more like Indian music, repetitive, ruled by mood.

## VI

*Apur Sansar* (1959) returns to the structural firmness characteristic of Ray, and continues and surpasses the purity of vision of *Aparajito*. The film progresses with natural logic which makes its poetry completely authentic, arising entirely from the events themselves, and never appears to be imposed on them by the film-maker. The relationship of Apu and Aparna is one of the most perfect depictions of love in the cinema. In the scene in the carriage coming back from the cinema, as Aparna's face is lit up by the glow of the match stick, there is an ineffable feeling of evanescence; Apu watches this, and says: "You know how I love my writing; I love you even more". The way her face is lit, her eyes regarding the flame, and the way Apu says the words, slowly, with a complete inwardness, it is as if, in the prime of their youth, the two lovers have understood something of the impermanence of life, and therefore of love. Indeed, from the beginning, Aparna's fragile beauty has a touch of sadness about it, as if somewhere in it there is the shadow of a knowledge of mortality. It is as though happiness is not natural to human life; it is an unexpected bonus by nature impermanent.

Ray's way of slowly bringing about events, outward and inward, in perfect relationship to each other, gives the film, especially in its first half, a sense of inevitability. It fits the story's classic outline: Apu's frugal, lonely life as a student; his marriage by chance; his love, his inconsolable sense of loss on the death of Aparna; his waking up to the awareness of his son and reclaiming him. In Robin Wood's highly perceptive analysis of this film (*The Apu Trilogy*), he misses the point of Apu's tossing away the pages of his manuscript, perhaps because it is so bound up with the line of dialogue in the carriage I have quoted above. Apu has become a *sanyasi*; he has given up all claims to life, and he no longer needs his novel. His friend, the highly realistic Pulu, had praised it so; but what will he do with it without Aparna, whom he loved even more?

Hundreds of marriages like that of Apu and Aparna are known to have taken place, some within the living memory of older generations, and have been celebrated in literature. Once her wedding was fixed for an astrologically propitious hour, the Hindu upper-caste girl who was then not wed, had to remain unwed and held in contempt, along with her family, all her life. The strength of tradition in that period was such that it was, for the bride's family, a matter of life and death. Times were changing but tradition had not lost its force. With his Western education, Apu protested against "the dark ages," but when the moment came, a traditional sense of duty got the better of his troubled rationalist conscience. Besides, had his parents lived, Apu would probably have had to marry by their choice rather than his own. The question of his own choice had barely begun to arise in Hindu society in Bengal at that time. As far as Aparna was concerned, Hindu girls worshipped Lord Shiva from their childhood and prayed for a husband like him, monogamous, handsome, noble and strong, even though he was a bit of a vagabond bohemian, rode a bull and kept the company of ghosts. Whomsoever she married, in an event brought about more by fate than by free will, would become her Lord Shiva. The correct behaviour was to follow him to the ends of the earth, no matter what his circumstances. Aparna's behaviour in leaving her affluence to go and live with Apu in his attic was thus far from unnatural.

If Apu's flute-playing casualness before his marriage prospect carries a suggestion of Krishna by the riverside, his long spell of disconsolate grief after Aparna's death cannot but recall Shiva wandering from place to place carrying the dead body of his wife on his shoulder, neglecting his divine duties of keeping the cycle of creation, preservation and destruction, going. The other gods, perturbed by this danger to the order of the universe, cut her body into pieces, and each place where a piece fell became a place of pilgrimage. When he found she was no longer there, Shiva reluctantly returned to his responsibilities. After he has torn up his novel, his great act of giving up all for Aparna, Apu is persuaded by his friend to return to life and reclaim his son, for whose future he must now become responsible. In a sequence lit up by a marvellous understanding of the child mind, Apu, who acts as though he is a child himself playing a game with another child, gains his confidence at last, and goes away alongside the river, with Kajal hoisted on his shoulder. The choice of the location itself has a philosophic charge, conveying the endless ebb and flow of life, which must go on, no matter what. Fate had brought together a perfect lover after marriage for perhaps an inevitably brief idyll of happiness; then reality ended it (death in childbirth was a common fate of women in those days), and grief had to give way before duty.

*Apur Sansar* is Ray's most personal film in the nature of the emotional charge it carries within. It is informed by a deeply, freshly felt Indianness going back to the archetypes of tradition in a kind of personal rediscovery. It is suffused with warmth and compassion without any awareness of the old-wordly values it is internalising. The director is at one with his characters, reaching out into the heart of traditional realities through them, seeing them as a part of the great, timeless process of life. By comparison, the exquisite perfection of *Charulata* is less Indian in its restraint and has less of a personal sense of frank and open identification with the characters.

Ray's close sense of identity with Bibhutibhushan has had two consequences: one, the important changes he made in the storyline went unnoticed, and secondly, it has become well nigh impossible to separate the novel and the film, at least for the Bengali. The cinema has the advantage of largely overcoming the language divide and can therefore reach the world audience with one leap. The process of translation is slow and difficult and its reach is necessarily narrower. It is this that accounts for the impression of the film overwhelming the literary product in the international scene and therefore literature buffs need not lose any sleep on that account.

VII

The trilogy consolidated, very early in his career, the nature of Ray's humanism. Living in an emerging Marxist intellectual ambience in Bengal, Ray held on to his Tagorean beliefs and rejected the methodology of Marxism. The crux of this social philosophy lies in the importance of the growth of the individual mind and the influence idealism exercises, through religion and art to prevent it from extreme self-seeking at the cost of the welfare of others. The goodness of the individual, in this view, is the basis of social growth. In the socialist view, the individual is a cog in the wheel of social engineering; the suppression of his ability to think for himself, to work out his own synthesis of personal and social welfare, becomes necessary in order to impose a uniform mechanism within a system of beliefs which is basically unalterable, unquestionable. In the Indian form of humanism, the poet is often described as a seer (as in the epic of the *Mahabharata*). His right to formulate his own idea of human welfare and the future of the race is not curtailed but listened to with respect even where it is not widely adopted. Indeed the intellectual or the poet or the seer is free to propagate his world view in competition with those of others. In the systemic view of socialism, the thoughts and acts of the individual are of little significance; it is the larger pattern of self-interest and social welfare that gains ascendancy to the point of reducing the individual to a cipher useful only for organising collective action. What is asked of him is conformity, as in religious orthodoxy governing all behaviour and leaving nothing to the secular will.

At the heart of the Indian renaissance, there was this emphasis on the moral and intellectual growth of the individual activated by literature, the arts, the social sciences, and the reform of religion to rid it of its accretions of self-interest leading to large scale ignorance and inability to think. In its development, this humanism later on accepted much of the analytical aspect of Marxism rejecting the validity of its prescriptive impositions. Hence one found among intellectuals and artists in Bengal a widespread affinity with Marxism's social goals without accepting its principles and practices particularly where they elevated the end over the means.

২২/৭/৮৪

শ্রী[illegible] বন্দ্যোপাধ্যায় সমীপেষু —

সবিনয় নিবেদন,

আপনার চিঠি [illegible] পেয়েছিলাম, কিন্তু তখন [illegible] তাই এত দেরিতে উত্তর দিতে হল।

[illegible]

২।

[illegible] Doppel-Gänger [illegible]

[illegible]

[illegible] Science Fiction ও Fantasy [illegible] Staples - [illegible]

[illegible] limitation আছে। [illegible]

[illegible]

# The Rest of the First Ten Years

*Pather Panchali* is the most openly, universally appealing of the three films, but *Apur Sansar*, with its more personal, romantic but controlled feeling, its perfect structure and fine, even craftsmanship, is the masterpiece of the trilogy. And no wonder, because after *Aparajito*, Ray had made two films which refined his craftsmanship further before turning to the third part of the trilogy—*Parash Pathar* and *Jalsaghar*.

*Parash Pathar* shows a poor bank clerk, pot-bellied and bold with bulging eyes and an awkward gait, who on a monsoon day, finds lying in the rain, a shining little ball which he puts in his pocket. When he gets home, tired and wet, and gives the "marble" to a boy but discovers that it turns iron into gold. He recovers it and becomes rich overnight. He goes on a taxi ride past British statues and scrap-yards which rouses bizarre visions of whole iron structures turning into gold. He acquires a secretary, servants and a mansion, makes speeches, gets invited to a cocktail party where the disdainful attitude of the big shots towards his lowly manners provokes him to demonstrate his power. This brings nemesis upon him; the party-giver demands the stone, threatening exposure to the Press unless his demand is met. Newspaper headlines threaten a financial crisis and Paresh Babu takes to his heels. But his car stalls near the Victoria Memorial, that Calcutta monument to the British Raj, and he is taken to the police station. But the police doctor finds that Paresh Babu's secretary has swallowed the philosopher's stone in order to prevent the police getting hold of it. What he finds more amazing is that the young man's metabolism is so vital that he has digested the stone. The gold lying on the police officer's desk turns back into iron. Paresh Babus sighs in great relief, and his wife's face breaks into a smile as warm as sunshine, celebrating the proverbial goodness of simple people. Ray called the film a "combination of comedy, fantasy, satire, farce and a touch of pathos".

With all its comedy, *Parash Pathar* is Ray's first foray into the contemporary urban scene. His understanding of the clerk Paresh Babu is as complete, and as fully derived from literary models as the characters of the trilogy, though not nearly as individualised. The story is one of the most timeworn, but it obstinately refuses to assume the universality of the more regional stories. It is directed more to the Bengali audience and is conceived on a less universal plane. Unlike the trilogy or *Jalsaghar*, the spoken word plays a more important part than most Ray films of this period. One of the exceptions to this is in the purple patch which dims the rest in expressiveness—the taxi ride and the walk across the scrapyard. The look on Tulsi Chakravarty's face—dazed, dreary, pathetic—is perfectly matched by the violins sounding like a thousand bees singing in unison in the poor clerk's heart at the sight of the giant iron structures which one touch of the stone in his pocket would turn into gold. As the nineteenth century cannon balls clatter on the steel sheets in the scrap-yard, we are awakened from a dream that lives secretly in all of us—the dream of the lottery ticket that pays off.

As a necesary adornment of his newly rich status, Paresh Babu of course acquires a secretary appropriately named Priyatosh Henry Biswas; appropriate because his middle, Christian, name adds a piquant touch of irony to his character as to his employers and to the ambience of the *nouveau riche* household. The emphatic enunciation of the Christian name imports a shade of the British sahib and lends an anachronistic glow to Paresh Babu's new status. Ray gives the character some individuality through his love affair carried out entirely on the telephone. We never see the girl, emphasising the secretary's redundancy and his position as an ornament for Paresh Dutt's establishment. But Ray lavishes attention upon him to emphasise his vitality which is such that he eventually digests the philosopher's stone, an achievement of no mean significance that makes the police doctor call it "amazing".

We do not identify ourselves with the character; it is someone else's dream come true; yet we share it with him, not without a shade of regret that it is not our own. The clerk turned millionaire is a lonely man.

In his anxiety to keep our attention concentrated on the middle-aged couple who form the centre of the drama, Ray dismisses the episode of love and youth in a one-sided telephone conversation. The interminable phone calls are staged with a brittle cleverness that robs the love episode of value and reduces it to mere news. The result is a certain strain against which even a competent actor like Kali Banerjee is somewhat helpless.

In fact, from this point, the film loses much of its vigour and revives only in flashes, like the bedroom scene opened by Ranibala (the wife)'s song, the morning after the cocktail party, the drive at dawn along the deserted road to capture and the scene in the police-station. These are on the same level as the opening, which shows the business centre of the city so vividly from the point of view of the pitiful clerk. The scenes of the rain, the limping return to a dim household ruled by an irate wife—here Ray is in his element, his neo-realist best. The two most difficult scenes, the first in which the philosopher's stone is introduced, and the second where the clerk's laughter turns into sobs when he discovers the effective-ness of the stone, are brought off with marvellous ease.

In contrast to these, the cocktail party, filled with celebrities of the Bengali screen and played almost impromptu, does not fulfil its grand promise. As Bansi Chandragupta, Ray's art director, remarked. "I think Satyajit has preconceived notions about the rich—their propensity for drinking, gambling etc. They appear as caricatures and types rather than people. It is this prejudice against drink that has influenced the scene." Ray's teetotaller self gets the better of his natural capacity for observation; he always avoided going to cocktail parties.

The "fall of the gold standard" scenes are pastiche. The Police doctor, oblivious of the financial aspects of the case in his obsession with science, is one of the brilliant cameos that enrich Ray's films with the warm glow that they cast on them. His affection for the character is obvious. Similarly acute and amusing is his observation of the policeman's resentment in the police station scene that instead of his worthier self, 'this silly fat old bank clerk with his ugly wife should have found the very touchstone to wealth.' The family servant is banal, ever showing the sudden pitfalls that face Ray when he tries to move from irony and gentle humour to slapstick. Yet one will always remember the scene in which the couple go through the long wait at the police-station; as the clerk explains the pitiful limits of his ambition, his pathetic, impossible desire to stop at the end of his needs, and shows his knees full of injuries received in alighting from overcrowded buses, the dialogue reaches a rare poignancy. And, finally, the film is lit up by a wonderful smile from the wife as the gold turns back into iron. It is a charming comment on the simplicity and absence of real greed in the old couple. This is quintessential Ray, expressing his sense of values through a warm, affectionate observation of human foibles.

But the film would not have been possible without the brilliant comic flair of Tulsi Chakravarty, a much underrated actor of Bengali cinema until *Parash Pathar*. He was so typecast in the so-called comic interludes of Bengali films and so ubiquitous, that no one before Ray had taken serious note of his genius. His bulging eyes, his pot-bellied figure, his bald pate, his forever open mouth and his foot-splaying walk—all of which he was well aware of and utilised to the hilt with uncanny intelligence, made him the very stuff of comedy. One of the high points of the acting comes where Paresh Babu's wife (played by veteran actress Ranibala) sings and her husband playfully goes round the bedstead with a necklace in his hand, saying with a teasing lilt: *aami debona debona mala* (I won't, won't put the garland around you—which can also mean a playful refusal to marry her). The theatrical style is evocative of stage conventions that husband and wife must have seen in their youth. The image of the fat, aged couple romancing once more as they bask in the glory of their new-found riches is unforgettable. Like many other Ray finds, Chakravarti died not so long after his performance of a life time—he had never had such a rich part to play, not even in *Pather Panchali*, where he was the village school master-cum grocer.

## II

*Jalsaghar* (1958), a marvellous evocation of dying feudalism further develops his powers taking Ray beyond the neorealist confines of his first two films, both realistic, largely location-shot, played by non-professionals. In *Jalsaghar* he takes on the studio environment with vengeance, and directed one of the most formidable personalities of the Bengali cinema— Chhabi Biswas. Here he came closer to Visconti and his fascination with actors playing aristocrats in sumptuous traditional interiors, abandoning the tenets of neo-realism. Working in Calcutta's oldest and most decrepit studio, Ray creates the period flavour and the decaying splendour of aristocracy in the vault like hall, lined with his ancestor's portraits and the music room with its chandelier in the middle which Ray uses first in the titles and later as a symbol, a key to the man. The mastery of mood and atmosphere is at its height in this film, never to be so consistently pursued in any of his other works. Indeed *Jalsaghar* is primarily a film of mood. Like Indian classical music, it establishes the dominant notes of its visual melody and rhythm through repetition and variation until it pervades the whole experience at the film. The mood is elegiac but not unmixed with irony. Ray establishes it through a variety of means. Firstly he makes this a virtually one actor film, subduing all other characters to shadows like his wife or his manager or cariacaturising them and cutting them down to size as in the character of his adversary, Mahim Ganguly, the *nouveau riche* capitalist without taste. Ray makes the man's vulgarity so obvious that it is difficult to take him seriously.

The portrait of Bishwambhar Roy is created in the very first scene on the terrace where he sits with his back to camera and, in the twilight, his servant handing him the mouthpiece of his winding waterpipe, while he asks: "Ananta, what month is this?" Ray takes a story with great dramatic potential and consistently plays down the drama and the song and dance component. One is reminded of Auguste Renoir's statement in *Renoir, My Father* by Jean Renoir:

> The hero portrayed at the moment when he is defying the enemy, or a woman, shown in the hardest pain of labour, is not a suitable subject for a great painting, though men and women who have passed through such ordeals—become great subjects when later on the artist can portray them in repose. The artist's task is not to stress this or that instant in a human being's existence, but to make comprehensible the man in his entirety.

To those who think of the cinema mainly as a vehicle of action, this concept of portraiture must be its total antithesis. The cinema shows what the camera has recorded—the surfaces of reality; the popular way is, therefore, to treat the cinema as a medium of action. But for the same reason, expressing what is behind the surface is the cinema's most important challenge, and when successfully met, its chief claim to art. To Ray, the cinema is like the Greek theatre; the action takes place off screen, while on screen, we see the reaction to it. He has seldom been really comfortable with the direct depiction of action scenes. In *Jalsaghar*, not only is the sinking of the boat not shown, but even the suggestion of it in the upturned model boat on the shelf, the insect struggling in the landlord's drink, the dead body of the boy brought in, are awkwardly achieved. What is magnificent is Bishwambhar Roy reclining on cushions in the *mehfil* or sitting on the verandah in moonlight, or watching himself in the tall mirror under the chandelier, riding to his death on his white horse.

Curiously, neither the music nor the dance scenes quite come off. Begum Akhtar's song is evocative only when heard off-screen; she never becomes a part of the whole scene. Roshan Kumari's Kathak is, as always with dance sequences in Ray, observed from a distance (a technique that has never worked except in *Shatranj ke Khilari*), with the result that her personality does not come through any more than Begum Akhtar's, and the complex traditional relationship of such characters with the zamind-ari environment is completely missed. In Tarashankar Banerjee's short story, the singer is a mistress of the zamindar; Ray takes the love interest out, thereby perhaps sacrificing something of the complexity of the story. What he gains is in concentration on the absorbing portrait of a grand obsession. Ray does not allow even the music to dominate the film even though there are twenty minutes of it, and classical music has a life of its own which asserts itself at once. He avoids close-ups of the musicians as far as possible as also quick changes of angle which would give them a strong three-dimensional presence. She becomes a somewhat shadowy figure because the *mise-en-scène* underplays her personality. He could easily have shown a young woman with the famous Akhtari Bai of Faizabad playing back for her instead, he has the great musician, ageing at the time and unprepossessing in looks, to sing herself, on camera. The purpose one can read into this is to subdue the effect of all personalities other than the zamindar's. The device also ensures that no impression of any liasion between the musician and her patron can be inferred. All other musical roles are also played by famous musicians themselves, like Salamat Ali Khan, but without bringing their personality to the fore.

His sympathy for the character is evident. In one of the most extraordinary changes he ever made from a literary original, Ray totally ignores the sudden awakening of Bishwambhar Roy's soul in the last few paragraphs of Tarashankar Banerjee's story. Ray's zamindar dies unrepentant.

Unlike his elaborate explanation of every change from the Tagore story he made in *Charulata*, Ray never said a word about the extraordinary imposition of his own will on a great literary original. Not that he was obliged to; nonetheless it was a striking departure from his normal habit of logically working out every change in the interests of his medium as well as of clarity, accessibility and a certain element of contemporisation.

In *Jalsaghar* the major change is as brutal as it is wilful. Obviously Ray saw a grander design in retaining the mulish one-dimensionality of Bishwambhar Roy till the end. Tarashankar Banerjee's ending which redeems the character, did not fit the image Ray had formed of the proud, noble but foolish aristocrat. Probably Ray's film gained in unity and in the deep impress made by the zamindar's unshaken obduracy. Even so, it would have been interesting to have Ray's explanation. No critic ever asked him for one, and he did not volunteer any.

At the end of Tarashankar Banerjee's short story, a drunken Bishwambhar Roy gets off his old horse after a long ride that has exhausted both the rider and his mount. The old man apologises to the horse saying—"it's foolish, both of you and of me".

Next he walks into the music room where, at dawn, the lights are still burning, empty bottles roll on the ground, the portraits of his ancestors staring at him and presiding over the picture of ruin.

"Struck with fear, Roy stepped back. He felt he was looking at himself in a mirror. He turned from the door and in a stricken voice cried— Ananta! Ananta!

"Ananta answered his call and rushed towards him. He had never heard his master cry out so. The moment he came, Roy shouted—'Put out the lights'. Put out the lights! Put out the lights—close the door of the music room—the music room!

"No more was heard. Only the riding crop smashed down on the door of the music room". The End.

Tarashankar's zamindar suddenly comes to his senses. Satyajit Ray's does not. In the film Bishwambhar Roy sees the lights go out one by one and takes fright. Instead of asking his servant to put out the lights, as in the story, in the film he asks why the lights were going out. To the end he clings to his illusions of glory and hurtles to his death.

Ray's ending is at once more realistic, true to type, and has tragic undertones. Perhaps he did not want to change the mood of the film so abruptly and wanted to stay with the decadence in order to emphasise the fate of the whole class of zamindars, a tribe eliminated by independent India in its anxiety to abolish feudalism.

Certain age-old but nonetheless effective symbols and devices are used to heighten the drama. The chandelier is a living symbol of an era, of the final incandescent glow of feudal aristocracy, almost of the zamindar himself. It is the visual centre of the film. The huge mirror is, as it were, a doorway into the past. The storm accompanying the music concert during which the news of drowning of his wife and child arrives is an ancient literary device, the pathetic fallacy, expertly utilised. The chandelier reflected in a glass of liquor is the luminous side of aristocratic splendour mixed with a suggestion of drowning as much as the fly fluttering its wings in the dark liquid bears the portent of death. Similarly there is the old elephant manipulating his huge bulk and the old horse, the two contrasted to the capitalist's car and lorry, new to the countryside. The decaying mansion is itself a picture of desolation, heightened by the sounds of great chunks of earth falling into the water as the notorious river Padma, known as the devourer of villages on its banks, changes its course. The faded portraits of the ancestors also bear the imprint of an obsessive doom brought about by the spendthrift ostentations of past generations. Music and dance too are photographed with a detachment that does not allow them to occupy the centre-stage and prevents us from turning our attention away from the hero for even a brief moment. If some of these symbols are simplistic, they are effective nonetheless and make for a sharp clarity in the positioning of the forces. Ray lays it all on thick and leaves his hero no route for escape. No wonder after that structure he finds it impossible to retain the original ending of the short story whose protagonist wakes up to his ruinous condition.

*The Music Room* thus becomes one of the most compelling portraits of obsession in the history of the cinema.

Marxist critics in India were quick to condemn what they saw as Ray's sympathy for the feudal lord and antipathy for the capitalist whose rise falls into the classic pattern indicating a stage of historical inevitability mapped out by their ideology and therefore the rightful claimant to the director's sympathy. They contrasted the film with his first two, both of which according to them showed an empathy with the underprivileged. Ideologues of this persuasion have for a long time been the most vocal in the intellectual ambience of Bengal. Coming just over ten years of India's Independence, and not long after the abolition of the zamindari system by the new government of India, their criticism carried a certain amount of bite. Consequently the film has not had an adequate appreciation on its home ground. Its artistry in the weaving of the spell of a mood did not make quite the mark that it could have if political correctness had not been the prime consideration of the critics.

In both *Jalsaghar* and *Parash Pathar*, Ray is trying his hand at things as different as possible from his first two films, refusing to stereotype himself as a melancholy neo-realist chronicler of poverty. Yet *Jalsaghar* is as much a story of social change as the first two films of the trilogy, and it is as the poor man that the clerk in *Parash Pathar* wins our sympathy. The clerk's home is as good an essay on urban suffering as *Pather Panchali* on the rural. The search for Indian reality and for identification with it remains alive in particular dimensions of *Parash Pathar* and *Jalsaghar*. The gains made from them, and before them, the first two parts of the trilogy, must have provided the assurance that went into the smooth flow of *Apur Sansar* and gave its controlled passion a fullness to the brim.

### III

Somewhere around the 1830's (writing in the 1930's, Prabhat Mukherjee, the author of the short story, places the action a hundred years ago), a drama, by no means unfamiliar in those times, takes place in a village in Bengal. We are in the heart of the twilight age lying between the total eclipse of Mughal glory and the flowering of the nineteenth century renaissance. The Mutiny of 1857, the last big uprising against the consolidating power of the East India Company, is yet to come. The burning of widows is still to be banned, female infanticide is a familiar occurrence, human sacrifice is by no means unknown. Religious prescriptions for marriage and the daily acts of life have reached a fearfully complex and totally meaningless state. Education, confined to an infinitesimal minority, is traditional to the point of absurdity and its concerns are inane, totally irrelevant to the state of society. Raja Rammohun Roy is campaigning for the abolition of *"Sati"*, and Pandit Ishwar Chandra Vidyasagar for the remarriage of widows. An inward-looking society fervently protects its religious identity through centuries ruled first by the Muslims then by the Christians. The shock waves of these blows against age-old practices hardly reach the recesses of the village, although they stir much debate in Hindu College, founded in 1817, by now the centre of "Young Bengal".

As in *Jalsaghar*, Chhabi Biswas plays the feudal landlord Kalikinkar masterfully and without any hint of decay. His younger son, Umaprasad is married to Daya, (played by Sharmila Tagore with unavoidable shades of Aparna upon her face and manners). Kalikankar, always a devout man, has recently lost his wife which has made him lonely and drawn him more and more to religion. He is devoted to his younger daughter-in-law who in traditional fashion comforts him by rubbing his legs, bringing him his medicines and generally looking after him and his religious rites. His son, Daya's husband, is away pursuing his somewhat unorthodox studies in Calcutta. His elder son, Tarapada is cast in the orthodox mould and follows his father blindly even though his wife is more realistic and rational in her ways. One night Kalikinkar has a dream in which Daya's face is transformed into Goddess Kali. He proclaims her a Goddess and sets her up for worship by the faithful who begin to throng the mansion. Daya seems to have cured an apparently dying child. Umaprasad tries to persuade her to escape with him to Calcutta but, assailed by self-doubts, Daya refuses to accompany him. While Umaprasad goes back to Calcutta to his studies, Daya fails to cure his elder brother's son. When Umaprasad comes back to confront his father and take away his wife, she has gone mad and disappears into a misty forest of flowers.

The period is created without recourse to the physical specifics of the times, which are, in any case, almost impossible to find; the action is staged, as it, were, in a lighted area encircled by darkness. The village is not established; its inhabitants are as distressed spirits hovering around the only reality, the landlord's mansion. The title music itself sets the tone, with heavy brass cymbals signalling doom from underneath the apparent joy of the annual ritual of worship and the immersion of the Goddess Durga. The entire film is enveloped in a Bergmanesque gloom dominated by night scenes, dark silhouettes, and deafening temple music. The style in which the atmosphere is developed and the drama unfolded itself is reminiscent of the silent cinema of the great Russian masters, full of long shots, low angles and wide angles with depth of focus, big close-ups, heavy movements and formal grouping of figures. To this is added an evocative use of sound, like the menacing echo of the old zamindar's wooden slippers as he walks down the staircase or the corridor, forever coming towards his young daughter-in-law. The howling of the jackals makes the silence eerie. Much of the style is special to *Devi* and not to be seen in other Ray films.

The newly-wed couple, Umprasad and Dayamoyee (played by Soumitra Chatterjee and Sharmila Tagore) kiss like shadows dimly perceived through white mosquito curtains, and even the shots of them in bed are overladen with a foreboding silence. Overtones of both films that preceded it are present in *Devi*; again we have the sumptuous zamindari home, evoking aspects of *Jalsaghar*, and the young husband and wife brought together and carried by fate reminiscent of *Apur Sansar*. The paterfamilias is the Chhabi Biswas of *Jalsaghar* as Kalikinkar ("servant of Kali") Ray, obsessed with the Goddess Durga (Kali) instead of the classical music and dancing of the previous film. The image of the young couple haunted by tragedy is rich with the underlay of *Apur Sansar*, the film which immediately precedes *Devi*, and is played by the same performers. Besides, Sharmila's face has the classic outlines of the traditional image of Goddess Durga, here enveloped in an intense inwardness, and entirely suitable for the aged father-in-law's Freudian dream.

The development from the scene of young Dayamoyee massaging her father-in-law's feet to his dream of the Goddess's eyes inexorably turning into the face of his son's wife is achieved with great fluency and exactness. The dream itself is one of the finest ever in the cinema, with the eyes coming forward in the darkness, the menace of the third eye in the middle (the visual concept is clearly a designer's and goes back to Ray's training in the economy of advertising techniques). Kalikinkar is convinced that the goddess appeared in his dream to tell him that she was none other than his son's wife, descended in human form. When Dayamoyee, in the midst of the weird but sincere worship of her by thousands of people, faints from sheer shock and exhaustion, old Kalikinkar bends over her face, and decides that she is in a trance. Umaprasad, taught by rationalist teachers in college, goes back to the village to rescue his wife. Secretly, they go out to the riverside, talking softly while the tall grass sways in the moonlight, reflecting the agitation in their minds behind the calm faces and the still bodies. Dayamoyee spots the skeletal image of Durga, half immersed in water, and is tormented by doubts. She goes back, turning away from the vast landscape with the escape boat shining in the distance, and closing all avenues of retreat. Torn by the conflict between her husband and her father-in-law to gain dominance over her, she goes mad and dies. When Umaprasad makes his second and more determined bid for rescue, it is too late.

In his belated confrontation with his father, Umaprasad tells him sharply: "You are not the only one who knows her, I have known her for three years. She is not a Goddess. She is a human being." The Oedipal triangle is now explicitly stated. It is sharpened by the way the scene is shot, using a wide-angle lens which emphasizes father and son's distance from each other in a very formal, alienated arrangement. The way Kalikinkar constantly addresses his young daughter-in-law as "mother", following a general custom, serves in his case as a device for deflecting and sublimating the sexual attraction which makes him elevate her to the Great Mother and thus alienate her from his son.

The moment of the son's decision to take his wife from his father is built up with exact logic with typical Ray devices. Umaprasad is at first confused to find Nibaran's son cured of his illness; he sits in the dark, thinking. At this point, a servant enters with a lamp with a large white shade and places it on a side table in big close-up. It is as if the light of reason has dawned. Umaprasad gets up from his chair, goes out with firm steps towards Dayamoyee's room.

There are interesting echoes from Ray's earlier films. Umaprasad is akin to Apu in his affiliation to Calcutta and the new education taking him farther and farther away from traditional stereotypes. The scene of the teacher advising him to assert his right against his father's wrongs recalls Apu's meeting with his headmaster in *Aparajito* at the end of which Apu comes out globe in hand and later tries to explain its mysteries to an uncomprehending Sarbajaya. Kalikinkar refers to his son as Dayamoyee's "Christian husband", because he is taught by Christian Europeans or westernised Indians. The Bengal renaissance is never far away from Ray's films of the nineteenth century Bengal. Later, in *Charulata* we are even to hear a song written by Rammohun Roy, the "Father of Modern India", at the celebration of the electoral victory of the Liberals in England.

Although *Devi* raised some protests from the orthodox and embarrassed some of the liberals as well, it does not take sides with "progress". It only shows the inexorable process of change. The superstitious zamindar is not seen as the villain of the piece; he has his own reasons and as much right to sympathy as his victim. The song in praise of Kali, written by Ray himself and sung by the poor old man (played by Mohammad Israil) sitting on the steps with his grandson, is charged with feeling, evoking all the passionate devotion it is capable of.

There are innumerable songs by the eighteenth century Bengali poet Ramprasad all set to a fixed tune. In spite of this, Ray wrote the song himself and set it to the traditional tune; for this the only motivation one can formulate is that he was trying to identify with the devotion and not judge it from the outside. Invariably this brings to mind the maxim pronounced by Gora, protagonist of the eponymous novel by Rabindranath Tagore, that no reform is possible without first identifying with the "superstitious" beliefs and the people who hold them. Kalikinkar's faith in the Goddess is shown with complete sincerity, without a hint of the falseness which would have made the attitude to the characters a polemical one. Ray's outlook here is rather more compassionate than that of the author of the story, whose idea had been suggested to Prabhat Mukherjee by Rabindranath Tagore. Being a leader of the reformist Brahmo Samaj, Tagore did not want to write it himself. It apportioned blame more than the film does. In the outcome, it is the film which gains in depth. In the literary original, Daya hangs herself; in Ray, she gets lost in the mist in a meadow of flowers, inevitably evoking Sita in the Ramayana, who at the end re-enters the earth from which she had been born.

The character of Tara Prasad, the elder son, casts an oblique light on Ray's attitude. When he comes back somewhat early in the night, his wife is surprised. She berates him on his drinking and he says: 'It's not liquor, it is *Kaaran* or Shiva's sacred drink imbibed by the sect cultivating the demonic, Dionysian aspects of Shiva, drinking and keeping the company of ghosts, roaming in the cremation ground, going into strange *Tantrik* sexual practices etc.

Ray's distaste for the Bengali mother cult underlies the film. It is a disapproval he shares with Rabindranath Tagore as opposed to Bankim Chandra Chatterjee. The Brahmo movement leaned heavily on the Vedanta which repeatedly uses the world *Purusha* (male) in the sense of the cosmic being who pervades all time and space. This perception of God almost as an abstraction, a creation of the intellect as it were, is the exact opposite of Bankim Chandra's God as mother cast in a material image, an idol true to *Puranic* Hinduism. Bankim was the first of the modern Hindu fundamentalists; Tagore was in the line of great social reformers, advocates of rationality and the intellect in which the intuitive and the instinctual was deeply embedded but never became the dominant force.

Clearly, Ray's attitude to the mother Goddess myth is tempered by his rationality. The view that underlines the films is that India lives too much by myth and too little by fact; unless a balanced interaction between the two could be restored, myth would do more harm than good.

### IV

The year 1961 marked the birth centenary of Rabindranath Tagore. Ray celebrated it with a feature as well as a long documentary. It was a homage to the mentor of a few generations of Indians, particularly Bengalis. Many of Tagore's vast mass of short stories are finely crafted, and yet have an earthiness and humanity which has endeared them to a wide readership. Often, they suffer when expanded to full-length features; the decision to treat them as short features is thus very apt.

Like *Parash Pathar*, an exercise in comedy, *Monihara*, one of the three short stories filmed in *Teen Kanya* (Three Daughters) is another attempt by Ray to test the reaches of his ability, this time in the macabre.

The story of an affluent young wife's obsession with jewellery is treated with claustrophobia and suspense. As a craftsman, Ray justifies himself well enough, but it is an area in which he has formidable competition, from the Nordic masters Carl Dreyer, Paul Wegener, Robert Wiene *et al* to latterday experts like James Whale and Alfred Hitchcock. The reading out of the story on the steps of the tank is beautifully lit and has an eeriness not fully matched by the events it describes. Neither the obsession with jewellery nor the scenes of blackmail are altogether convincing. The film serves more as a forerunner of *Charulata* in terms of treatment of interiors than as an indication of Ray's ability in a new direction. One cannot help feeling that forays into such uncharacteristic areas have not been rewarding either for Ray or for his audience. It is interesting to note that the film was sent abroad with two stories, *Monihara* being left out.

In *Postmaster*, Ray is once more in his element. The forty-minute film is full of human warmth nestling inside its brief but well-moulded form. The servant girl is like a little mother with a store of outgoing love; a tight-lipped dignity protects her soft heart form showing the hurts it sustains. The young postmaster from the city takes a casual interest in her, spends his spare time teaching her the alphabet and chatting generally. To the orphan child, unused to such attention in the midst of her hard life of child labour, it becomes a real relationship, as though she has found someone who values her. She looks after him with a singlemindedness and care that one extends only to close relatives. She is not therefore prepared for the way he gets himself transferred and abandons her without a thought. All he can think of is to give her a tip that she is too hurt to take. Such casual mobility is not part of the world she inhabits, surrounded by its bamboo groves, stagnant waters "breeding malarial mosquitoes, and a lone madman breaking the silence".

At the turn of the century, when the story takes place, the post-office is not a very old institution and, along with the railway, provides a tenuous link with the world outside. The village is a self-contained unit; relationships here are more enduring than the postmaster conceives them to be. Ray achieves the sense of the early hiatus between town and village perfectly, and contrasts the two world-views with a compassionate irony. Apu went from village to city; Nanda, the postmaster, illustrates the reverse traffic. Tagore's vision of rural Bengal is not nearly as romantic as Bibhutibhushan's. Nanda slips in the mud, shudders on seeing a snake skin, and the madman symbolises for him all the terrors of the village.

Ray changes Tagore's ending with superlative effect. In the original the little girl begs the postmaster to take her with him and he refuses. In the film, Ray prefers to use the wordless expressive power of the cinema and enhances the girl's emotional maturity by making her turn away from him in her wounded pride. His casualness, so self-evident on the screen, hurts her deeply; at that stage, for her to beg him to take her along would have been incongruous and made it unduly sentimental.

Another change from the original is no less significant. The Tagore story makes Chandana, the young girl, about twelve or thirteen, in that period a very suitable age for a girl's marriage—a fact explicitly mentioned in the text. Indeed the story makes the relationship between the girl and the postmaster an implicit and understated expression of sexual love. The film disregards this angle completely; it contemporarises the age relationship, situating it far away from the possibility of "love". Ray shifts the tension by making the postmaster compose a doggerel which declares Chandana to be "like a sister". The axis of tension is now vested in the question: "is she a servant or a sister?" which results in a tiny explosion in Chandana's heart, at the end of the film, making her turn away from the postmaster as he tries to pay her a tip. The Tagore ending is now made implicit: she had expected him to take her away from her little life stifled in the village: he wants to end his responsibility by paying her some money. Much of the poignancy at the end arises from the post-master's indifference to all the emotional trickery he had played on her in order to make him look after him well and to provide the warmth of a relationship as long as he was there. Only at the very end he realises that there had been a real human relationship between the two that will stay with him. In other words, he is not cynical, only thoughtless and emotionally somewhat irresponsible. (This question of male responsibility in creating an emotional relationship reneged afterwards comes up repeatedly in Ray's films.)

The dark, shadowy tones—there is hardly one sunlit scene in the film—the long night shots, the shabby interiors, the camera's avoidance of large open spaces that abound in rural areas, subtly convey the spiritually limiting effects of the environment in the village, so far removed from the city from which the postmaster comes, bringing something of that space with him as he sits with the local group with its discordant, outdated type of singing.

The treatment of space in *Samapti* is the opposite of *Postmaster*—wide, airy, sunny, with the river and the great tree with the swing strung from it. The rooms have large windows in them through which the nature outside is visible. Even the slushy village paths are wide and have a depth of perspective. But again, the wide windows belong only to Amulya's house and he is fresh from the city, akin to Umaprasad in *Devi* and Apu in Calcutta in *Apur Sansar*, more of a piece with 'Young Bengal' of the Hindu College than the village. However, unlike them, Amulya has no conflict with the village. His return to it, down the path leading to his village only affirms his affinity to it and connects it with the new culture developing in the city.

*Samapti*, the third and longest of the triptych, is less of a short story. Its theme of the rebellious young girl who refuses to give up her tomboy life and matures after marriage forced on her, could well have become a full-fledged film by itself. Handling it in an engagingly light vein, Ray brings to it a gentle warmth and humour unique in his work so far. At the same time, the town and country relationship is further explored, and the cultural mores of the times are evoked in Amulya's treasured portrait of Napoleon, his tartan socks, and the Oxford shoes which slip repeatedly on the village's slushy paths. The contrast between college-educated Amulya's sense of importance and uneducated Mrinmoyee's free spirit is piquant. The wedding of the two is an early instance of a young man asserting his own will in the matter of his own marriage; also his marrying a girl as grown-up as Mrinmoyee is a sign of changing mores. Amulya's choice of Mrinmoyee the tomboy, is itself unusual, apart from her age, for the girl has a will of her own and is not the obedient shadow that the bride his mother had chosen would have been. Amulya's absence awakens in Mrinmoyee a need for him and his return finds her grown from a girl to a woman. We are left with the feeling that she will keep with her something of her sense of independence and make her more of a companion than a pliant slave so common in the absoluteness of male domination in that age. Amulya had been attracted by her freedom and is not likely to try to suppress this streak in her or to succeed altogether, even if he tried. As in *Postmaster*, the characters are authentic and the rhythms of life in the village perfectly achieved. Ray's return to the rural scene since *Pather Panchali* (except for the sequences in *Aparajito*), is easy and full of charm. Free from the intensity of the trilogy, he is here at his Chekhovian best—in the two stories that are characteristic of him. Its deft lightness of touch makes *Samapti* one of his most engaging films, and complements the gentle pathos of *Postmaster*.

## V

The documentary on Tagore does not share this mood of celebration. It is a serious homage, trying hard to provide a rounded image of the poet-philosopher-composer-painter-educationist, the final outcome, and last architect, of a renaissance that had been building for over a hundred years. Ray was so directly and completely a product of the Tagore era that this film is something of a consolidation of his knowledge of himself, an acknowledgement of the tradition which his own talent was taking forward, in the classic Eliotian definition, into the new medium of the cinema. In a great melange of still photographs, live shooting of re-enacted scenes from the poet's early life, newsreel clippings, drawings, shots of landscape, paintings, songs, evocation of political events, constantly moving by means of quick dissolves and held together by a narration written and read by himself, Ray created a massive tribute, and perhaps the best biographical film yet made in India. He was able to give it the historical perspective and magnitude that such a film demands. In doing so, he made no interpretation of his own, but took the prevailing view established by scholars and commentators. This he informed with a narrative clarity and a quiet sense of reverence which is all his own without being hagiographic.

The word "Rabi", the first syllable of the poet's name, means the sun, and the setting sun is shown after shots of cremation of Rabindranath's body, attended by a huge mass of humanity live to a sense of loss. From this effective, if literal, opening, the film goes into a flashback of his life and his achievement. In his only explicit homage to the Brahmo, reform-ist-Hindu movement Ray was himself heir to, the film maker's reverence serves as an acknowledgement of his cultural patrimony. As Ben Nyce shrewdly remarks, Tagore's return home from England after giving up his studies at London University "to write operas which incorporate English music of the Gilbert and Sullivan variety and Indian classical music. This mixture of Western and Eastern cultures is a central trade-mark of Tagore's work and, one might add, of Ray's as well". It is in this respect that the Tagore documentary becomes a testament of faith, a pivotal text in the study of Ray.

"In a recreation of Tagore leading a demonstration", Ben Nyce goes on to say, "The man playing Tagore looks very much like Ray himself, and though it is not Ray, perhaps it is significant that Ray chose a look-alike to play Tagore at this moment".

One of the most succinct, most telling sections of the film is the one depicting Tagore's emergence as a painter, graduating from sketches made out of corrections in his manuscripts to strange, shadowy figurative paintings in dark colours, making him one of the progenitors of modern Indian painting, coming after Amrita Sher-Gil.

Ray never alludes to his own closeness to Tagore through his grandfather or his studies at Santiniketan. His emphasis is clearly on his homage to an omniscient objective influence that helped to create him, independently of all personal recollections and relationships. Ray makes clear in the documentary how Tagore embodied an emergent new India that avidly sought to utilise the British conduit to the Western civilization in order to modernise India and at the same time remained eventually and proudly affirmed in its Indianness. The rational and the intuitive, the modernist and the mythopoeic blend together in the best works of both Tagore and Ray and the generations of talented men and women who helped to create the dominant stream in the modern Indian outlook.

Ben Nyce argues that unlike Tagore, Ray never took upon himself the role of the educator. These are, however, some indications to the contrary Ray's satirical treatment of India's godmen, his cultivation of a scientific temper in his stories and films for children (which are at times quite didactic despite their sense of childlike fun) point to his identity with his father and grandfather both of whom were dedicated reformers, working expertly through the medium of literature for children.

## VI

*Kanchanjungha* (1962) was Ray's first colour film, the first based on his own story, first also to tackle contemporary society. *Parash Pathar* does have glimpses of Calcutta's life, but its blend of reality and fantasy sets it apart, and it can hardly be described as a comment on contemporary social mores. But like some sequences of *Parash Pathar, Kanchanjungha* also brings about a confrontation, between different classes of society. The Rai Bahadur is a slightly simplistic stereotype of the servant of British colonialism holding on to his values, and imposing them on his dependants, long after the masters have departed. His social code is also simplistic; his wife must be an obedient shadow without a will of her own; marriage in the family must be willed by him to enhance its fortunes and prestige, which are to be held above everything; he must spurn all else, even an interest in birds; it must be impossible for him to conceive of a young man who turns down the offer of a job, a daughter who turns down a suitor with money and position. This rigidity is made more brittle by the preponderance of dialogue, albeit well written. On top of this, the entire story takes place within the film's own length of the hour and forty minutes before the family's departure for the plains. Unity of time, place and action could not have been more severe. What softens all this, tones down the stiffness of the very symmetrical arrangement of relationships, is Darjeeling—its gentle tones, its interplay of sun and cloud and mist. The treatment of colour in *Kanchanjungha* is delicate and fragile; it plays a vital role, as of an invisible omnipresent character in the story, constantly colouring moods, affecting outcomes, now turning grim, now creating mystery, and the next moment breaking into a smile. Ray uses this mercurial play of nature with great deliberation, staging certain sequences in one kind of light, others in different kind, making his colour both attractive and meaningful. Had he been able to get the country house near Calcutta where the film was to have been shot as a picnic, the changing dimension of light would have been absent. Would the severe symmetry and rigidity of the story then have stifled the film?

The rather four-square story is about Indranath Chowdhury, a retired petty officer of the British Raj who is on a holiday in the hill resort of Darjeeling in a foothill of the Himalayas along with his flock, consisting of his wife, eldest daughter and her husband, his son, his younger daughter as well as his wife's brother. All the events take place in one day. Kanchanjungha is the Himalayan peak hanging magnificently over the town on a clear day but invisible on this day which is marked by subtle changes in mood reflected by the weather. Will the youngest daughter agree to wed the engineer who is courting her with her father's evident approval—is the question at the centre of the film dormant under her father's complete conviction which takes her assent as a matter of formality. Into this situation walks a young unemployed man, a bit of an intellectual who gains the respect of the girl by impulsively turning down her father's help in getting a job. The self-important relic of the Raj upsets him by his pompous speech glorifying money and power and British rule. At the end there is a casual conversation between him and the Rai Bahadur's daughter about the possibility of meeting sometime in Calcutta.

*Kanchanjungha's* light-seeming story orchestrates and encapsulates a number of conflicts; conflict between the older and the younger generation, between the British India and independent India, between male supremacy and the beginnings of feminine assertion, between the people of the hills and the plains, between the corporate executive and the dissenting youth. It plays upon these contradictions with a deftness of touch, avoiding high drama and yet waking us up to the multiple dimensions of change taking place in society and holds up all pompousness to subtle ridicule. Rai Bahadur Indranath Chowdhury, a petty title holding relic of British rule totally unaware of his irrelevance, proclaims his self-importance with the same ridiculous righteousness as the young engineer hectoring the young girl he has been encouraged to court by the girl's father about the importance of money, position and security. The girl's mother is an embodiment of woman in a totally male-dominated world. She has suffered all her life at the hands of the imperious pettiness of her husband but never even thought of divorce, which comes easily to her eldest daughter's mind. In rejecting her affluent suitor, Manisha, the younger daughter, strikes a note of defiance impossible in her mother's time. The poor little Nepali boy embodies the neglect that the hill district of West Bengal has suffered in the hands of the plainfolk who run the government, which would later fester into an unresolvable conflict alienating the hills from the plains. This was perhaps not consciously in Ray's plans but appears to have acquired a new meaning which may have been lurking somewhere at the back of his mind.

I don't remember *Kanchanjungha* being revived, even for a casual show, in Calcutta. It was shown in New York at the Ray retrospective at the Museum of Modern Art. At this and subsequent viewings, I found the film more and more captivating in its charm, its wit and its exquisite timing. The scenes of the ponderous yuppie executive assiduously wooing the young imp of a girl who seemed perpetually to slip through his confident fingers are full of sunny humour and fine observation laced with mild satire. The placement of camera and the timing of dialogue, the circular movements interacting with other circles now and then, have an inevitability about them as though nothing else was possible. The paralleling of real time and screen time added an extra dimension of authenticity. Indeed *Kanchanjungha* is one of the most enjoyable things Ray ever made outside his children's films. It has a gossamer lightness of touch and is at the same time meaningful and fully in line with his social commentary in other films. Only the divorce episode does not quite have the sureness that other scenes do. The Rai Bahadur's reduction of his wife into a non-person is tragic; her song eloquently expresses her predicament but of course its import is lost on the vainglorious husband. Similarly, her anxiety that her daughter should not suffer the same fate as her elder sister and her mother comes through delicately. The uncle forever looking for birds and the son chasing girls provide contrast to the redoubtable business at hand of the marriage arranged elaborately by the father. The film captures a certain new mood, delicate and fragile, never again seen in Ray, before or after.

## VII

*Abhijan* (1962) represents a departure in Ray's career which can only be explained in terms of his periodic urge to break out of the confines of what he is best reputed to do, and to try hand at something unfamiliar. The world of taxi drivers and smugglers and kept women as far removed from Ray's middle-class experience as anything could be.

Narsingh, the taxi driver, owns a 1930 Chrysler and runs it in a small town area of West Bengal. His ancestors had come from the distant state of Rajasthan and belonged to the warrior caste. Narsingh (Soumitra Chatterjee) tries hard to act up to his heroic antecedents, and suffers what he considers his fallen state with an aggressively stony silence. He gets involved with a smuggler who tempts him to join him as a partner in a transport company. Meanwhile, the smuggler's mistress Gulabi (Waheeda Rehman) finds herself attracted to Narsingh, who in turn falls for a Christian schoolteacher (Ruma Guha Thakurta) from a family that comes from the same town as his. She is, however, committed, against her family's wishes, to a one-legged, pious-looking son of a Christian priest, and eventually uses Narsingh, whom she considers a friend and no more, to elope with her lover. Meanwhile, Narsingh has grown used to, and fond of, the smuggler's mistress. When his ambitions of learning English from, and perhaps gaining the hand of, the Christian girl are foiled, and the smuggling activities of the merchant about to be exposed, Narsingh takes the option offered by Gulabi to go away and set up a farmstead, and finally accepts her into his life.

In Tarashankar Bandhopadhyay's novel, this story is garnished with drunken brawls and much racing and rivalry amongst the drivers—all of which Ray translates faithfully to the screen. Charu Prakash Ghosh as the smuggler and Bombay's front-rank star Waheeda Rehman as Gulabi turn in excellent performances. Gulabi's seduction scene in which she sings, dances, cries and tells her life story—all within a few minutes of long takes—is memorable. Robi Ghosh, whom we later see in a number of Ray films, is engagingly real. So are the Christian family and the group of drivers. But Ray's apprehension of the milieu and the motivations is at best incomplete, at worst extremely awkward. For the maker of the trilogy, *Devi* and *Jalsaghar*, the unsureness of motivation proves to be a great handicap. To avoid the problem, Ray goes for the externals of the action rather than the mental events, and spells out more than he suggests. The result is predictably banal; he is obviously in territory to which his talent is not suited. To compound the problem of his choice, Soumitra Chatterjee's affinity to the urban literati is so marked that to make him put on a long beard, a permanently afflicted expression and false accent is one of the most uncharacteristic casting decisions Ray ever made. It simply does not ring true, ever. Seen again today, it sticks out like a sore thumb in a row of master-works. The fact that it was followed by *Mahanagar* (1963) and *Charulata* (1964), probably indicates a conscious return to the natural character of Ray's creativity, and an acceptance of its limitations.

Ray repeatedly acknowledged the limitations of his film in conversations, some of them with the author of this book. He explained with some care that the film was to have been made by an assistant of his for whom he had written the script. But as the work progressed he was persuaded by the producer to make the film himself. This explains the simplistic nature of the treatment and its lack of "suspension in a larger context" (Kael's phrase). Conceptually, and in treatment, there is an unexpected ordinariness about the film which is hard to understand without knowing the genesis of the project. A belated and somewhat strained effort to give the basic tawdriness of the concept some significance shows through the texture of the work. To compound the problem, Ray personally knew the Bengali small town ambience even less than the rural in which he was able to build upon the abundance of literary models and his own rural experience which grew rapidly through his work. Nothing betrayed the lack of depth of exposition more than the scene of the fight between Narsingh with other taxi-drivers. The reasons for this inadequacy have been explained by hagiographic writers in terms of the physical conditions in which it was shot. But the critic is more concerned with what actually appears on the screen and it is impossible not to see in the failure of many of the scenes the basic lack of empathy with the characters and the milieu.

## VIII

Until now, the protagonists of Ray's films have been men. In the trilogy, Sarbajaya is heroic in her husband's absence; in *Apur Sansar*, Aparna becomes, for a while, the centre of Apu's existence. Nonetheless, they are shadows to their men. They do not live by their own will. The wife in *Parash Pathar* finds joy or sorrow in accordance with her husband's actions; in *Jalsaghar*, she has even less importance in herself. *Devi* finds her a plaything, an object of psychological tussle between father and son, a sacrificial victim. In *Teen Kanya*, the rich woman is abnormal, the servant girl is a little mother from childhood, caring for others, secretly hungry for affection; the tomboy submits against her will to marriage and finally embraces fulfillment in a traditional role. There is a hint of revolt in the Rai Bahadur's younger daughter in *Kanchanjungha*, perhaps in reaction to the abject humility of her mother and sister's suffering from the disastrous marriage arranged for her by the dominating father.

In his next three films, *Mahanagar* (1963), *Charulata* (1964), and the short feature *Kapurush* (1965), has a new concern with woman, not as the shadow of man, but as an individual. It is in *Mahanagar* that, for the first time, we come across a woman who awakens to the possibility of determining the course of her own life. Typically enough, the awakening touch comes from the husband, for men have traditionally liberated, just as they have enslaved, women. But traditionally too, they have retracted when they have seen the consequences of their action. It is the husband who mentions to his somewhat timid wife the possibility of her working for a while, like some acquaintance of theirs, in order to tide over certain financial difficulties. Arati rises to the challenge; with all her apparent shakiness she is strong and sincere, and makes a success of her job— success that goes a little to her head, like a first taste of champagne. With nostrils flared, she shows her money first to herself in the bathroom mirror, then to her husband. She offers some, with a conspicuous lack of grace, to her father-in-law who needs money for new spectacles, but does not approve of her working for them. It is her own sense of independence that gives her the strength to resign when her Anglo-Indian friend is eased out by the boss, actually in order to reduce his overhead, but with a show of contemptuous disapproval of the supposed immorality of all girls of that hybrid community. In the simplicity of her indignation at the slander, Arati produces the resignation letter her husband had drafted when he found her growing so independent. In the meantime he has lost his job and is trying to reach her and prevent her from resigning.

As the traditional middle-class housewife finding a new worth in herself, Madhabi Mukherjee is the perfect embodiment of the woman, torn between self-abnegation and self-respect. Even her looks are of the housewife lost in her chores who has, secretly in her somewhere, all the enticing mystery of woman. The enticing aspect is to unfold itself further in *Charulata*; but the possibility is indicated here, where Madhabi strikes the perfect note of hesitant emergence from behind the curtains of tradition. Faced with the sureness of her feelings, Anil Chatterjee, an experienced actor who plays the husband, is not quite as confident of himself.

The family life is vividly brought out, full of cross currents between its members of three generations cramped into the three rooms. The plot is complex and falls into three closely inter-related sections: there is the home, the office and the subplot of the father-in-law's doings. The film lives because its foreground action of Arati finding, doing and giving up her job is embedded in the family's life and its complex web of relationship, attitudinal and generational differences, all of which are acutely observed and take up a good deal of its length. For instance the sub-plot of the father-in-law's doings such as his awkward visits to his ex-students has an important function in the film.

The camaraderie of sales girls, developed within the privacy of the restroom and largely in their reflections in a mirror, is a first essay to be further developed later in *Ashani Sanket* (Distant Thunder, 1963). It is in the large mirror that Arati first really sees herself in a new light, as an independent person, no longer defined solely by her relationship with the men who rule her life. She embraces the female company avidly, finding in them a warm supportiveness she has not encountered before. The fact that she is drawn to a warm relationship with the Anglo-Indian girl Edith, who could not have been more different from Arati in her habitual independence (not shared by her other colleagues), is very significant. It is she who introduced her to the use of a lipstick, an event of great import for Arati in her new awareness of herself in the mirror and her nascent sense of independence. The mirror vanishes, at it were, when she resigns her job; but something of the image she had seen in it persists, and reveals itself in her sense of equal responsibility for the family, along with her husband, at the end of the film. As an essay on the emergence of the new woman in India, *Mahanagar* is a work of a very subtle and delicate perception, guided by a fine sense of identity with the female protagonist for which Ray must have summoned up feelings from the depths of androgyny within himself as an artist.

In the office relationships and ambience, the sense of camaraderie of the sales girls as they talk in the washroom and accept the leadership of the only Anglo-Indian among them and the only one with a carefree sureness about her, is very convincing. The psychological developments have a seamless organic wholeness about them.

The texture of the film is too complex to be as influenced by neo-realism as Ben Nyce has suggested in his otherwise admirable book. The relationships in *Bicycle Thief* or *Umberto D* are more linear and lyrically treated where Ray's more real and complex. But the scenes of bank failure and the beating up of the husband signal, as usual with Ray, a hesitant and gingerly handling of overt action. Calcutta, the big city after which the film is named, remains rather dimly in the background; its crowds and its tensions are far from fully communicated. The opening shot of the film showing the over head pantograph of a tramcar passing below is attractive, suggestive, but conveys the careful avoidance of actual street level reality. The office sequences, realistic enough, do not suggest the depths of cynicism, corruption, and complexity that Ray is later to master in a film like *Jana Aranya*. Technically too, it is not as evenly realised as some of his other films; the back projection in the boss's office, for instance, leaves much to be desired. The ending with its mild and charming assurance of one of the two finding a job in the vast city, is a little too four-square, a shade too glib, as a solution to a problem that is going to plague us for a long time.

Actually the ending suggests a sort of surge of optimism about the emergent Indian woman in Ray who realises anew that with all their gentle charm, traditional Indian women have a great deal of strength and resilience. They can cope better with change than their men. Ray seems to have learnt this from his exploration of Arati's mind and the unravelling of her behaviour, preparing him for his next venture into that territory in *Charulata*. In terms of chronology, Ray had thought of *Charulata* earlier, but the film came to be made after *Mahanagar*. Yet in terms of psychological progression, the second film is like a development of the first, in terms of a woman's discovery of herself.

Ray's analytical method, his ability to reveal the mental event with exactness and with few words reaches its height in *Charulata*. His method justifies the dictum that in the Indian tradition decoration and expression are not two different things but one. His craftsmanship reaches a fineness of detail which turns skill into art, quantity into quality, decoration into emotional expression. Perhaps that is a perverse way of putting it; it is the emotional rightness which translates itself into perfection of detail, transforming every little thing into a means of expressing not mere fact, but a certain tone of feeling. To turn from contemporary western cinema to *Charulata* is like shifting the scene from tall, crashing waves on high seas to reflections in the cool, clear water of a pond stirred by a pebble. If one is prepared to abstract oneself away from everything else and concentrate on the reflection, the stir within it is no less disturbing.

The story of *Charulata* takes place in 1879, at a time when the Bengal Renaissance is climbing towards its peak. Western thoughts of freedom and individuality are ruffling the age-old calm of a feudal society. Thinking men have already responded to it and set changes in motion. The liberation of woman is being talked about, but not much beyond a few cases of widow remarriage and some education, has been achieved. In Madhabi Mukherjee, Ray finds the embodiment of the Indian woman poised between tradition and modernity. Deeply intelligent, sensitive, outwardly graceful and serene, inwardly she is the kind of traditional woman whose inner seismograph catches the vibration waves reaching from outside into her seclusion. The world outside is changing, and down below in the drawing room, the victory of the Liberals in Britain is being celebrated, nineteenth century western social philosophy and Rammohun Roy's ideas are inexorably working towards the future liberation of woman.

Charulata's husband, the suited, bearded Bhupati, is inspired by the gospels of Mill and Bentham, by ideas of freedom and equality. He spends his feudal wealth and his waking hours on the propagation of these through *The Sentinel*, an enterprise which is destined to flounder by the very fact of the single-minded enthusiasm of its editor. But the winds of change are not only stirring him; unknown to herself, his good Hindu wife, conveniently childless, is no longer capable of treading the beaten path of the ideal wife who wants nothing of life but her husband's happiness. She longs for his company and is bored with his attempts to supply diversions in which he is himself not involved. One of these diversions is her husband's cousin (in Indian languages, brother and cousin are indistinguishable), who is served to her on a platter by the trusting husband as her friend, philosopher and guide. In him she finds one with whom she can share her thoughts and on whom she can bestow her affection. Slowly, inexorably, and without her knowledge, the traditionally "sweet but chaste" relationship between wife and husband's younger brother turns into one of sexual love. In his youthful narcissism, Amal encourages her to fall for him, but when his object is achieved and his ego satisfied, he flees in dread into marriage and a distant city. Bhupati, who sees in her closeness to his brother only a traditional bond of affection, suddenly comes face to face with the truth when she breaks down on receiving news of Amal after his decision to marry and go away to England, not knowing that her husband has come back into the room. Tagore's short story finds the husband departing at the end, leaving the wife to her grief. Ray opts for the more realistic solution of bringing them together again to live for ever in a state of suspended animation. Suddenly, as their hands are about to meet, their movements freeze, making their inner separation permanent, as it were.

Ray had misgivings about the subject while making the film. How would society take this "transgression?" *Devi*'s gentle pointer at the price of superstition had come to grief at the box-office; had the Freudian undertones in the father-in-law's outlook on his son's wife been widely understood, there might have been a minor riot. Indeed, there were murmurs during the making of *Charulata*; but they died down when Ray's triumph came in the enormous critical and box-office success of the film. One was not surprised either by the Catholic award at Berlin for a film on a woman's movement towards adultery or the sight of old women coming out of the theatre wiping their tears. The secret of their identification with an otherwise uncomfortable theme lay in the state of innocence of the characters caught in the web of forces greater than themselves. Their lack of conscious knowledge of what is happening inside them gives them a certain nobility; it is in their awakening that their tragedy lies. Amal, the younger man, is the first to realise the truth; for Charu it is an imperceptible movement from the unconscious to the conscious; for the husband, it is a sudden, stark, unbelievable revelation of truth. All three wake up, as it were, into the twentieth century, the age of self-consciousness. The rhythm of the unfolding is so gentle, impeccable and true that there is no sense of shock even for the conservative Indian, although Ray's film was as daring for the wider audience as Tagore's story had been in its day.

Ray's "calm without, fire within" concept of eastern art is most serene outside and smoulders most inside Charu herself; she is the only one of the three who has no crisis of conscience. Bhupati feels guilty for not having devoted enough time to her, and blames himself more than others for his predicament. Amal realises that he was about to betray the trust of his cousin and benefactor and beats a hasty retreat. Charu alone never turns back on her passion. Her eyes are tranquil and without much accent until that swing scene in which she dimly senses within her, for the first time, the onrush of a forbidden love. When Amal, in his vanity, flaunts his attraction towards Nanda, she goes beside herself in passion and her lips are drained of colour; in later scenes, as her realisation grows, the eyes go dark and her pupils shine (a clever trick of make-up and lighting), like a tigress's. In her reconciliation with her husband there is no sense of guilt, only a recognition of reality.

The film, flawless as it is throughout, yet has some purple patches that should be highlighted. The opening scene establishing Charu's loneliness is a superb example of wordless characterisation comparable to *Jalsaghar*'s. Here it is achieved by the inspired device of an opera glass. The swing scene, the *piece de resistance* of the film, lit with a Renoir-like chiaroscuro, has a minute piece of cutting which shows Charu's foot touch the ground for a split second every time to give that extra energy to the swing's movement. Then there is the moment she slows down the movement of the swing, trains her opera glass on Amal, and, with a darkening face, realises that she is falling in love with him. In Ray's style of wordless communication, it is a highwater mark. The long sequence of her recalling her childhood days has an exquisite rhythm produced by a combination of the gentle rocking of the swing with the rocking of the boat with its elaborately designed sail into which her face slowly dissolves. It is a rhythmic transition that puts us exactly in tune with Charu's mood of nostalgic remembrance which she is going to write about.

Another remarkable visual element in *Charulata*, not known for its use in contemporary Indian homes is the wallpaper. It lends a graceful texture and a rich background against which the contrast or consonance of the costumes, the furniture, the floor, the delicate tonality of black and white photography, are measured with obvious care. The decorative texture enhances the feeling of Charu as a bird in a gilded cage, a rich woman encased in a large jewel box. Perhaps it also suggests a western tinge in the mind of the very Bengali owner of the house as well as of his cousin. The victory of the Liberals in England is clelebrated with some elan; the two songs sung in the film and echoed in the background music, are derived from the west; the possibility of Amal's getting married and departing for England plays an important part in the drama of relationships.

Ray always looked for devices to relieve the uniform blankness of walls so commonplace in Bengali cinema despite the occasional break provided by a framed picture, calender or a window which often emphasis, rather than relieves, the drabness of the surroundings, even in a rich home. The lime-coated finish of most houses is hardly conducive in any way to the use of wallpaper which would dry up in summer and get damp in the monsoon, causing disfigurements. The use of the wallpaper is thus a deliberate departure from the conventions of Indian interior design in order to achieve a tonal richness.

It is the fine quality of the delineation that raises Ray's film aesthetically way above Tagore's short story, told in simple outlines. Looking at a contrasty print of the film once, I suddenly realised why it seemed unexpectedly mannered. It was because the relative absence of tones had taken away something of the visual content of each shot which now therefore seemed to linger on the screen longer than necessary. The next time I saw the film in a good print and proper projection, the feeling disappeared.

There is a passage in Tagore's short story (*Nashtanir* or *Broken Home*) which reads: "Perhaps Bhupati had the usual notion that the right to one's own wife's affection does not have to be acquired. The light of her love shines automatically, without fuel, and never goes out in the wind."

In words like these, which are interjected here and there in the story, Tagore sums up the condition of woman in a feudal society. In Ray's film, it does not take us long to see that the husband's preoccupation and the wife's boredom are merely outward instruments of plausibility which do not obscure the inner change of attitudes and aspiration in woman in a society in transition. The urge for freedom to love, the need for companionship in place of mere loyalty, the sense of being an individual being— these forces are all there underneath the play of events.

Ray had already touched upon it in *Mahanagar* and recorded the hesitant winds of change. In both films, the instrument of change is provided by an unthinking husband who takes his wife for granted and cannot see her as an individual. In *Mahanagar*, the instrument is the job which is to give Arati a brief but lingering taste of economic independence. In *Charulata*, it is the cousin who opens Charu's young mind not only to the joys of literature, but to those of a youthful companionship which she cannot have with her husband. In both, the husbands are theoretically modern, but in practice unable to foresee the consequences of their action in disturbing the status quo of their homes. Of woman's new urge for a happiness of her own making, both are blissfully unaware. But when the change comes, both husbands accept it with wisdom.

*Mahanagar* is a contemporary story, *Charulata* a period piece. Yet Ray's statement comes out with greater depth in the latter. Its miniature-painting-like images have an exquisiteness, autonomy and poise. Its rhythm never falters, and Ray's own musical score, competent and interesting in *Teen Kanya* and *Kanchanjungha*, for the first time becomes a major instrument in making the statement of his film. Its title theme (variations of which recur in the film) is derived from the melody of a composition by Tagore. The words of the song are so apt for suggesting the restlessness in Charu's mind that one would think it was the words which made Ray think of this particular derivation. Another musical tune in the film is taken from a Scottish melody which Tagore had earlier used as the basis for a song sung in the film by Amal and Charu together. It is the first Tagore motif that makes the predominant impression, like the folk melody of *Pather Panchali*.

The exquisite period flavour is Ray's own, and distinguishes the film from the story in which Tagore takes it for granted. The sunlit garden, the swing, the embroidery, the floral motifs on the doors and the walls, the horse-drawn carriage, the evocative settings created by Bansi Chandra Gupta are, however, more than exquisite decorations, they frame the action and set it at a distance—the distance of contemplation.

শ্রীযুক্ত জয়ন্তকুমার সরকার —

২২/
২/
৬৪

সবিনয় নিবেদন,

আপনার পূর্ববর্তী চিঠির সিদ্ধান্ত এতে নিন সেই
মত ফিরছিনি, তাই সময় হাতে আছে।

আপনার লেখাটি খুব সুন্দর এবং বিষয়টি
ওলা লেগেছে। সাথে সকল লেখা মাঝখানে ওতে ভালো
ইত এর মিল এমন, কোন এক সিন্ধা আমর সব বিষয়,
এ সব এই বেদনাটি ভুকে সাগরিক মোটামুটি বিষয়-
বিষয়ী হয়ে নাই ইত কোন সমস্যা নাই
বিষয়বিষয়ী এলো কিছুটা কম খুবই মাঝখানে
সুধর আগ্রহণে, এ পর মুকুট অমলা নিয়ে সমঝোতার
আসবেন — এ মুখেই আমর মতে খুব মনে একই অমলার
বিষ, এই রখা এই জনমনর মুখী মোটা খুবই এই
সকল-ওতু মধ্যকার হিন্দি নই নতুন সমস্যাকে
মূল আর এই খুবই। কোন সমঝোতা সুপাতর হিন্দি
বিষয় সম্বল।

২।

সময়গুলি এটি সমঝুত মুখ্য বিষয় সুবল লেখা মনে ঐ
সমনি এই মর মিল সমঝোতার খুবই ঐ আমর এই —
মোটার সমাজন ভীষভি তর্কিকের (বিষয়র সর্বির)
সাগরিক সমঝোত সমনি। Dokhel-Ganger (সমন
মিলানে প্রবিন্ন এই) বিষে সকল নাই এই সমল এই
সমান মিলানি।

মুখ্য মৈথিলী এই সমঝোতার নিয় সকল এই নই মর
ভুল মর সমঝোত মুলে ভুই সমঝোত মুল এই মর
শিয়ন। এই সিদ্ধান্ত সমঝোত মুলে এই সমঝোত,
এই সমল সমঝোত লোন সমঝোত মুলে সম-সমঝি এ
মুই সমন এই সমল মত মুই মরে ঐ। মর মুহি
সমল মুঝ মেঘা এই সমল সমাধানমূলক এ সম্ভব
নই হইল।

সমী এই সমল সমঝোত এই সমঝোত সমঝ মরি
মুই ও বিষয় সমঝোত সমঝোত সমন সমল এই বিষয়।
Science Fiction ও Fantasy সমঝোত সমন সমমনি এই
staples — এ সমমন সমঝি সমল সমনই মনি সমঝোত,
সুমর, সমঝোত নিম নিম এই। সমঝোত সমঝোত নম
এই। বিষয়মি সমঝোত সমমনি সমমনি সমঝোত

# Uncertainty and a New Search:
# The Period after *Charulata*

## I

Madhabi Mukherjee's eyes shine as darkly in *Kapurush* (the first story in *Kapurush-O-Mahapurush*, 1965) as they did in *Charulata*. The same central character is projected, in the same situation. She is now married to a vapid tea planter and lives in modern, instead of period, luxury, continuing her life of suspended animation in marriage to a man she does not love. Her old lover suddenly reappears by a coincidence. It is almost as if Amal of *Charulata* is reincarnated and has come back to her after she had reconciled herself to her husband. Once more, she is drawn towards him, and once more, he finds himself incapable of defying society. She, on the other hand, has become stronger with time; in the flashback of their days in college, she is the one to propose marriage, and he to shy away from it. When he sees her again by accident, he again tries, with the same casualness and male vanity as in *Charulata*, to make her fall in love with him once more. This time she is wiser; she knows how weak he is. She turns up at the station, only to see if he would be relieved to know that she is not going away with him, and realises how right she was. She merely asks him for the pack of sleeping pills she had earlier given him; then she disappears into the darkness. Madhabi Mukherjee's acting here is as firm as ever; Soumitra Chatterjee's is wooden by comparison. The film-making is also indifferent by *Charulata*'s standards. It is listless, mannered, although it still has a great deal of poignancy. The exquisite interiors of the aristocratic house have given way to a brittle, *nouveau riche* milieu. Altogether, *Kapurush* is a weak restatement of the earlier film's ending with a final rejection of the romantic lover by the wounded and wiser woman, thwarted in her search for independence. It is as a part of the series on the theme of the emerging woman that *Kapurush*'s chief interest lies. In *Mahanagar* she had found, and sought to keep, her economic independence; in *Charulata* her right to love. *Kapurush* reflects her failure to find either. It is no accident that Madhabi Mukherjee plays the woman in all these films; she has come to represent in them the middle-class Bengali woman who is taking a good look at herself, her rights, her position in a changing society. At first sight she suggests the wife next door, but soon turns out to be powerfully attractive, with great hidden reserves of strength that lead her nowhere as yet. But more than that, *Kapurush* emphasises the man's weakness and regret at being what he is in a sort of self chastisement. This theme of the male's facile effort to rouse a woman only to decamp thereafter was to surface again in *Aranyer Din Raatri*. Fear of society, the discovery of cowardice within oneself and a sense of obligation to make overtures to a woman are among the causes of abandonment of responsibility. Sanjay is totally discomfited when the lonely widow offers herself to him with frank abandon; Ashim tries to make Aparna come to terms with him sexually, but she too is aware of the casualness and irresponsibility of male overtures especially in the isolation from society that the men's holiday offers. It is almost as though she was Charu and Karuna in her previous incarnations; only the role is not played by Madhabi Mukherjee. How would it have been if she had in fact played it? One will never know, for Madhabi never appeared in any Ray film after *Kapurush*. She went on acting, and in fact some of her roles were vaguely reminiscent of *Charulata*, as in Purnendu Patrea's films, but never again in a film of Ray's.

Although overshadowed by *Charulata*, *Kapurush* has its moments. The flashback to Karuna and Amitabha's love affair is brilliantly realised with as fine a feeling for contemporary modes of sexual interaction as with the more Victorian in *Charulata*. Karuna's shadow moving back and forth in the light under her door is a fine piece of cinematic observation and signals Amitabha's keen awareness of her presence so close to him in the dead of night, and the last scene at the station is poignant; it is a great moment of lovers parting for ever, after fate had brought them together a second time.

Even after the near-sardonic ending of *Kapurush* it is difficult to accept the half-hearted and inept horseplay of *Mahapurush* (the second story of the film). Ray's irony is always telling but his sense of humour always lacked his father's genius for the delectable mix of fun and nonsense, the absurd, the sardonic, the satirical. It is more akin to the rather literary and affected humour of Tagore, ever unable to cross the barrier of self-consciousness. A gentle warmth, incidental situational humour mingling laughter and sadness, as in *Parash Pathar* or *Samapti*, would come to him with ease; but whenever he tried to be funny in action in a slapstick style, the result had a certain awkwardness and childish simplicity—the servant changing clothes repeatedly in speeded-up action in *Parash Pathar*, the would-be-bride-groom coughing up food on to grandpa's balt pate in *Samapti* are examples of this. In *Mahapurush* he simply failed to match the magnificent verbal slapstick of Rajshekhar Bose, Bengal's other great humourist besides Ray's father. Bose could invariably conjure up a magical contrast of the ponderous and the down-to-earth, at the same time charging it with satire or sardonic humour with an ease that Ray could never equal. Usually, Ray's films turned out to be improvements on their literary originals, even of writers like Tagore, Bibhutibhushan or Tarashankar; in Rajshekhar Bose, particularly in the *Mahapurush* type of direct and forceful belly-laugh story, he meets his Waterloo.

    *Mahapurush* marks the beginning of a low point that Ray was to reach in *Chidiakhana* (1967), a phase of spiritual exhaustion after a series of magnificent and masterly works. It is as if he had finished all he had to say. Except for a mildly charming sequence around a supposed old film song as a clue in the detective story, *Chidiakhana* is hardly recognisable as a Ray film, almost in any respect.

## II

But before reaching the nadir of his career, Ray made *Nayak* (1966), from a story he himself wrote and with Uttam Kumar, Bengal's talented matinee idol, as its hero. Like *Kanchanjungha*, he again creates a highly symmetrical, tight and four-square framework. The entire action takes place during the hero's one-night train ride to Delhi to collect an award for a performance. Uttam Kumar, an actor of considerable intelligence, sophistication and popularity, is, as it were, playing himself. Sharmila Tagore, who later became a big star of the all-India Hindi film, plays her own opposite number, a journalist who interviews the film star, while travelling on the same train. Although a bespectacled highbrow, some-what contemptuous of popular film stars, Aditi Sen Gupta is induced to interview him by her fellow travelling friends, who are thrilled to find themselves in such glamorous company. At first returning her contempt with its kind, Arindam Mukherjee, the alcoholic and insomniac actor who comes face to face with his dreaded self every night, volunteers the interview and is charmed by the interviewer's freshness. She too is attracted by the human core revealed from behind his brash exterior. But the train reaches its destination too soon, and the young interviewer, having extracted highly personal revelations from the star, tears up her notes. She has discovered a vulnerable and attractive human being, and has no wish to run an exposé of his private problems in her magazine. Arindam's personal life is pieced together expertly through the interview, seven flashbacks, two dream sequences, and brief encounters with fellow passengers—all with their little side stories.

*Nayak* has a strong similarity to *Kanchanjungha*. The glamour of the mountain is replaced by that of the film star, almost as legendary in relation to the characters in the film and the audience seeing it. The place, instead of Darjeeling, is the train, both isolating the characters from everyday life and bringing them together for a brief while. The isolation, in both cases, helps to bring their personal problems to the surface. In place of the colour and the constant changes of light, there is the perpetual motion of the train, with its fascinating, ever-changing sounds, as the extra dimension.

The film is structured and developed with much skill. It has a pace as brisk as the speeding train on which its action takes place. The sense of timing and the ear for sound are superb. The illusion of the train is perfectly created in an almost completely studio-bound film. The visuals are less delicate, more firmly etched. There is nothing decorative, and the whole feeling is refreshingly "modern"—the shooting has new elements too, in the camera's swing back and forth between the star and the interviewer in the dining car, the trains crossing in the night, the shining railway track speeding past while the hero has thoughts of suicide, the endless stare of the sick girl from the upper berth.

It is in turning the hero from a type to an individual that Ray reveals, behind the expert craftsmanship, the inner emptiness which appears to plague him in this period. The individual whom he tries to reveal in the star-type of Arindam Mukherjee is even more typical than the exterior of his personality. The alcoholism, the death wish, the guilt over deserting the purer art of the theatre and the early leftist links, are all more or less part of the popular mythology of the film star. The ingredients are made up of the predictable and the commonplace; there is no personal vision. The two dream sequences are banal exercises in pop psychology. They are not Arindam's dreams; they are what his public thinks he ought to dream. From the beefcake poster to the popular postmortems of Marilyn Monroe, the full spectrum of already-existing reactions to stardom is here, laid for one, defying the discovery of one trait that one had not suspected. Alongside the star, there are some of the other typical products of our times—the brash advertising executive, the globe-trotting business-man, the throat-spraying, perfume-splashing salesman of religion. As usual, these types are well observed and brilliantly cast; the cameos of their relationships—as between the ad-man and his wife, the sick child and its mother, both fascinated by the film star, the husband and wife who are friends of Aditi—are expertly etched and have moments of warmth (although the ad-man's use of his wife's charms is overdrawn). But they do not rescue the film from its brittleness, due to the lack of a warm personal understanding of the central character; the matinee idol is a type that Ray does not like, and he cannot overcome this barrier. He is a little like the Rai Bahadur of *Kanchanjungha*, representing values that his maker does not approve of. In the best of his earlier work, Ray dealt with people to whom he is naturally drawn or for whom he feels compassion and can, therefore, see from inside. In *Nayak* he seems to concern himself rather more with externals, and to try to invest them with a meaning they do not fully express.

However, in *Kanchanjungha* he had made us laugh good-naturedly at the pompous Rai Bahadur, at the same time making him completely believable. In *Nayak* the problem is that Ray wants to make the matinee idol both laughable and sympathetic and the man ends up being neither. The effort to explore the character below the surface is falsified by cliches. Only in the attitude of the fans towards their star does Ray's observation sight its targets perfectly; the star himself is unable to fathom as a human being except in his relationship with the young journalist which he develops with a fine mix of understated understanding and ambiguity. Ray himself never understood why western critics rejected the film. He told me just after the showing at the Berlin film festival: "They don't like us making films on contemporary subjects"—a misgiving that was proven wrong with *Days and Nights* and the three city films that were to follow. At the festival (1966) Ray was given an award for the totality of his work and not for *Nayak*. It had embarrassed his admirers after the glowing achievements of *Mahanagar* and *Charulata*, both of which had won the Best Director Award at Berlin.

It is important to note here that *Nayak* was the last film in which Ray worked with Subrata Mitra as his cameraman. After the parting of their ways, it must be acknowledged, Ray's films never achieved that opalescence of photography, although it continued to be not only acceptable but good.

### III

Along with *Mahapurush*, *Chidiakhana* (1967) is a film that one must find difficult to accept as Ray's work. It was to have been directed by an assistant of Ray's but he had to take it up due to pressure from the producer. As noted earlier, it moves on an entirely commonplace, average-Bengali-film level, except for one sequence. If *Nayak* has a commonplace core behind its brilliant craftsmanship and aspects of humanity, certainly what follows it is devoid of them. *Chidiakhana* is a signal of an arid season in Ray's creative evolution. Perhaps he took on the simple detective story as an escape and, having done so, could not summon the creative energy to make anything of it (compare the charm of *Joi Baba Felunath*, made in 1978, also a crime story). For ten years he had turned out outstanding films of some moment, socially, emotionally, formally. Some of them, like the trilogy, *Jalsaghar*, *Devi*, *Mahanagar* and *Charulata* are master-works of the cinema. A certain inner glow had lit up the earlier films; suddenly , it seemed to have dimmed.

But what Ray faced in the period after *Charulata* was more than spiritual emptiness and exhaustion. It became clear that his universal vision was an extension of a pre-Independence outlook shaped by the Indian renaissance. He was the great chronicler of social change over a canvas of more than a century; he saw it whole because he saw it from a distance. But the distance also kept him away from the immediate reality of things, particularly in contemporary society. To quote from my own writing (*Sight and Sound*, Winter 1966-67):

> The Calcutta of the burning trams, the communal riots, refugees, unemployment, rising prices, and food shortages, does not exist in Ray's films. Although he lives in this city, there is no correspondence between him and the "poetry of anguish" which has dominated Bengali literature for the last ten years.

This complaint grew from a murmur to some stridency as time went by. *Kapurush-O-Mahapurush* was dismissed as inconsequential; *Nayak* was seen to be a concession to the box-office, and *Chidiakhana* as unworthy of comment. Certain groups in Bengal and elsewhere began to see a more living immediacy in the work of Ritwik Ghatak. His *Ajantrik* (1958), with its very (compared to *Abhijan's*) credible taxi driver, *Meghe Dhaka Tara* (1960), with its poignant picture of life among refugees from East Pakistan and the loud cry at its end: "I want to live," and finally *Subarnarekha* (1965) with its forceful directness and its bitter irony of the fallen revolutionaries, had made a profound impression on the Bengali mind. As Ray's inspiration flagged, vociferous claims were made to build up Ghatak as the greater figure representing the true future of Bengali cinema. Ghatak had little standing abroad, where Ray's seemed to grow, on the strength of his earlier films, rather more than at home. Mrinal Sen came into the limelight in the all-India scene with *Bhuvan Shome* (1969), in Hindi, his love affair with the French *nouvelle vague* finally yielding a style markedly different from Satyajit Ray's.

How far all this affected Ray is difficult to say, and useless to speculate.

After *Pather Panchali* and *Aparajito*, Ray had turned to the comedy of *Parash Pathar* and the atmospherics of *Jalsaghar*. Both films were outstanding in their ways, but could be seen as lighter exercises than *Apur Sansar* and *Devi*. But the young Satyajit was then cutting his teeth on different material, to test his powers. One might say that, having found out his own predilection, he then stayed with them faithfully in the period upto *Charulata*. All the films have evident social significance, bear clearly a humanist outlook (with the possible exception of *Monihara*, which was his first and only exercise in the macabre), and are marked in the seriousness of their intent. They engaged all of his being, as it were, and in their own different ways, are fiercely uncompromising. All this appeared suddenly to go slack, and threaten his very future as a great film-maker.

In 1961, four years before *Kapurush-O-Mahapurush*, Satyajit, at the height of his glory, had decided to revive *Sandesh*, the famous children's magazine founded by his grandfather and continued by his father until his death. Generations of Bengalis had been brought up on this magazine, written largely by the editors and other members of the Ray family and richly illustrated by them, mainly Upendrakishore and Sukumar Ray. Indeed the family had for generations contributed richly to children's literature in writing, illustration as well as publication, achieving high standards of creativity in all the three. Satyajit Ray probably stumbled on the idea of breaking out of what looked like an impasse by turning to the family heritage. Himself an accomplished draughtsman with illustrations of many children's books (including an abridged version of *Pather Panchali*) to his credit, there seemed no reason why he should not direct the great tradition into the cinema. It could well become a refuge, an earthy material to touch Atlas-fashion in order to revive the inspiration when it flagged, or to wait for it to return, as far as weighty problems of the adult world were concerned.

The result was *Goopi Gyne Bagha Byne* (1968), based on a delightful fantasy by Upendrakishore Roy Chowdhury.

In the world of children, the values that Ray derived from an earlier world made up of Tagorean ideals, had not been altogether lost. Ray's films for children have the innocence and integrity of being that his earlier films about adults celebrated. The absence of self-consciousness is perhaps the common trait of Apu and Paresh Babu, Bishwambhar Roy and Kalikinkar Roy, Arati and Charulata. They are wrapped up in their being, like children and animals, totally true to their respective destinies. The only monsters we meet in the children's stories are fairy-tale ones. Ray's children's films have a secret core of joy, a Mozartian Magic Flute quality in which the children are little Papagenoes, unimpressed by evil, which is a cloud that only makes the sun shine brighter. They are in tune with the human warmth and grace that are probably the deepest characteristics of Ray's work and never get altogether lost even in his least consequential exercises.

Adults in Bengal, baffled devotees of *Hamlet* more than of *Midsummer Night's Dream*, were not sure what to think; but children loved *Goopi Gyne Bagha Byne*.

Kanu Kyne's son Goopi's great ambition is to be a singer, but he does not have a voice. Egged on by neighbours, he tries to sing to the local king but ends up by being expelled from the village on a donkey. In a jungle he meets Bagha, the drummer, who has suffered the same fate. The two strike up a friendship which is strengthened by their encounter with a tiger. As night descends on the forest, the image goes into negative, ghosts come out dancing under the trees, black, shadowy figures hovering around in a grey darkness. Then, out of an advancing star with flashing lights emerges the king of the ghosts, and a weird dance starts. Black on white, white on black are varied with optical effects. The groups represent the British, the Indian rulers, Indian people, priests of various religions, who fight—the British and the Indians fight, the Indians fight among themselves, and are arranged in strata, as their movement ceases. The ghost king is pleased with Goopi and Bagha and gives them three boons they want: the two should merely clap each other's hands to get any food, travel anywhere, and they will be master musicians. They meet a group of musicians going for a contest to the land of Shundi. They instantly go there and, of course, win the contest. The good king of Shundi has a brother who is the king of neighbouring Halla, but a wicked general has turned brother against brother by keeping the king of Halla on certain drugs which make him aggressive, the drugs being made by an evil magician. Goopi and Bagha, through their tricks, foil the general's plans, re-unite the brothers and marry their only daughters.

The first half of the film is highly inventive, the dance of the ghosts being the high watermark which provides a lesson in Indian history along with its visual and aural thrills. The sets and costumes are brilliantly designed and succeed to some extent to compensate for the lack of colour, which Ray wanted but could not manage financially. The songs are brilliantly written, composed (by Ray) and sung, and both the film and its songs are a favourite with Bengali children, who love seeing it and hearing its songs again and again. Tapen Chatterjee as Goopi and Robi Ghosh as Bagha bring an irresistible simplicity and charm to their roles. Shot partly in Rajasthan, it brings, like all Ray's films for children, a sampling of people of different places and kind and habits. But the film runs out of inventions after some time and loses some of its interest when it gets down to plain story-telling. It promises the constant addition of new dimensions which cease to come forth. In spite of this, and the rather obvious anti-war sentiment, it adds up to a wealth of entertainment which, as always, adults enjoy as much as children. It is Ray's best children's film, inventive and joyous; it is a pity that it could not be made in colour (except for the last scene).

IV

By the time Ray began a search for a new understanding, a new identity, in the adult world, the seventies had begun. In 1969, when *Aranyer Din Ratri* was made, the adult world in Bengal was up in flames. "The Calcutta of the burning trams," never seen in Ray's work, had turned into a conflagration. Murders were taking place everyday, pipe guns and bombs were common sights and sounds, seething discontent among the youth was manifest in the Naxalite movement which many of the best university students joined. It was necessary to understand, not only this new phenomenon, but the sea-change that had taken place in the new generation, now well past the residual glories of the Bengal Renaissance, and impatient with them anyway.

Such understanding does not come easy, and Ray was in no hurry. As usual with him he began, not with the Naxalities, but just a sample of the older younger generation in its least politicized state and in an earlier point of time. Four young men set out to escape the monotony of Calcutta and land up in a tribal area. They travel in the car belonging to the more affluent and sophisticated Ashim (played by Soumitra Chatterjee), bribe their way into the government forest house that they have not booked. Nearby, there is the holiday residence of a prosperous old man from Calcutta who is staying there with his daughter Aparna (Sharmila Tagore) and daughter-in-law (Kaberi Bose), who is a widow. The women are attractive in different ways: the daughter is slim, beautiful, petite, the daughter-in-law bigger built, with large features and a sexy languor about her. Ashim is soon attracted to Aparna and the daughter-in-law to Sanjay, the tall, shy and laconic member of the group. One of them is an easygoing sportsman who eyes and finally buys the favours of a tribal girl (Simi Garewal) in a stereotypification of tribal women that evoked protest. It is only the clownish Shekhar who fawns on all but is left out of the mating game. There is much drinking and merrymaking at a tribal joint and civilised conversation at the neighbour's house. As the mating game progresses, it brings about the moment of truth for each character; Ashim is attracted to Aparna but discovers that she has a greater depth than he had suspected and to develop the relationship will require a growth of his own personality; Sanjay, who goes along thoughtlessly with the young widow, finds himself too weak and disconcerted when she offers herself to him simply and without pretence. The sportsman, Hari, succeeds in buying the favours of the tribal girl and has sex with her in the forest, only to be beaten up afterwards by the man, also a tribal, whom they had earlier hired, and fired, as their factotum. It is the clown, Shekhar, always uninvolved but hovering around, who escapes unscathed from the encounter with self that the isolation of the forest imposes on the city-bred group.

For the three who make the encounter, the lesson is of responsibility for their action. Their "unauthorised" occupation of the rest-house through bribery gets the caretaker into trouble; they know the possibility, but do not care. Since it will happen, if it does, only after they are gone, their consciences will remain untroubled. Even Ashim, least irresponsible and most perceptive of the lot, knew about it but had not cared to find out how ill the caretaker's wife was. In the midst of his emission of delicate signals of his attraction towards her, Aparna asks him how he is, and he confesses that because he had known something was wrong, he had not pursued the enquiry. Responsibility also sits heavy on Sanjay, who had realised that the young widow, hungry for love, was falling for him, but he had done nothing to warn her off, and does nothing when, as the outcome of a growing proximity he had listlessly encouraged, she offers herself to him. The sportsman recklessly pursues his prey, finally buying her into submission, and pays for it. The forest has brought out their true selves, and made them face much they did not know or, knowing, had not faced up to before. Their knowledge of each other and finally of themselves is gradually intensified, and the web of attractions and disillusionments beautifully woven.

But the lesson in responsibility is the least part of the enjoyment of *Aranyer Din Ratri*. In every way so different from *Charulata*, it has the same perfection of structure and a musical rhythm, with melodic themes, varied repetitions and resonance, exactness of progression. The form of the film is in many ways reminiscent of Jean Renoir's *Rules of the Game* especially in investing and following the fortunes of a set of characters of virtually equal importance. To the Indian, especially the Bengali intellectual, content easily separates itself from form and he seldom sees structure and observation of detail to be as essential to art as its content; his favourite Bergman is *The Seventh Seal* and he has little time for the magic charm of *Smiles of A Summer Night*. When it was first released *Aranyer Din Ratri* was dismissed by many as trivial. It is not Ray, but his audience, that often proves too literary. His brick by brick building is as perfect here as it was in *Charulata*. Its rhythm is more varied, each character bringing his own style and pace of movement, emphasising the casual and disparate nature of the group, its lack of internal bonds, despite the characteristics shared.

Like the house in *Charulata*, the forest is a character in *Aranyer Din Ratri*. Indeed, Ray has always needed an inanimate character as a silent participant, sometimes to provide the pathetic fallacy as well; the village in *Pather Panchali*, Benares in *Aparajito*, the railway track and the forest in *Apur Sansar*, the mansion in *Jalsaghar*, the mountain in *Kanchanjungha*, the train in *Nayak* and so on. Later, when making films against the background of Calcutta, this is to cause him problems, as in *Pratidwandi*. But of that later.

In *Aranyer Din Ratri*, perhaps also in many of the later films, the quality of Ray's relationship to his content is profoundly changed. Behind *Charulata*'s formal beauty there was an intense apprehension of character. With Charu, and Bhupati in particular, there was a passionate identification. The characters, especially of Charu, were seen completely from inside. *Aranyer Din Ratri* shows a colder although as thorough, analysis of its protagonists. They are, like the hero of *Nayak*, foreign to the Tagore-Bibhutibhushan-Tarashankar typology, and Ray's effort in these post-*Charulata* films is not to express his passionate identification with them, but to try to understand them in order to relate to them or discover his relationship with them. It is a new search for identity with the post-Independence generation which does not share with him the full value of the Indian renaissance, perhaps not even its mildest resonance. The factors that determine the character of this generation are new and require a new understanding. Perhaps this is why he had to take it out of its normal setting, making, as it were, a laboratory analysis. However, the women are distinctly more real than the men in *Aranyer Din Ratri*; Aparna has a greater sense of reality and responsibility; the young widow has a certain animal sureness, although she is emotionally so vulnerable.

In the films from *Aranyer Din Ratri* onwards, with the exception of the fantasy of *Goopi Gyne Bagha Byne* and the children's stories, there is a progress in the effort and the understanding. But all understanding is not love, and the film does not escape a certain coldness. The new search for understanding, and identification, does not bring forth quite the human warmth that the earlier did, when the Brahmo found his rapport with Apu in his Hindu priestly duties in *Aparajito* or Kalikinkar in his religious obsession in *Devi*.

২২/৩/৮৪

[illegible] সমীপেষু —

সবিনয় নিবেদন,

[illegible]

[illegible]

২।

[illegible] Doppel-Gänger [illegible]

[illegible]

[illegible] Science Fiction ও Fantasy [illegible] staples [illegible]

[illegible]

# Grappling with Contemporary Reality

## I

Ray attempts a more direct approach to the problem in *Pratidwandi* (1970), again from a story by the contemporary novelist Sunil Gangopadhyay.

In the early 1970's Calcutta's increasingly volatile politics built up a critical mass and threatened to explode. That in the end the city did not destroy itself proved its infinite capacity for survival, for preserving its inner care of delicacy. Communist extremism had taken hold of the best minds among the students, "the flower of Bengali youth" the urge to destroy the citadels of the middle class, the greatest betrayers of the revolution, burst forth into murder and mayhem and police brutality on a scale that changed the feel of the city forever. Every street corner carried menace. Murders in broad daylight, bomb explosions, took place everywhere with impunity and erupted with a suddenness that instilled fear in every heart. But the film makers, like everyone else, kept working despite the threats and interruptions that were visited upon them. Ray faced up to the Calcutta of the burning trams, the angry political processions, the agonies of the unemployed—for the first time in his film making career.

The film opens with pre-title shots, in negative, of Siddhartha's father's death, the transportation and the cremation of the body. As Siddhartha (Dhritiman Chatterjee) stands by the side of the burning body, the negative image turns to positive and the titles appear. In what must be one in a series of unsuccessful interviews for a job, the hero make a somewhat impassioned reference to the courage of the Vietnamese and this does not endear him to his prospective employers. His good-looking sister (Krishna Bose) has a job in which she spends such a lot of time with her boss after office hours that his wife comes to the house one day and gives the family a piece of her mind. Siddhartha has an argument with his sister when she returns home but defends her to his mother, and goes off to the boss's house in order to teach him a lesson. But Siddhartha is so hesitant and embarassed himself that the visit fails to have any effect on the boss. A communist leader known to Siddhartha suggests that he should take up a medical representative's job in a small town in West Bengal, but the thought of leaving Calcutta horrifies him and he finds the leader a bore anyway. His brother (Raja Roy), tight-lipped political-minded young man, and a very good student, has turned Naxalite (left extremist). His friend (Kalyan Chatterjee) from the medical college induces him to go to see a nurse who makes some money on the side as a prostitute, but Siddhartha runs away from the scene in nervous embarrassment. As he wanders off, he comes across a girl (Joysree Roy) whom he had known slightly before, and over the next few weeks, finds himself in love with her—a love she reciprocates. The girl's mother is dead, and the father is going to marry her aunt, much to her disgust. Towards the end of the film, Siddhartha goes to another interview for a job, where he, along with hundreds of others, is kept waiting for hours in intolerable conditions in spite of protests. When one of the candidates is taken ill, Siddhartha bursts into the interview room and overturns the table, loudly protesting against the inhumanity of the interviewers. He then takes the medical salesman's job and lands up at a small town hotel to be greeted by the ritual cries of a party carrying a dead body for cremation—*Ram nam sat hai!* (Glory to Lord Rama).

For this fell encounter with contemporary urban reality, Ray chose the story of Siddhartha, in whom we rediscover the mind of Apu, sensitive and delicate and made for the life of the imagination (Apu's father, let us not forget, was a poet, elated by the slightest praise of his work even in the midst of his hardships). Ray forces Siddhartha to encounter every-thing that is contrary and demeaning to his temperament—greed, lust, brutality, injustice, violence, humiliation—with none of which he has been trained to grapple. The world has no use for his gentleness, his capacity for love, for flights of the imagination, for his longing for peace; what it requires of him is violence, competition, musclepower, ruthless-ness, cunning. He knows he does not have these in him and his spirit is cowed down, it withdraws into its shell with hurt even before his joust has begun. He is not incapable of anger, as the interview scene shows; suddenly he comes out of his shell to attack, even as he knows its futility. Yet he never really arrives at the centre of the stage to play his part; he skirts around it, senses his failure in a context that is not his, and withdraws to escape into the birdsong of a dim past and into a peace of doubtful value for which he has had to pay an unfair price. For even in his withdrawal he must give up on his potential (whose presence he has always sensed within him) and everything within him that would have been of value in a better, more just, society. It is the poignancy of this denial that lies at the heart of Ray's *Pratidwandi*.

Significant in the treatment is the lack of Ray's customary use of participating background to interact with the human predicament: the village and Benares in the trilogy, the house in *Charulata*, the mountain in *Kanchanjungha*, the train in *Nayak* and so on. There is a half-hearted attempt to create the background of a living city which does not quite succeed (success is to come later, in *Jana Aranya*). As a result, the characters and incidents, compared to Ray's other films, *Aranyer Din Ratri* for instance, seem to drift indeterminately in a rather undefined environment reflecting the protagonist's distaste for it. Ray's first attempt to explore the seamy side of the city in the visit to the nurse-prostitute is very well realised but Siddhartha's character is conceived as a hesitant in-between without either the nobility of Apu or the determination of Somnath in *Jana Aranya*. His sister's commitment to her amorality is quite firm, and so is the medical student friend's and the brother's Naxalite. Siddhartha himself has lost his innocence but chosen not to acquire the capacity to tolerate, not to speak of embracing, evil.

Thus Siddhartha is meaningful in showing the transition from the Apu inheritance, residual traits of whose moral goodness and contemplative nature are present in its latterday version in a colder, harsher world. It is a very real transition in Bengali middle-class society brought up on Tagore and a dream world of truth and universality conceived in the island of beauty and culture at Santiniketan, belied more and more in contemporary post-Independence India. Ray himself refers to this residue of a bygone world by repeated flashbacks to Siddhartha's childhood days in the country with his brother and sister, whose lost togetherness is rather simplistically and somewhat awkwardly symbolised by the call of a particular bird. The flashbacks to the latterday Apu and Durga convey no warmth and are altogether too abrupt to integrate with the rest.

The interview at the end shows Ray's characteristic talent in structuring an event and a state of mind. The slow build-up of the impatience and the final explosion of anger are perfectly realised, and the image of the skeletons waiting for their interviewer is memorable. Likewise, the closeness between Siddhartha and his girl-friend is carefully developed and credible; the girl has a freshness and charm and the suggestion of a saddened innocence about her. In contrast, the meeting with the sister's boss is poorly conceived. One has only to think of the landlord's visit to Apu in *Apur Sansar* to realise the curious vagueness of the scene in *Pratidwandi*.

*Pratidwandi* has more of a charming, rambling quality than the films that precede and succeed it. Although there is a dénouement, it is not the sole reason for the existence of all that goes before it, as later in *Jana Aranya*. We have time to be fascinated by the charm of the girl who calls Siddhartha in when the fuse has blown; the way they meet is itself full of a gentleness that belongs to an older world. The camera swings slowly from one end of the terrace to the other and back again with her walking while the sky is rent by the voice of the political orator coming through a vast public address system below. As Siddhartha and the girl emerge from the top of the skyscraper, slanting sunlight frames them in a moment of ineffable sadness and charm which has no "dramatic" meaning. The boy and the girl seem to feel that they belong to a private world, far removed from the crowd stirring below. These aspects of *Pratidwandi* seem to carry resonances of Ray's earlier films, even though the nostalgic but abrupt flashbacks to the bird songs of a happy childhood that we have not seen, seem somewhat mannered devices to create script balance.

*Pratidwandi* marks many firsts in Ray' career. For the first time, he uses what, in rather acrimonious public debates with Mrinal Sen, he had earlier condemned as "gimmicks." The film opens in negative, and goes into it at many other points, notably where the nurse-prostitute is about to take off her bra. There are sudden, brief flashbacks to Siddhartha's medical education; for instance, when a well-endowed girl crosses the street, there is a cut to a medical diagram of the female breast, together with a technical explanation by a teacher. There are flash-forwards of wish-fulfilment scenes, such as of Siddhartha beating up his sister's boss. It is as if Ray is out to prove that when it comes to gimmicks, he can invent them just as well as anyone else, perhaps better. It is worth noting that they are never again in evidence in Ray's later films, including the ones built around the predicament of Calcutta's youth—*Seemabaddha* (1971) and *Jana Aranya* (1975). Even in *Shatranj-ke-Khilari* (1977) where Ray orchestrates a wealth of situations and devices—the animation sequence on Lord Dalhousie's swallowing of Cherries, the black humour in the visit to a dying man's house in search of his chess set, the farce in the discovery of a lover in the wife's bedroom, the rare overtness in the attempted sex scene—the *Pratidwandi* kind of "escape" hatches are not used. They represent a turning away from confrontation with ugly or "unchaste" reality that goes very well with Siddhartha's inability to take a clear stand, unlike his successful sister or his idealist brother.

*Pratidwandi* was released virtually alongside Mrinal Sen's *Interview*. Both dealt with the problem of the educated unemployed among middle-class Bengalis. Partisanship of their respective admirers ran high, often divided according to political affiliations, the radicals favouring Sen's treatment, and criticising the weaknesses of the Ray hero and his escape from the battle-front. Sen's film has a certain youthful freshness and vigour and perhaps a greater sense of overt affinity with its protagonist; but in retrospect, despite its obvious faults, and its uncharacteristic gimmicks, the Ray film emerges as the more serious in tone and has greater integrity. The strongly built final interview helps to reinforce its reality, and the vacillations of its hero seem true to a stage in the social evolution of the more sensitive sections of the educated middle class. His defeat seems to have more reality and substance than the defiant gesture of Sen's protagonist. In the event, both heroes are proven weak; one in his retreat, the other in the fruitlessness of his defiance. The Sen hero throws a stone at the store window housing a tailor's dummy; Ray's Siddhartha upturns the interviewer's table, perhaps an act of greater courage, but equally fruitless in the outcome. Sen expresses his own attitude more forcefully, where Ray remains the chronicler of the times, a firm but quiet believer in the worth of the individual human being and his integrity as the basics of social good.

In the next year, Ray turns, in a more clinical, well-structured, clearly integrated narrative, from the employee to the employer. Except for the misty glimpse in *Kanchanjungha*, and the comical cocktail party in *Parash Pathar*, his first essay on affluent contemporary society is in *Seemabaddha* (1971). It is the story of an ambitious young executive, Shyamalendu (Barun Chanda), well educated and suave, who is willing to trade his moral and cultural values for a seat on the Board of Directors. His company has a valuable order for the supply of ceiling fans to Iraq but runs into a manufacturing defect which there is no time to correct without attracting severe penalties. Alongside the tensions of resolving this problem arrives another—in the comely shape of his sister-in-law Tutul (Sharmila Tagore), whom Shyamalendu soon begins to prefer to his attractive wife Dolan (Paramita Chowdhury). Tutul had always admired him and now is attracted to him all the more. She belongs to Shyamalendu's earlier, less affluent milieu and is as attracted by his personality as she is repelled by his ambition and the ways of his jet-set crowd. Shyamalendu is elevated to the Board when, with the help of his Personnel Officer and his agent-provocateurs, he is able to provoke labour trouble and declare a lock-out, thus buying time on the contract and escaping its penalty clause. After being whisked for a while from club to race course to cocktail party, Tutul observes how firmly Shyamalendu's mind is set on the rat race, and leaves.

The film opens where *Pratidwandi* had opened and closed: with the unemployed. Over shouts of them thronging the street and cars passing in front of them, Shyamalendu's first person introduction records his satisfaction with the act that he is not one of them. A biographical introduction shows how, one rainy day, a thoroughly drenched postal peon delivered his appointment letter for an executive job in Hindustan Peters, makers, among other things, of fans. Promptly he got married, moved into a high-rise apartment and started playing boss-cultivating golf. Ray describes his position in the company with documentary precision, including information in split-screen, an organisation chart and inset shots of his bosses and himself. The circle in which he is inset grows bigger and we find him sitting inside a moving car driven by a chauffeur. Telephones ring and car horns honk over the small typographic titles, with a roughly played flute introducing a touch of music.

Telling strokes sketch in the atmosphere. A decrepit old director who invariably sleeps at Board meetings recounts his prowess in refusing to pass Field Marshal Auchinleck's bill for travelling expenses for a long time and finally signing it on high-level intervention. The English, however, are so civilised that Auchinleck never held it against him. Shyamalendu keeps himself informed of his workers' temper through a young man for whom he finds a job among them. We are taken on Cook's tour of high life in Calcutta and see an advertising film on fans with Shyamalendu and his advertising agency discussing it. He tells his sister-in-law of his problem in the office, but not his wife. During the cocktail party at his flat, his parents arrive unannounced, and are led through it, without introduction to the guests, into a bedroom where husband and wife take turns to leave the party and converse with them. When a guard at the factory is injured by a bomb thrown by agent-provocateurs, Shyamalendu promptly visits him in the hospital; swathed in bandages, the guard tries to sit up and salute him. The cold, suave cynicism and the machinations behind the polite smiles are brought out to perfection. Shyamalendu speaks chaste Bengali with his fellow Bengalis and good, clean English with others without any affectations in accent. There is nothing simplistic about him, nor about the set-up in which he operates. There is little that they do without fully knowing what they are doing. So much so, that Shyamalendu enjoys, and is attracted to, the reminiscences of his student life that Tutul's idealistic innocence brings. It amuses him that Tutul should remark on his annual salary as equal to what Rabindranath Tagore had received as the Nobel Prize.

With all his perfection of structure and detail, Ray's distaste for the affluent, phony ambience is such that he is unable to summon up a little warmth even for the innocence of Tutul and the little drama between her and her brother-in-law. Played with a rather self-conscious gentleness by Sharmila Tagore (as also in *Aranyer Din Ratri*), her acting is excessively aligned to Barun Chanda's in its controlled coldness. The only one who reveals the person behind the role he plays is the Personnel Officer (Ajoy Bannerjee); the rest present dead fronts, pieces in Ray's jig-saw puzzle that, at the end of the film, fit so perfectly. Gone are the days when the persecutor and the persecuted were both objects of compassion; here both are regarded with indifference, if not distaste. There are villains aplenty, even if they have their reasons, making it one of his less readily attractive films.

Nonetheless, there is a fascinated, microscopic examination of the characters and relationships carried out with much subtlety. Very probably what Ray saw in Shankar's short novel of the same name about a young upwardly mobile executive rising out of the ashes of an intellectual and student of Shakespeare, is an interesting set of dichotomies. On the one hand there is the outstanding student's dilemma of pursuing his intellectual abilities and his desire to achieve money, power and a kind of social prestige; on the other there is the typical, alignment of intellect with a left-of-centre political attitude up against an anti-labour stance considered mandatory in a yuppie. A moral polarity between intellectual pursuits and success through trade and industry is posed repeatedly by Ray except late in his career in *Shakha Proshakha* where the honest business man is contrasted to the dishonest. In between, there is *Jana Aranya* which highlights the compromise with evil that a sensitive young man (another incarnation of Apu) must face in order to achieve even moderate success as a businessman. This somewhat simplistic stereotype is transformed by Ray into very subtle shades of progression in which the protagonist veers away from the life of the imagination to the harsh realism of commerce in which two women represent the two moral poles—the wife who wants a life of comfort and the sister-in-law who values an intellectual-artistic life above material success. Tutul, the sister-in-law, is fascinated, even attracted at times to this "boxwallah" (Indian executive in British firm) life style and has an unspoken relationship, entirely in the sphere of the mind, with her yumpic brother-in-law; yet she is never dislodged from her basic anchoring in a different value world. If she is attracted to him, it is because she sees other possibilities in him than the, to her, rather crass one he has chosen. This accounts for the silent give and take between the two which Ben Nyce analyses with much finesse.

As a matter of fact in Shankar's short novel, Tutul, the sister-in-law, gets selected for the Indian Administrative Service, the highest administrative cadre, and embraces a 'life style' very similar to her brother-in-law's, thus wiping out the polarity between her world and his. Ray rejects this ending: the poles remain apart, despite the fascination each feels towards the other caused by the very fact of the difference between them.

II

Ray's next significant work was a documentary on his erstwhile teacher at Santiniketan, the painter Binode Bihari Mukhopadhyay, who continued to paint ever after he went blind. In the 20-minute space-regulation of the Governmental documentary, *The Inner Eye* (1972) marshals the major facts of the painter's life and work with Ray's characteristic thoroughness and clarity, without sentimentalising his blindness. As a result the build-up of facts becomes moving when we arrive at the blind phase and see the painter moving around the house, making his own tea, and working all by himself without the use of his eyes.

Ray avoids pontificating about Binode Behari's style of painting, the influences on him, his revolutionary differences from the revivalist and idealist trends of the "Bengal School" and several other aspects of his work as a painter on which commentary would be relevant. As in his film on Tagore, he is content to show what he has seen and to let his audience savour the flow of the film, the vision placed before it and to draw its own conclusions. As always, he wrote and narrated the film himself with characteristic detachment. Alongside the Tagore film, it is his best documentary, a genre of which he was not overly fond. His rich voice and his firm English accent (which never stressed the purely phonetic aspect with over-enunciated dipthongs, and always sounded perfectly natural) helped the credibility of the films. The writing was invariably objective and not opinionated, allowing the subject to come through in a transparent manner. Perhaps this is why the films worked best when they were subtly imbued with respect as in the case of Tagore and of Binode Behari.

Ray had for a long time wanted to film Bibhutibhushan Bandyopadhyay's novel *Asani Sanket*, dealing with the man-made famine of 1943. Perhaps the idea had come to him during the severe drought of 1967, which had claimed innumerable lives. In 1943, millions had died while the harvest was good and the food plentiful: a mystery few of those who died for the lack of it were able to fathom. All the food they had produced was taken away to feed the British army and they saw little of it. They never understood how it went or where. In hordes they trekked to

Calcutta, begging from door to door; they died without raising a hand at the people who had everything. They stood before food shops and did not loot them. They just died on the streets, like flies. All this neither the novelist nor the film-maker dealt with. The thunder they heard was a distant one. Bibhutibhushan saw an age-old way of life crumbling before the cynicism that hunger brings. A Brahmin priest (very sensitively portrayed by Soumitra Chatterjee), typically ruled at once by his intellect and his greed, savouring every good thing in life—plenty of well-cooked food, a sexually appetising wife—scrounges on his devout clients and lives happily enough on the outcome. Suddenly, portents of change begin to appear. Food goes scarce, the women begin to gather edible roots that they normally spurned, sleep with strangers for a kilo of rice; unknown to her husband the priest's wife is raped by one of the strangers who have appeared out of nowhere and are hovering around the village. Events are seen from the point of view of the village-folk who do not know who or what is causing this bizarre problem of shortages in the midst of plenty. Vaguely they hear of fighting in Singapore, without knowing where that city is or what connection the war being fought there has with the rising prices they encounter. The *modus operandi* of those who spirit away the grain is as unclear to the audience as it is to the villagers. In one last Brahmin-feeding ritual, at a time when food is already beginning to get scarce, Gangacharan (our priest) finds it hard to eat the delicacies thinking of his starving wife. Soon after this, hell breaks loose. The rice-dealer who has loads of it stashed away will not sell it to the villagers (obviously because he will sell it at a much higher price to the war authorities and one large-scale operation is more convenient to him). In the resulting riot, the Brahmin's soft skin gets bruised. With a shock he realises, suddenly, that the fact that he is a Brahmin and a priest has no value; his livelihood has vanished into the thin air, along with an age-old tradition of reverence for his kind in all circumstances. The Brahmin's person is no longer inviolable.

In the mounting famine, it is an outcast who dies first, with a casualness matched by the indifference of passers-by. Gangacharan's wife is pregnant; to compound the problem, another Brahmin whom they have occasionally fed—one who is denied the good looks, the elegant mud hut and the beautiful wife of his fellow priest—lands up with a number of dependents. This too, Gangacharan accepts with good grace. But then grey hordes of humanity appear on the horizon marching towards their death. Over this apocalyptic vision, a title tells us of the number of people who had died in 1943: five million.

In the years since *Charulata*, this is Ray's first period film. It is also Ray's return to the rural scene, and is marked by a surprising sureness of touch. Surprising because there must have been somewhere deep down, a need to be different from *Pather Panchali* which, apart from two stories in *Teen Kanya*, had been his only rural film in the years from 1955 to 1973. In that context, it is possible to see *Postmaster* as an exquisite but all-too-brief exercise in which the village is never established, and the villagers are only a part of the local colour that surrounds the main protagonists, the servant girl and the postmaster from the city. Along with *Samapti*, it is concerned with showing the predicament of the city-bred in the village situation and is not a film of rural people, seen from the inside as *Pather Panchali* was. So *Asani Sanket*, postponed many times before it was finally undertaken, was Ray's first substantive return to the Bengali village scene, burdened with the fearful problem of achieving the reality of *Pather Panchali* without the benefit of the primitive passion of the "first fine careless rapture".

Ray adroitly avoids the problem of comparison with the earlier work by opting for colour and by a change of context. Unlike in *Pather Panchali*, he goes in for vast shots of the landscape laden with dark clouds, taken with a wide-angle lens; it helps to create the canvas that would take in the traditional Bengali village and the invisible international forces that bring about the famine. In this, as in the use of lush colour, Ray seeks a contrast between the bounty of nature and the terror of man-made famine. The "distant thunder" of the title frees him from the need to confront the action required in depicting the terrors of famine. But the combination of the palpability of colour and the "distant" thunder of the suggested famine tends to reduce the impact of the tragedy. Nature and the people are brought into a more living presence by the way in which heightened rather than muted colour is used; in contrast with this, the famine, seen from a distance, does not impinge sufficiently on the consciousness, and the severity and mordant irony of the contrast that Ray seeks does not materialise. The moral burden placed on that last shot of approaching people turning into grey hordes is a little excessive, too preciously conceived to have the impact that the title tries to reinforce. It is not sufficient by itself, to convey the cruel irony of contrast with a lush nature. The problem comes precisely because Ray raises the expectation of an indictment, raising the threshold of the tragedy himself from the individual to the social-political plane, at which his ending becomes a little half-hearted, almost an afterthought. Had he stayed with an intense observation of the individual tragedy, leaving it to the audience to infer the social statement, the film would perhaps have been more characteristic of himself.

But this rather schematic evaluation of the ending tells us little of the extraordinarily living presence of the characters or the sense of reality of the change that comes about in them and their society. If one is prepared to forget the famine as such or the device used for a great pay-off in terms of indictment, one begins to see the film's real strengths.

*Asani Sanket* shows more of the village and its life on a much larger-scale than any of Ray's previous rural films. Every scene rings true, including the ones with overt action, such as the clashes between the grain merchant and his customers. The pitiful helplessness of the villagers suddenly hit by an invisible enemy comes through tragically. The camaraderie and the immense strength in adversity that the women display is extraordinary, and strikes a new dimension in Ray's work although there is an inkling of it in *Mahanagar*.

The women here know that the menfolk can't feed either themselves or them, that they have been totally defeated by circumstances and have no reserves of strength to rely on. The women fend for themselves, forage for food, protect one another, even kill a rapist totally in secret. Both the attempted rape and the killing are conveyed more by suggestion—especially brilliant in the killing with blood flowing down the stream alongside them. Not a word about this is whispered to a living soul, least of all the husbands. One of the women gives herself to a (rather melodramatically) disfigured man—something the others know but will never mention. What is more, the women are observed in their rich sensuous presence in a manner never seen before or after in Ray's work. They are as beautiful as the lush nature around them and have the same secret will and power to survive. Not once do they appear as helpless and vulnerable as the men.

In Gangacharan, the handsome young Brahmin with a beautiful wife, we see the age-old Brahmin idyll broken to pieces by forces of change which had actually been gathering power for a long time but are suddenly unleashed by the prospect of famine. The last full meal Gangacharan has on his journeying around for rice which had been earlier so easy to get, sets the limit beyond which traditional reverence for the Brahmin is not going to be of any help. The Brahmin in Gangacharan wakes up to the reality of a change capable of wiping out caste distinctions and levelling all. At the end, totally unmindful of the prohibition against touching a low caste woman Moti, whom they have fed before from a non-polluting distance, Gangacharan holds up her wrist in big close-up to see if she still lives. Convinced that she is dead, he slowly lowers the hand and lets go of it. It is an act that would have been unthinkable in normal times. But something in him is changed, for normal times in the sense in which he has known them, safely divided amongst caste and class, is not going to come back again, not fully anyway. The prospect of famine has, in a way, changed everything.

The visual beauty of the film had put off many at the time of the release of the film; Ray had thrown too many things unexpected from him at his audiences for them to cope with the film. Seen today, the beauty of the film is poignant with humanity.

By now, the situation in the Bengali cinema, changing for some time, had begun to indicate the difficulty of satisfying the urbane audience with black and white films, especially if it was not the strictly commercial variety, loaded with song and sentimentality. The all-India film in Hindi, made in Bombay, had made such inroads into the Bengali audience with its colour spectacles that good black and white cinema was well on its way out. Hardly any new talents had emerged since the halcyon days of the late fifties and sixties which had borne high hope of an up-swing in creative cinema led by Ray, Sen and Ghatak. The year 1974 saw the making of Ritwik Ghatak's last complete feature film, *Jukti Tarko Gappo*, two years before his premature death. Only Purnendu Patrea had made some claim to distinction with his *Strir Patra*.

Ray returned to children's cinema, this time in colour and detective fiction in place of fantasy, with *Sonar Kella* (1974). A young boy who remembers the location of his previous birth in which he was the son of a jewel cutter, becomes the target of hunters for secret treasure, whose machinations are foiled by Ray's Poirot, Pradosh Mitter (Soumitra Chatterjee), his adolescent assistant, Tapash (Siddhartha Chatterjee) and their inseparable companion, the crime-fiction writer Lal Mohan Ganguly (Santosh Dutta). As usual, Ray's story (written by himself; by now he is a prolific writer of such stories), takes the character on a tour of some parts of India, and plants general educational material all along the way, rather more than his father and grandfather did. There is an admission of the possibility of reincarnation, quite a concession for a rationalist to make. But the suspense of detection never becomes too intense; everything flows at a fairly even rhythm, a childlike charm, simplicity and sense of fun taking precedence over twists of plot and technical subtlety. Not only violence but even shock cuts are studiously avoided. The result is as agreeable if not absorbing to children as it is to adults. The warmth now relatively lacking in his films about the adult world seems to have taken refuge in the world of children. Not only the warmth, but the values as well—values that he cherished but were disappearing fast from the environment around—were now finding a haven in the children's films.

The next year saw the making of *Jana Aranya* (1975), marking Ray's return to the urban scene, and continuing the rather unfinished business of *Pratidwandi* and *Seemabaddha*. In the meantime, Calcutta has changed. The bombs and the terror of political murder are gone; but the quality of life has gone down further; prices and unemployment, are up, and there is little hope for a better social order left in the educated middle class. Political stability in the absence of better prospects of unemployment has brought in its wake some amount of despondency and apathy; idealist enthusiasms have led nowhere, and are giving way to cynicism.

Somnath (newcomer Pradip Mukherjee) lives with his elder brother and his wife and his retired father. His examination results come out; he has passed, but without the honours which he was certain to win. There has been obvious negligence on the part of the examiners, and his father (Satya Banerjee) fumes in protest, but Somnath's elder brother (Dipankar Dey), as always, mocks these old-world expectations of rectitude. There is nothing to be gained by protest; things are as they are and the sooner one accepts them and gets on with whatever can be done in self-interest, the better. Somnath, applying for job after job, soon gets converted to this philosophy. His despondency and cynicism are helped by his girl-friend's marriage within her higher social strata, for she can no longer resist the pressures of her family and wait for Somnath to get established in life. He meets an old acquaintance (played by Utpal Dutt) who is in business, and willing to help the young man to do something on his own. He becomes a middleman, buying from one and selling to another, and has some success on a small scale. The crunch comes when a bigger deal, which would really launch him on a career, requires the provision of a shapely female for a sex-obsessed client. Somnath faces the choice of either yielding to his moral revulsion or losing his career. Egged on by a "public relations agent" who is experienced in such manoeuvres, Somnath chooses the latter. At the last moment he finds that the girl he is offering to the client is his erstwhile best friend's sister. She does not shy away from the situation; her resolve firms up his. As he goes back home and announces he has got the contract, his father remarks that hard work is still rewarded. Only his sister-in-law (Lili Chakravarty), self-effacing mother to the three men, knows that he has paid some unknown but enormous price for that success.

Somnath is almost a re-incarnation of Siddhartha of *Pratidwandi*. The very first page of Shankar's novel of the same name has the protagonist in the middle of a traffic mess in Calcutta made up of the wild movements of slow and fast traffic and a mass of humanity trying to make a progress that seems impossible to achieve. As Somnath, participant and observer, looks on, he thinks of the city as a prehistoric, sick dinosaur driven out of his safe habitat and groaning, caught in the vast web of Calcutta. "Had it been a few years ago, Somnath would have later written a poem from his notes and read it out to Tapati (the girl he loves). But poetry has departed from his life". Despite his obviously contemplative bend of mind, Somnath has no time for poetry, for he is busy looking for a prostitute he must procure for a client from whom he needs an order for office supplies. He is unable to achieve this by himself, and is waiting for a "public relations officer" who is adept at such manoeuvres and will help him out of his predicament. The novel flashes back from this point, to explore the transformation of the poet into a procurer, a pimp.

Obviously, Somnath has slid a much longer way down the moral path than Siddhartha of *Pratidwandi,* the literary original of which had been written by another writer, Sunil Gngopadhyay. But in the two novels, Ray saw a process of further decline of his archetypal character, Apu. Characteristically, Ray rejects the flashback, and goes for a straight, chronological unfolding climaxed by Somnath's success in finding a girl for his client and the first notable success in his business.

Ray's repeated effort, from *Aranyer Din Ratri* onwards, to come to terms with the new post-Tagore, post-Independence generation, carried on in *Seemabaddha* and *Pratidwandi,* reaches its peak in *Jana Aranya.* There is now a determined attempt to come face to face with the reality of the times, without hesitation or obliqueness. For the first time, Calcutta comes to life. Its grime and dirt are established with the very first shot. The camera tracks down the city's narrow by-lanes laden with their *pan* and *lassi* stands and their little ramshackle shops huddling together. The crowds are seen, not from above as in *Pratidwandi,* but at eye-level. Power keeps going off, telephones do not work, exams are a farce. There is a veritable Cook's tour of the call-girl establishments as Somnath and his public relations agent go in search of one for his client; each visit is brought off with subtle variations and with greater cynicism than in *Pratidwandi.* In both, an innocent is inducted into the mysteries of an underworld of sex; but in *Jana Aranya,* it is not a youthful yet morally ambivalent desire for initiation into sex, it is instead a cold decision to use it for making money. Neither Somnath nor his P.R. expert want any of the girls for himself—indeed the thought does not enter their heads. The unemployed has become as hard-headed as *Seemabaddha's* employer. Somnath's hesitations stem more from his inexperience than his lack of decision. His innocence does not have a chance to be shocked; it turns straightaway into full-scale corruption. He has realised that there is no other way. Each one must fend for himself as best as he can.

*Jana Aranya* epitomizes not only the mood of the seventies, but the failure of earlier values celebrated in so many of Ray's films. The moral centre of the film is the father, from whose point of view the values are seen. Even father's attempts to discuss the need for a higher set of values are dismissed by his elder son with an abruptness that hurts him, and shocks his daughter-in-law by its thoughtlessness. When an acquaintance calls with an offer of marriage for Somnath, with a string of benefits attached, the father dutifully informs his son, but is relieved when he refuses. He wants to call for Somnath's examination paper and have it re-examined, only to be assured that the examiners will not admit their error. He does not know what the film-maker has told us; that the examiner could not read the paper for lack of his neighbour's spectacles, because the neighbour was out of town (we are not told that it is Somnath's paper that he reads perfunctorily, with tired eyes; but the inference for the particular case is obvious). He keeps insisting that protest and moral sense should prevail, but this only sets up a communication barrier with his sons. At the precise moment that Somnath takes the vital decision to arrange a woman for his client, Ray cuts to the father, sitting in candlelight in the absence of electricity, and a Tagore song issues out of the radio like the voice of doom, saying "Darkness is gathering over the forest". Tagore never wrote the song for such a context; but in Ray's juxtaposition it acquires a shattering impact. Significantly, it is not a young person (the boy throwing a stone in the last shot of Shyam Benegal's *Ankur*, the young man in Sen's *Interview*, the boy at the end of Ghatak's *Ajaantrik*), but the old man who protests and refuses to give up hope. Ray, whose work shone with faith in his earlier films, sees in the present an erosion of the values that made life meaningful to him. Pauline Kael shrewdly compared Ashim in *Aranyer Din Ratri* to a corrupted Apu; indeed all urban heroes in Ray's contemporary films are—Siddhartha in *Pratidwandi*, Shyamalendu in *Seemabadha*, Somnath in *Jana Aranya*— in their different ways. They are all intellectuals in their mental make-up, introspective in nature. They are latter-day Brahmins, and the residue of their privileged inheritance has not been wiped out altogether. Somnath's associates in his business environment are wiling to help him because they are attracted by his innocence and his good looks, his cultured, soft-spoken, introspective personality. Yet this also invests them, wily as they are, with some humanity.

The film has a brisk pace, unlike *Pratidwandi* which is somewhat discursive in comparison. Its structure, too, is more carefully built up, brick by brick, towards the shattering climax at the end. The situations and relationships are sketched in, one by one; so painstakingly that the audience wonders why Ray is taking so long over it. Suddenly, from the point where Somnath slips on the banana peel and meets the businessman, the film begins to gather speed, and then takes off. Everything over which Ray had taken time now begins to pay off. Everything except the episode with Somnath's girl-friend (Aparna Sen). Unlike the rest of the film, this scene never rings true. It is schematic, fitted into the structure because a certain weight was necessary in the direction of his personal affections to balance the preoccupation with career in the rest. It had to be done and got over with. Almost every other scene comes off, including the delightful one of Mrs Ganguly (Padma Devi) presiding over her menagerie of call girls. And the technique, with its harder lighting, hand-held shooting, trucking along crowded lanes, fits. Taking a lift with the client, Somnath repeatedly closes the glove compartment which falls open, revealing the picture of a semi-nude girl. When Somnath comes home after making sure of his contract, his dark shadow from a light outside enters first. No film of Ray has an equal sense of the complexity and depth of evil as *Jana Aranya*, his most important statement since *Charulata*, and the peak of his new search for understanding, the peak also of his three city films examining the world of business and employment.

After the major effort of *Jana Aranya* in 1975, the only film Ray made in 1976 was a half-hour documentary on the famous prima ballerina of Bharatanatyam, Balasaraswati, then 59 years old. Like *The Inner Eye*, this film portrays an artist past the prime. What the eyes are to the painter, youth is to the dancer. The tragedy of the performing artist is instantly revealed in the limpid eyes of the dancer as she is making up before a mirror, and Ray's voice says something like this: "Balasaraswati is now 59 years old. She still dances. This evening, she is making up to dance the *varnam*, the most complex form in the repertoire of Bharatanatyam." With that he cuts to photographs of Bala in her youth, and traces her career, rising to fulfillment as the greatest exponent of Bharatanatyam acclaimed in India and abroad. It is a fine moment in the film. Some of the dances themselves, however, leave one a little dismayed. The rendering of the *padam* "*Krishnani begani baro*" is staged on a beach, with the obvious intent of suggesting something cosmic in the vast expanse of the sea and sky behind. But the effect does not quite come off because of the difficulty of dancing on sand and the wind running away with the dancer's sari. Similarly, Ray's usual style of filming the dance, in the final *varnam*, from one set-up without change of distance or angle, purist as it is, fails to realise the values of a three-dimensional experience in a two-dimensional medium. The dancer's age compounds the problem. One is reminded of the curiously flat dance and (on camera) singing in *Jalsaghar*.

It is in *Shatranj ke Khilari* (1977) that the technique succeeds, perhaps because Shashwati is a younger dancer and Ray is not as rigid with an unmoving camera. The dance is extraordinarily beautiful, its fragile charm perfectly setting off the fall of India's last Mughal ruler. The Nawab's minister has just returned from a meeting with British resident, General Outram (played with great assurance and a sense of guilt-laden history by Richard Attenborough), who has demanded that the Nawab of Oudh surrender his Mughal crown to the British. Finding the Nawab thus occupied, the courteous minister, on the verge of breaking into tears, watches the exquisite movements of the youthful dancer, the rich, soft voice of Birju Maharaj providing the perfect accompaniment. There is nothing depraved, contrary to the fulminations of General Outram, in the music and the dancing. It is in perfect taste. Only the time is wrong. The forces of history are too great for the Nawab. He is by nature a poet, a learned and cultivated man, a connoisseur of things of beauty. He is intelligent enough to know that he was not born to set right what had gone wrong over several decades, perhaps a whole century, in the sunset of the Mughal empire.

Ray had for years resisted offers of making films in Hindi, a language he did not know, whose unfamiliarity would hardly suit his *auteur* style of film-making. So far there had not been one line of dialogue in his films that had not been written by himself. Now there was going to be. Partly driven by the need to work in colour already discussed, partly perhaps by the attraction of the period setting and the largeness of the canvas, Ray accepted to make a film not merely in Hindi, but in the exquisite Urdu of the Lucknow of Nawab Wajid Ali Shah.

*Shatranj-Ke-Khilari* forms a unique event, a landmark, in Ray's oeuvre. For the first time he has a literary original by a nationally famous writer in a language he does not know, which presents him with the barest of outlines, which he must fill in himself in order to make a film of acceptable length and substance. He has done so before, enriching a literary narrative with plenty of detail, something that comes naturally to him, but here he must construct the story itself almost completely.

He meticulously recreates the interiors of Lucknow, Muslim mansions, bringing to life their elegant, frivolous denizens with the perfection of Mughal miniatures, whose colours and designs he evokes with great skill. Very often the narrative engages us so that we do not realise the fineness and the richness of the period texture laid before us.

In doing so, he alters even the thin story line given by Premchand, with marked freedom. In the original, the two noblemen actually watch the British take away their ruler and turn back to play chess and finally shoot each other, instead of the British. The irony is heavy, the contrasts are rough and broad. Premchand clearly condemns and satirises the regime of the Nawab. Ray introduces much subtlety; the irony is gentle, the force and the black humour are all clothed in the elegance of a long and rich tradition. The two noblemen only see the British army enter in procession, in the distance, like a long row of toys moving forward against the sky. The nobles do have a quarrel and one of them does shoot, but the shot only grazes the other's skin. The grandeur of the British entry is avoided: it is never shown in close up and is infact reduced to a mere historical fact. It is the tragic elegance of the nobles and of the court that remains with us. Ray relies less on the original's succession of events and more on Premchand's own description of the age of decadence sketched by the writer in the opening paragraphs:

> It was the age of Nawab Wajid Ali Shah, and his capital, Lucknow was steeped in subtle shades of decadence and bliss. Affluent and poor, young and old, everyone was in the mood to celebrate and enjoy themselves. Some held delightful parties while others sought ecstasy in the opium pipe. All of life was charged with a kind of inebriated madness. Politics, poetry and literature, craft and industry, trade and exchange, all were tinged with unabashed self-indulgence. State officials drank wine. Poets were lost in the carnal world of kisses and embraces. Artisans experimented with lace and embroidery designs. Swordsmen used their energies in partridge and quail fights, while ordinary people indulged in the new fashion for rouge and mascara, and bought fresh concoctions of perfume and pomade. In fact the whole kingdom was shackled to sensuality, and in everyone's eyes there was the glow of intoxication caused by the goblet and the wine flask. About the rest of the world, the advances and inventions which knowledge and learning were making, how western powers were capturing areas of land and sea, no one had the slightest idea. They cared only for the quail fights and the bets being laid while partridges parried and thrust in the ring. "Chausar" a kind of Monopoly, was played with great zest— people endlessly discussed manoeuvres and counter-manoeuvres, and great games of chess. Whole armies were lost and won but only on the chessboard.

Clearly Ray's film maintains much greater distance from the narrative than does Premchand, whose condemnation of Wajid Ali Shah's regime is far more absolute than Ray's perception of the inevitable tragedy. His detractors obviously had not read the Premchand original when they charged him with being pro-British.

Much has been made of the effeminacy of the men, including the Nawab's. However, as Premchand's opening tells us so clearly, it is the decadence of the late Mughals, their inability to stand up against the British not only in Lucknow but almost everywhere, that makes their men act and appear in an "effeminate" manner. The equation of effeminacy with decadence is itself a Western construct; the business of ruling a territory and people is too serious to get mixed up with art and culture which are by themselves somewhat "effeminate" occupations. The image of the artist as a weak man dies hard. That cultural leadership is something that a ruler can offer his people was inconceivable to the British. But it is not, to Satyajit Ray. The dance sequence (with Sashwati Sen as the dancer) is the most exquisite passage in the whole film leading us into the very heart of the culture at its most refined. That the king's minister (Victor Banerjee) has to wait to give his master the worst news of his life until the dance is over itself signifies the respect given to the cultural event at hand.*

There was superficial indications to the contrary, to subsume Ray into the British point of view on effeminacy. There is the heavy metaphor of Mirza's impotence and Mir's cuckoldry. There is also the demonstration of the strength of woman in the Queen Mother's proud and aristocratic reprimand of Outram, a mere servant of the alien ruler, citing the perfidy of the British:

Outram: I have come to you, Beghum Sahiba, because I know I can trust you to give your son good counsel, as you have done in the past.

Beghum Aulea (from behind curtain):

What if Begum Sahiba were to advise her son to order his troops to take up arms against the British forces?

And again, later:

Resident Sahib, how can I ask someone to sign a treaty which I myself do not understand? Wajid Ali Shah was enthroned with the full consent of the Company Bahadur. If he proved to be a bad ruler, why did the company not do something about it? Why did it not guide him to correct the administration? Why this sudden drastic step after ten years?

And further down:

| | |
|---|---|
| Aulea: | Is not the Governor-General a servant of the Company? |
| Outram: | Yes he is! |
| Aulea: | Is he also not a servant of the Queen of England? |
| Outram: | Yes |
| Aulea: | Does the Queen of England realise how her servant is treating His Majesty...... Resident Sahib, tell the Governor-General we do not want money. We want justice. If the Queen's servant cannot give us justice, we shall go to the Queen herself and ask for it. |

---

\* See Ashis Nandy, *The Savage Freud and Other Essays,* Oxford University Press, 1995, for a discussion of the issue of effeminacy. Nandy appears to over-emphasise this aspect at the cost of the issue of decadence so clear from a reading of the Premchand original.

Munshi Premchand's famous story is very brief, merely describing, with great irony, two noblemen devoting their lives to chess while the British conquer Lucknow.

With his lack of knowledge of the language, Ray not only surrounded himself with others who did, but called in actors of known, and considerable talent. The Nawab is played with great dignity by Amjad Khan, the most stereotyped villain in contemporary Hindi cinema, given to constant ranting as the man you love to hate. Sanjeev Kumar and Saeed Jaffrey play the two noblemen; both act extremely well, but Jaffrey has much the truer feel of the civilised wit and refinement of Lucknow.

There are two distinctly different intervening strands in the film; the documentary, and the fictional. Ray painstakingly researched the history and the background himself, going into exact details of Lord Dalhousie's series of annexations, of the army that entered Lucknow, and the exact manoeuvres of General Outram that led to it. The British action is developed with greater narrative emphasis and analysis of motivation; the Indian side, perhaps less documented, is relatively more impressionistic. It is here that a certain structural weakness rare in Ray's cinema, leads to the lack of a unified impact. The feeling in the Indian side of the story is exquisitely perceived; but the facts are not equally detailed out or inexorably built up.

For the first time in his career, Ray strays outside his strictly narrative style. Except for *Nayak*, there are few flashbacks in his films (how easy it would have been for Sarbajaya to indulge in reveries of life in Nischindipur!); except for *Pratidwandi* there are no flash-forwards in wish fulfilment. His best films are chronological in structure. The subtlety of treatment is held up by a strong, continuous base. Given this characteristic of his work, Ray was possibly juggling with too many balls at once in *Shatranj ke Khilari*.

Even so, the sense of historical happening is always present, and the largeness of canvas is well related to the details, in emotional terms. In the General's encounter with the queen mother behind the purdah, the invisible voice speaks with a historic dignity before which Outram becomes painfully aware of his low cunning. In his confrontation with Outram, the king humbles him too by offering him his crown, but refusing to sign the demeaning "treaty". The farcical quality of the lust of the two wives, one's for her husband, the other's for her lover, complements the irony of their husband's obsession with chess while the kingdom, the basis of their courtly elegance, passes to the hands of the enemy before their very eyes.

The impotence of the noblemen in the hour of their eclipse is shown with mordant irony in the unfulfilled (unfulfillable?) sexual appetites of their wives. Mirza's impotence is as funny as Mir's blissful ignorance of his wife's affair, complete with her lover under the bed. The impotent and the cuckold play chess, Indian style, as the kingdom collapses. At the end, as the British enter Lucknow, they continue to play, but have changed to the British rules of the game.

His wife wants sex; Mirza wants to finish the game, which he had left at a very interesting point. The conversation with his wife is full of pathos, irony:

*Khurshid* (the wife): That game, I curse that game.

*Mirza*: But why? It's a wonderful game—you know—it was invented by an Indian, now the whole world plays it.

*Khurshid*: Then the whole world is stupid.

*Mirza*: Stupid? You know ever since I started playing Shatranj, *my power of thinking has improved a hundred times* (Italics mine).

The wives want sex; the husbands want chess. Both are escape routes from the thought of the world collapsing round their ears. Mirza's impotence and Mir's wife's exploits are both equally funny. The sexual comedy makes *Shatranj* a unique event in Ray's career; so does the complexity of the narrative style.

Ray's first foray into Hindi was clearly calculated to secure a foothold in the middle class segment of the vast Hindi market. Hence the array of stars, Amitabh Bachchan as commentator, Birju Maharaj's song, Sashwati's dance, sexual games, farcical scenes (including the black comedy of the visit to the dying lawyer in search of a chess set) — all marketable elements are assembled together without sacrificing Ray's artistic integrity. The Bombay film industry was evidently well aware of this possibility and decided to nip it in the bud. In Delhi, the film had a "fixed booking" of four weeks regardless of how well it ran; in Bombay it was reduced to morning shows as a signal to the filmmaker to stick to awards for his Bengali films, leaving Hindi commercial cinema severly alone. While this is naturally not documented, it appears to be well known in the industry.

It also attracted a lot of criticism, mostly from people who would have preferred to have seen Wajid Ali Shah glorified as India's last independent ruler. Commenting on this, Ray said in an interview:

One can well imagine a treatment of the annexation with Wajid painted whiter and Outram painted blacker, which would automatically enhance its popular appeal. My treatment avoids this falsification. It also discourages the stock "approved response" to feudalism and colonialism, not by condoning them or underscoring their evils, but by investing their representatives with certain human traits. These traits are not invented but backed by historical evidence. I knew that this might result in a certain ambivalence of attitude, but I didn't see *Shatranj* as a story where one would openly take sides and take a stand. I saw it more as a contemplative, though unsparing view of the clash of two cultures—one effete and ineffectual and the other vigorous and malignant. I also took into account the many half shades that lie between these two extremes of the spectrum.

The film is a work of remarkable depth of vision, narrative skill, wit and subtle historical understanding. Bansi Chandragupta returned to Calcutta briefly to work on the film and left his mark on the pellucid, lived-in interiors where every inch is perfectly weathered. Yet it so foiled the grander expectations of its audience, even the sophisticated sections of it, by its miniature-like exquisiteness, that the truth of its feeling and statement will probably have to await rediscovery at a later time.

The next film, *Joi Baba Felunath* (1978) continues the style and the characters of *Sonar Kella*. The story is this time laid in Benares, giving Ray the opportunity of revisiting it after *Aparajito*, this time with colour in his camera. Utpal Dutt plays the villain with great relish, Kanu Mukherjee as Arjun throws knives with a quiet, squint-eyed malevolence, his body racked by a cough. A good time is had by all. The writer, Santosh Dutta has a marvellous ability to say the obvious with earnestness and conviction. Jit Bose as the young addict of the comics, is adorable. As usual, the suspense is mild, the violence of fairy-tale quality, the events enjoyable. The film has more charm and ease of flow than *Sonar Kella*. It is helped by the unity of place, and Benares, Ray's old hunting grounds in *Aparajito*, plays its role admirably.

Ray's predilection for such delightful exercises for children is now more marked. The film that follows *Joi Baba Felunath* is *Hirak Rajar Deshe* (1979), a sequel in colour to *Goopi Gyne Bagha Byne*.

The enormous popularity of *Goopi Gyne* among children may have prompted Ray to fill a long-felt gap since the demise of his grandfather and father as also of some later writers for children. In *Hirak Rajar Deshe* he introduces the additional device of rhyming the dialogue. Ray copes with this self-imposed restriction quite well, his perpetually inventive mind revelling in juggling with one more ball. The songs are written with the same aplomb as in *Goopi Gyne Bagha Byne*, using simple words with great effect. His knowledge of western opera helps him to structure the songs dramatically and making the melodies adroitly reflect the meaning of the words. The melody sources are various types of Indian music ranging from the classical, folk and religious.

Despite the inventions, however, the film is weighed down by an excess of didactic emphasis and an overly simplistic and schematic revolutionary figure injected into the innocent world of Goopy and Bagha, making it perhaps the weakest of Ray's childrens' films, less enjoyed by adults than his other works in this game. The children's world now ceases to be the last hide-out of innocence, for the child in Goopy and Bagha has turned too didactic. A note of falsity has entered their voice.

This loss of innocence finds a different expression in *Pikoo* (1980), a 25-minute short made for French television. The child is now caught in the meshes of the adult world and alienated from it by the bitterness between his parents and his mother's affair with a lover, neither of which he is able to understand. He also has to contend with the closeness to death of his frail grandfather. In a telling moment he compares his right arm with the old man's and wonders why his own are smooth and round and the grandpa's so emaciated, with the veins sticking out fearfully. All of this oppresses his mind into a silent communication with his painting. The contrast between childhood and old age had always fascinated Ray as an unfathomable, constantly repeated mystery of nature and of life. We had first seen it in *Pather Panchali*, where the decrepit old aunt's death came immediately after the children's first sighting of a railway train, in a shock of total contrast. Here it reappears clearly, not in terms of contrast, but as part of the mysterious inexplicability of the flow of events around the child. Pikoo has an inkling of the inexorability of the processes of life and death that envelop us and reduce the importance of the happenings we encounter. The unspoken questions in Pikoo's mind are as basic to him as they are to the adult world, when it stops to think. Indeed it is through him that we are forced to ponder the same questions that we constantly try to escape. It is a poetic evocation of what the archetypal child mind of Nachiketa articulated in his philosophic enquiry in the *Kathopanisahd*: What is death? The resonance that issues from Pikoo's encounter is wordlessly pervaded by the same enquiry. It affects us because it is unspoken.

This is the aspect of *Pikoo* that stands out and gives the film its depth. We share the child's inability to understand, and it silences us. Where the film disappoints is in the brazenness of the husband-wife-lover triangle. It does not evolve; it has no inner logic. It is just there, as a vulgar fact. It is not even seen from the child's point of view. It passes a moral judgement on Pikoo's mother because of what is seen as just plain lust, unrelieved, unaccompanied by feeling. There is a bare hint of bad blood between husband and wife but it is not explored at all, not even by silent suggestion as in the opening sequence of *Charulata* ending with Charu regarding Bhupati with a lorgnette as he passes close by without being aware of her. Here Ray does not want to give a reason for the mother's infidelity in order to condemn it as totally as possible. Only as the reflections in Pikoo's mind does the love affair—which consists solely of getting into bed—have any significance. The attitude is alien to the early Ray, for whom, like Renoir, everybody had a reason. If Aparna had flashed a marriage certificate at the camera as her head emerged dramatically from behind Victor Banerjee's, would the situation have become more moral? Would husband and wife keeping son at bay while having sex in the afternoon been less vulgar? Ray obviously had a St Augustinian horror of "illegitimate" sex.

Despite this shortcoming, if that's what it is, the film remains telling in its effect. It is because of the depth in the concept of Pikoo's character and his relationship with the people and the things—like the flowers, the paint, the car, the sounds—that surround him.

*Sadgati* is Ray's angriest film, sizzling with an ice-cold vapour that rises from it. Like most of Ray's masterpieces, the film has an absolute inevitability about every aspect of it, as though nothing else was ever possible. There are no surprises. The Brahmin couple are absolutely Brahmin, fair, good-looking but flabby, arrogant and lazy; the chamar couple are absolutely the untouchables, dark, muscular, handsome in a rough-hewn way; subservient and completely unsure of themselves. The contrast between the two is total, and is emphasised by the cross-cutting between the indolent comforts of the Brahmin and the weary chores of the chamars. The casting accounts for a good deal of the perfection of the film; Mohan Agashe is the classic embodiment of the Brahmin as is Geeta Kak as his wife in whom we find a female villain. Both husband and wife express themselves more in their body language than in words. Every action of their's is the exactly expected one and perfectly executed. And in Om Puri and Smita Patil one has again the basic image of the castaways of society. It is hard to think of a better embodiment of the poor rural slum woman than Smita. In the fineries of the upper class, she always seemed a misfit as in *Arth* and in the commercials she did towards the end of her unduly short career. At most she shone as the middle or lower middle class woman of *Ardhsatya* or *Subah*. But as the milkmaid of *Manthan*, the slum dweller of *Chakra* or the chilli sorter of *Mirch Masala* she really belonged. Her attractiveness was of a very earthy kind, the kind destined to attract the lust of the upper classes that seemed to hang over her perfect form like an unseen threat.

*Sadgati*'s network of inevitabilities includes the predominance of discreetly low-angled shots of the Brahmins so as to make them just a little larger than life size and high angles for the *chamars*, so as to make them seem imperceptibly smaller by comparison. Similarly, rain comes down as tragedy befalls the untouchable family is a familiar device of Ray's, the "pathetic fallacy", in which nature emphasises the condition of man. The mastery lies in the orchestration of the inevitabilities, the perfect proportion of form given to the structure, and the sureness of the rhythm (the *laya* of Indian classical music) which informs it, giving the whole a resonant musicality. What we see as a result is an invocation of the image of the oppressor and the oppressed playing out their classic conflict stretched across two thousand years of the caste system. (Recall the killing of Shambuka by Ramachandra merely because he was a Shudra who indulged in *tapasaya* that would have given him knowledge, and therefore, power).

But the film does not stop at the eternal sadness of the plight of the oppressed. In the scene of the Brahmin dragging the body that the untouchables would not remove from his path, Ray lays aside his conventional establishing procedures and takes the film ruthlessly to a height of emotional power. Two kinds of shots alternately suggest the timeless nature of the oppression and its immediacy here and now. The first kind is the silhouetted shot, low-angled against the sky; the second, the high angle grass and the mud, with the earth being marked with minute furrows by the weight of the body dragged over it. Even before this Ray gives us a powerful symbol of the inert force of tradition that the untouchable faced. The huge log of wood, a gnarled mass of a tree trunk, hard as rock lying there challenging the might of the muscles of the starving, bonded, untouchable *chamar*. The log constantly deflects and defies the axe. The Brahmin had obviously given this task to his slave so as to rest on his charpoy through the afternoon and accompany the man to prescribe an auspicious date for his daughter's betrothal after the heat of the afternoon had abated. He had not realised that the man would die; he had a vague faith in the man's muscles, a faith that might have been justified if the man had not just recovered from fever and gone without food on that particular day. This last fact had vaguely troubled the Brahmin; in fact husband and wife have a thought about giving him some food, only to find that it would cause too much work for themselves in the middle of a hot day. This passing kindness of thought does not mitigate the Brahmin's villainy; it only reinforces it by humanising him just enough to make him credible.

Premchand's story was written long before the country's independence. Ray's film underscores the reality that remains, in the main so tragically unchanged. Indeed the fundamentalist Hindu revivalism and the increasing rate of atrocities against Harijans today, gives the film a renewed relevance.

Ray changes almost nothing in Premchand's story; right from the title on, he follows the writer almost line by line—a very unusual procedure for him. But he invests it with the over-powering credibility that only the moving image in the hands of a master can bring. An invisible presence of the archetypal reinforces the credibility further. It is as though the *chamar*, his wife and daughter bear upon their mien and their movements the weight of two thousand years of slavery. The thought that they have been "untouchable" castaways of society for millennia sends a chill down the spine of the modern sector of India, the sector that solemnly aspires to a democratic society with equal rights for all. That aspiration itself is under threat today from forces that refuse to allow their right to exploit to be removed, even reduced. The recurrent caste warfare in a state like Bihar cannot but recall Premchand's story, and Ray's film.

## IV

Satyajit Ray's films since *Shatranj ke Khilari* had been either breezy or didactic tales for children (*Joi Baba Felunath, Hirak Rajar Deshe*) or telling but brief episodes for television (*Pikoo, Sadgati*). One had been waiting for him to make another of his in-depth charges into the human mind and bring forth a great work. Despite his illnesses at the time it finally arrived in *Ghare Baire* (1984). Again, he went back to Tagore, one of his major sources, this time to a novel built around trends and events emerging on the eve of the British partition of Bengal in 1905. Tagore ruthlessly examines the values of the rising nationalism, and finds it wanting; the British, to his alarm, are succeeding in their game of dividing Hindus and Muslims and driving the Swadeshi (nationalist self-sufficiency) movement into a terrorism they know how to deal with. The events in the larger arena of society are reflected in currents at home; the novel weaves the fine details of a triangular love relationship into a tapestry of the national context.

No film since M S Sathyu's remarkable *Garm Hawa* (1969) had dared to examine the relationship of Hindus and Muslims. Tagore's novel was a rationalist, secular counterblast to the aggressive Hinduism of Bankim Chandra Chatterjee's *Ananda Math*. (*Bande Mataram* is often used ironically in this film). It delves into the question of ends and means, and of truth, that evil means not only do not achieve the true end but corrupt the end itself. When Sandip (in the novel) gets ready to give false witness to get a poor seller of foreign cloth punished by the law, Nikhilesh points out that it would not serve the interest of truth. Sandip's reply is the classic one of those who rate the end above the means: "truth is not just what has actually happened, but what ought to happen". Tagore's (and Satyajit's) Nikhilesh is the Gandhian who believes in the purity of means to achieve the truth and in the role of the individual conscience in social development as opposed to a mechanistic faith in a "system"—a product of nineteenth century scientism. In West Bengal and in India of the 1980's as a whole, *Ghare Baire* sounds a deep note of warning against communal passions and the power of evil means to corrupt noble ends. It suggests the causes of communal tension, showing the role played by the British and by the rich Hindu landlords ruling over the poor Muslim peasants and traders which was eventually to lead to the partition of Bengal, not of 1905 which was repealed, but the inexorable one at Independence. In the novel, Tagore has Nikhilesh returning injured, unsure of whether he is going to live; to emphasise his Gandhian point, Ray has him die for his ideals. Like Gandhi, Nikhilesh gives his life to prevent a Hindu-Muslim riot.

But the microcosmic metaphor for this troubled world abroad is the home, and the relation of husband and wife. When Nikhilesh persuades his wife to come out of the zenana to meet his tempestuous friend, his principle is the same; his wife should love him of her own accord (as she does in the end) after knowing something of the world, and not because of his power over her ignorance—just as his poor Muslim traders who are his subjects should stop selling foreign cloth voluntarily, not by the Hindu zamindar's coercion. When Bimala returns to her husband's forgiving embrace, she comes out of her infatuation with greedy male macho parading as the turbulent saviour of the country and recognises Nikhilesh's inner strength behind his mild, androgynous exterior*. Truth is one and indivisible, and there are no short-cuts to it, either on the left or the right.

In the oeuvre of Satyajit Ray, *Ghare Baire* will come to occupy a very special place. He had finally grown out of the Apu mould; Nikhilesh is not a variation on him. For the first time, he has a villain; and this itself marks a sea change. Even the pimping "P.R.O." of *Jana Aranya* (Robi Ghosh) and the Madam (Padma Devi) of the whorehouse were not wholly evil; their sparkling humour gave them a human warmth. In Ray's early films up to *Charulata*, his characters were noble, unselfconscious animals of a pre-Freudian, pre-industrial age. His later films from *Days and Nights in the Forest* onwards, progressively noted the loss of innocence of the younger generation, culminating in the self-abnegation of *Jana Aranya*'s hero. Innocence and goodness had taken refuge in the

---

* What Godse saw as "effeminate" in Gandhi, as Ashis Nandy explains brilliantly in *At the Edge of Psychology*, Oxford, 1980.

children's films with their fairy tale heroes and villains. But in *Pikoo* the child too, comes to losing his innocence. And now in *Ghare Baire*, when Sandip bares his fangs from behind a polite mask, the villain at last emerges in Ray's work. The scene in which Sandip's eyes gleam at the sight of the gold is remarkable for its directness and force. Soumitra Chatterjee, the archetypal innocent of Ray's cinema, now gives off subtle vibrations of villainy. The noble protagonist, with the tragic flow of Hamletesque hesitation, is no longer the young man emerging from a cocoon of isolation; he belongs firmly to a bygone social order. Yet all is not lost to the younger generation; Sandip's young revolutionary pupil, like Bimala, turns against his charismatic guru in traumatic disillusion. The comment on Marxist ethics, with its traditional emphasis on the end regardless of the means, is unmistakable; so is its relevance in the Marxist-ruled state of West Bengal and the rise of Hindu fundamentalism which attempts to derive its legitimacy from Bankim Chandra Chatterjee's rabidly anti-Muslim tirade in his novel *Ananda Math* and its theme song *Bande Mataram*.

The film is Satyajit Ray's wordiest. This issues from the analytical structure of the novel which sees the narrative from the differing points of view of its protagonists. For the first time, he makes the whole film flow in a flashback. To give the words the full value of their import, Ray uses camera movements very sparingly, has many more close ups than he would normally, thereby achieving a stark if a little rigid simplicity. The film has no set pieces or flourishes like the swing scene of *Charulata* or the skeletons of *Paratidwandi*; it removes from its path almost everything that might distract us from the moral issues which it wants us to face squarely. Yet there are a few scenes in which we cannot help admire the artistry no matter how absorbed we are in the content; one is at the beginning, when Bimala, sequestered wife of a traditional zamindar, comes out of the zenana in subtle slow motion down a long corridor, for the first time to meet a man other than members of her family. The scene of Bimala learning to sing "Tell me tales that to me were so dear—long long ago" from Miss Gilby (played by Jennifer Kapoor who exudes a warmth that alas we shall never see again), is utterly charming besides evoking the period. Finally, at the end, when her husband's body arrives in a long, silent procession, seen from the window above, there is a moving sense of inevitability. The death is announced suddenly, after tense shots of long duration, with Nikhilesh slowly riding alone on horseback, sola topee on his head, to inspect the trouble caused by his Muslim tenants on the rampage. A short cry of *Allah Ho Akbar*, a shot, then the procession. The rapid-fire succession of suggestions graphically establishes the anticipated tragedy. The staccato rhythm spells action, the outside world, and the fate reserved for uncompromising honesty. Coming after the relaxed warmth of the reconciliation of husband and wife, it shatters our tranquil world of period make-believe and delivers us into the heart of contemporary India.

Although it has memorable passages, *Ghare Baire* is far from being a cinematically perfect film like *Charulata*, despite certain similarities between the two films in terms of period, class character and a triangular relationship. Swatilekha meets the requirements of the character halfway; her large, square shoulders and strong features have a curiously old-world feeling, suggestive in fact of some women of the Tagore family; yet she is totally without the mystique or the quicksilver intelligence of Madhabi Mukherjee. For a film tradition that scrupulously avoids the kiss, *Ghare Baire*'s pecks are bold but mechanical. As usual, Ray is highly uncomfortable with physical intimacy and gets it over with as quickly as possible without exploring the developing sensuous attraction which culminates in it—just as in *Pikoo 's* treatment of the lovers. Victor Banerjee's Nikhilesh brings out the essential nobility of the character despite the edge of absurdity to which it pushes some of the issues, such as his almost throwing his wife into the arms of his supposedly charismatic friend. This charisma is held back from Soumitra Chatterjee whose greed and pettiness is stressed to make him somewhat one-sided.

Yet the film is so powerfully conceived and so well structured that it consistently holds attention. What is more, it raises extremely important issues and examines them with much concentration and an extraordinary enmeshing of the personal and the universal. It is for this reason that it rises easily above its purely technical shortcomings which have sometimes been unnecessarily overemphasised. Like Nikhilesh, its hero, the film itself has a certain nobility, a high seriousness on some of the most important questions of our time.

## V

Without knowing this background, it is impossible to regard *Ganashatru* as anything but a tentative effort by Ray to break out of the confines of his illness to get back to film making. He is clearly not in full possession of the entire range of his creative faculties and nowhere near his customary control of every detail of film-making that we saw in his earlier work. As a matter of fact, due to his ill health, he was never to recover it fully in the three films he made before his death, in spite of the astonishing progress made in his last two films, in which he almost pulled himself up by his bootstraps with what must have been an enormous exercise of the will.

In *Ganashatru* for the first time he adapted a foreign classic (Ibsen's Enemy of the People)—something that Indian, avant garde theatre often does. But rather more than in today's theatre, *Ganashatru*'s characters sit down and talk. The script structure is somewhat simplistic and, except for Dhritiman Chatterjee as the town's Mayor, none of the actors have very much to get their teeth into. Nor is there the subtlety of mise-en-scene that would minimise the disadvantages of the simplistic theatrical structure. There is hardly one memorable scene. The optimism at the end fails to extricate itself from the naivety of the entire pattern to rise at last to a meaningful level. Although it is possible to deduce the origin of this decline from the minor awakwardnesses of *Ghare Baire*, its difference with the last three films, particularly *Ganashatru*, is enormous.

শ্রীসুকুমার চট্টোপাধ্যায় সমীপেষু —

২২/
২/
৬৪

সাদর সম্ভাষণ,

আপনার পত্রটি যথাস্থানে পৌঁছেছে, এবং তার
সঙ্গে চিত্রনাট্য, তার জন্য অনেক ধন্যবাদ।

আপনার লেখাটি পড়ে সম্মুখে এলাম বিষয়ে
আগ্রহান্বিত। আপনি জানা (কোনো পত্রিকায় ছাপা হয়নি
এই যে বিষয় প্রসঙ্গে, এই এক যদি আমার সঙ্গে মিলত,
এ রকম এতটা অসম্ভব নয়তো পারতাম। পরিমিত বিষয়-
বিধায়ী হয়ে এই বই এর কথা পরিমাণ — তাই
চিত্রধারা আমার বড়ো হলে যায়। নিজে সম্ভাবিত
গ্রহণ করতাম, এই সুযোগ অনুযায়ী বিষয় সম্ভাবিত
আমাদের — এ সুযোগ বিষয় করে খুব ঘটনা-বহ ঘটনা।
বিষয়, খুব খুব এই একটা ঘটনা আছে,
সম্ভাবিত-টুকু সম্ভাবিত সুযোগ এই বই
সম্ভবত ঘটনা বিষয় । তবে সম্ভবত
বিষয় সম্ভব ।

২।

বিষয় সম্ভাবিত হয়ে আমার বিষয় বিষয় বিষয় বিষয়
সম্ভবত এই বই বিষয় সম্ভাবিত বিষয় সম্ভবত।
বিষয় সম্ভবত বিষয় বিষয় বিষয় Dokhol
বিষয় সম্ভবত হয় ) বিষয় সময় সময়
সম্ভবত মিলিত।

বিষয় সম্ভাবিত বিষয় সম্ভবত
সুযোগ এই সম্ভাবিত সুযোগ সুযোগ বিষয়
বিষয় । বিষয় বিষয় সম্ভবত
এই সময় সম্ভবত বিষয় আমার । বিষয় সুযোগ
সম্ভবত সুযোগ বিষয় বিষয় বিষয় সম্ভবত
হবে ।

এবং সম্ভবত আমার সম্ভবত বিষয় বিষয় নয়।
বিষয় ও বিষয় সম্ভবত বিষয় বিষয় বিষয় বিষয় বিষয়।
Science Fiction ও Fantasy সম্ভবত বিষয় বিষয়
Staples — এ বিষয় বিষয় সম্ভবত বিষয় বিষয়,
এবং, সম্ভবত বিষয় বিষয় আমার । বিষয় সম্ভবত
এবং । বিষয় বিষয় সম্ভবত বিষয় বিষয়

# The Last Phase

Ray never fully recovered from the illnesses that began to plague him while he was still making *Ghare Baire* and caused a steady decline in his health. Except for a half-hour short on his father, he had been off film-making for a good five years. *Ganashatru* and its successors were made by a director surrounded by nurses and doctors with an intensive care unit in an ambulance standing by at the door. "My doctor is now dictating my style of film-making", he said, "I am ordered to work only within the studio". But getting behind the camera, he added, exhilarated him and made him feel much better than did his medicines.

*Ganashatru* (1989) makes a frontal attack, far more direct than *Devi*, on the disastrous effect of superstition. Here the consequences are not visited upon an individual or only a section of society. In a hospital in a small but popular resort town of West Bengal, suddenly many patients are found down with jaundice and other diseases related to water pollution. The doctor who spots this investigates and finds the source, leaking sewers contaminating the drinking water ingested by pilgrims as *Charanamrita*, literally water turned into nectar by the touch of a divine foot. When he warns people of this, the Mayor of the town and others with a vested interest in the temple and its influx of pilgrims, attack him for what they see as his anti-Hindu view. A local newspaper is threatened into refusal to publish the doctor's findings. *Charanamrita*, the vested interests say, taking a Hindu zealot position, cannot be contaminated. The doctor calls a meeting to explain his point but rabble-rousing demagogues turn his audience against him and the doctor is dubbed an 'enemy of the people'.

Coming at a time when religious fundamentalism was gathering momentum, Ray's film reasserted the need for the rationality promoted by the nineteenth century reform movement and denounced by many modern scholars as scientism and a denial of the intuitive side of life. However, the subsequent explosion of Hindu fundamentalism threatening the unity and integrity of the country gives a prophetic quality to the statement of the film. The demolition of the Babri Masjid by Hindu zealots climaxed a movement to place popular belief above fact by asserting that Lord Rama was born at the exact spot where the masjid had been built regardless of what archaeologists had to say.

The simplistic weakness of *Ganashatru* are so obvious and so plentiful that it is difficult to admit into the body of his oeuvre. It is best seen as an exercise of Ray's creative muscles during dire illness, a tragic attempt to recover from atrophy. What is astonishing is the extent to which he recovers in his two last films for which *Ganashatru* provides a starting block.

*Shakha Proshakha* (1990) lost little on its appearance on television—something uncharacteristic for Ray's work as we have known it. It is clear that the film is a great advance on *Ganashatru*; it is dramatically powerful, firm in its construction and has cinematic moments worthy of a great film-maker. Despite its dependence on dialogue and its confinement, for the most part, within the walls of a house, the cinematic thinking remains of a high order.

The titles signal a direct return to form. The camera travels laterally across a long strip of ECG print out; heartbeats begin to sound—lubdub, lubdub; music enters unobtrusively, reflecting the pattern of the heartbeats, then slowly superimposes a continuous tone—all of this suggesting the excellence of the opening *Devi* or *Charulata* or *Pratidwandi*. But what follows is a bit different. The long, silent, opening of *Jalsaghar* on the terrace almost wordlessly supplied the basic information about the man and his times as though in a painted portrait; here father and son, seated on chairs, engage in dialogue to establish the basis of the drama. The tenderness in the relationship between the two, one of them old and the other with his brain damaged in an accident, is at once apparent, but its manner is more of a play than of a film. The transparent device of the poor reporter arriving for an interview just afterwards makes things even worse; the poverty of the device is so unlike the Ray of old.

As always with Ray, the foundation is firmly laid so that the relationships that unfold can be understood without any vagueness. When the father has a heart attack, his other three sons arrive, two of them with their wives, at the huge house in a small town in Bihar. The stage is set. The first memorable moment comes with the entry of the decrepit old grandfather dressed in a brilliant red sweater; he has been so firmly relegated to the care of an attendant in a corner of the house that the sudden sight of him upsets the assembled family. There is instant relief when the servant comes in, picks him up and takes him back to his assigned place. It is one of the most funny and tragic moments in the film; the red sweater's incongruity on the decrepit old man declares his irrepressible urge to live, to belong to the family and bask in the warmth of their presence.

In the week that the brothers spend together waiting for the father to die or to survive, the tensions lying dormant among them come to surface, first at the huge, dark, dining table where they must meet for their meals, and then at a picnic in the countryside to celebrate father's recovery, complete with a tongue-twister game reminiscent of the memory game in *Day and Nights in the Forest*. In his classic manner, Ray builds his structure brick by brick. A sense of the inevitable attends most of the events. The relationship between the brothers and their wives is expertly developed, both at the large dining table and in the tête-a-têtes between the youngest brother and his sister-in-law whose ambiguity is delicately suggested.

True to the Dostoyevsky tradition, the idiot is the moral man, representing the ethics of the old father who had risen to wealth and fame through completely honest means that his two successful sons have repudiated as irrelevant to the realities of their time. They deal in black money, gamble and indulge in varying degrees of what was deemed sin in father's times. The women keep the company of the idiot, as it were; they are honest, sensitive and kind, and full of family virtues. The youngest son rejects the values of his 'sane' brothers and struggles to remain honest to himself. Ray uses the abnormal son as a sort of schizophrenic wrapped up in his own world except to pass non-verbal judgements on the doings of his brothers. His escape hatch is in the best of western music; at first we hear Bach and later, when the cynicism of his brothers is unmasked, the "Kyrie Eleison" (Lord, have mercy on us) section of a Gregorian chant which floods the night. The magnificent ancestral clock with its chimes, combined with the music coming from the 'mad' brother's room are among the most moving elements in the film. Besides the telling use of these excerpts, Ray's own background score is, if anything, richer than before. His sense of dramatic construction and musical relevance remain impeccable.

The autobiographical element in all this is of course hard to miss; the heart attack and the very credible details of the treatment, the alienation from the cynicism of the times, the solace in music, are all pointers to Ray's own experience. Ajit Banerjee, who plays the father, is at times uncannily like Ray himself, even in his features and the texture of his skin, apart from his mental make up. His shock is great on learning that his sons deal in black money and that even his little grandson is fully familiar with these terms of dishonesty. For all but the most morally committed of a somewhat older generation, there is a touch of naivete here that tends to make Ray's ethics *passé* to them. Indeed it is sad that there should be an unseemly anxiety among some Indian film-makers to relegate him to the past, almost as cynically as the two successful sons in *Shakha Proshakha* ("Its time for him to go, after all", says one of them). There is much in the film to nail the lie of such sentiments; we have few film-makers as yet to create the great moments of Ray's last films since his rise from the nadir of *Ganashatru*, even though they may seem a little 'preachy' compared to his earlier style of understatement.

The only distressing aspect is the fall in the quality of physical technique—the lighting, the sets, the details which obviously Ray could no longer supervise with the furious energy and jealous control he used to bring to these elements. If Subrata Mitra and Bansi Chandra had been with him, one can't help feeling, the texture of the films of this phase of his career would have gained enormously. The moral statements are now greatly disadvantaged by the obviously painted, unweathered walls, the stereotyped staircases, and the occasionally foggy shots with poor lighting. The contrast of this with the fineness of the sound recording by French technicians is marked. What makes this more regrettable is that there is no dearth in India today of sophisticated lighting cameramen and expert art directors or make-up men. The French-financed film had plenty of money to hire them. Soumitra Chatterjee' role as the brain-damaged son is dramatically well conceived but its mix with schizophrenic characteristics does not seem to be well-enough researched, and, on top of it, the make-up man gives him a very theatrical beard. In other words, the film is rich in drama but short on cinema, even though the outdoor scenes are very well realised and provide great relief from claustrophobic interiors, however large in size. Nevertheless, *Shakha Proshakha* was certainly an important step towards the recovery of Ray's form after his protracted illness.

In the unfolding of his creative thinking, *Shakha Proshakha* continued his increasing preoccupation with problems of individual ethics. Ever since *Ghare Baire*, this preoccupation had resulted in more and more overt statements directly made in words. One is forcefully reminded here of Pauline Kael's classic statement, made in relation to *Ashani Sanket*, that in Ray's work what is understated has great impact and what is forcefully stated diminishes him to the ordinary. Even so, in a film like

*Shakha Proshakha*, there is a certain power in the uncompromising moral stance, refusing to get involved in the rationalisations and the justifying philosophies of the corrupt. Directness of statement is closely related to this and is not entirely unlike Tagore's forthrightness in his last poems, in one of which he spoke of hissing serpents poisoning the air, in which delicate words of peace would sound hollow, and his call to future generations was for war upon evil.

*Agantuk* (1991) has a warmth reminiscent of the children's films like *Sonar Kella* or *Joy Baba Felunath*. In fact it has such good humour about it that but for it, the large issues on which it pronounces could have been reduced to mere clichés. Utpal Dutt, who obviously represents the author's point of view, radiates a sense of fun in the lift of his eyebrows, his gait and the knowing air of his constant exposure of the fruitlessness of the precautions his long-lost relations take on the way to placing progressive confidence on him. With his weatherbeaten look marked by the great load of experience it suggests, he is affectionately amused by what is to him the naivete of his flock including those who persist in suspecting his integrity. The character of the prodigal uncle returned home is central to the film and all its content is coloured by his personality. There is also the element of the informative and the covert moralising which has characterised his children's films as well as the books for children he wrote. It is the ever present sense of mild fun that tempers the educative aspect and makes the films as attractive to adults as to the younger audience. In *Agantuk* the difference is that unlike the other films for the young it does not declare itself as such, and that the major part of his (Utpal Dutt's) audience within the film is in fact adult, albeit less experienced than himself.

In treating adults somewhat as children, *Agantuk* situates itself in unfamiliar territory and its difference from other Ray films is not readily apparent. When they miss the tone of the film with its lightly tongue-in-cheek manner, adult audiences are unable to place themselves in the right angle in relation to the film and misread it as serious social philosophy casually thrown around. However, one cannot totally dismiss the didactic side of the "noble savage" philosophy. Although uttered tongue-in-cheek, Utpal Dutt's words have a serious content which can be criticised, especially if we miss or dismiss the charming lighter aspect. For instance, the glorification of the tribal people, who have been subjected to thousands of years of exploitation and corrupted thereby, must remain questionable. Besides, can we write off the massive structure of civilisation built up since the times when everybody was primitive completely, or should we reconsider ways in which some of the characteristics of the aboriginals can be absorbed into the education and the lives of the "civilised"? In India, the tribals have been exploited and subjected to pressures of Hinduisation (Sanskritisation, as some pundits will have it) through all of history and much of prehistory. Our epics bear ample testimony to the antiquity of the upper caste attitude and treatment of these indigenous peoples. Their inability to cope with ever developing technologies of the civilised must surely indicate a serious weakness in a Darwinian world, however sad that may be. To lionise them today despite the constant erosion of their wealth and their culture and to set them up as model for the rest of the world has its hazards. It may indicate a kind of patronising self-indulgence on our part.

Neither will today's anthropologist, more and more troubled by the problem of "the self and the other", the politics of observation, in which the act of observation affects the observed, take an approving view of Ray's social philosopher sitting in an armchair looking at a group of Santhals of Birbhum dancing, nor of his niece's joining the dance in a politically much-abused act of belonging. We have seen Mrs Indira Gandhi doing that several times on television. There may be some merit in asking ourselves to take another look at what we call civilisation and opting for a simpler way of life but it is too broad a prescription to internalise in a more than facile way.

The important point about the film is thus the fact that we can enjoy the film without taking its "message" too seriously. But this is something the message-mongering solemnity of the Indian audience is unable to accept. The sophisticated criticise the film both for its lack of textural beauty and the triviality of its philosophy; the general audience falls between the two stools and does not know whether to react as adults or as children. The upshot of this was that even though it was released very soon after Ray's death and widely billed as the master's last film, it ran to virtually empty houses in Calcutta, his city. In France it had a big run and even climbed into the top hits bracket; whether that makes the French more sophisticated or more naive than us is difficult to conclude.

Most of Ray's films are adaptations from the literary work of others; only a few—*Kanchanjungha*, *Nayak*, *Pikoo* among them, were written by him (*Pikoo* was made from one of his own short stories, the other two he wrote as original screen plays). With the exception of *Goopy Gyne Bagha Byne*, the children's films were all written by him. The characteristics of the children's films we have briefly touched upon. Of the rest, *Kanchanjungha* is the most successful, *Nayak* was rather schematic and trivialised by the naivete of the dream sequences with their pop psychology. But two qualities distinguish them one of which they share with virtually all his scripts, and the other is almost completely reserved for the children's films. The first is the perfect architectonics of his story structure and script development; the second, the warmth they radiate despite their penchant for covert edification. Only *Kanchanjungha*, among his films for the adult audience, has a unique combination of wit and charm, and an amused contemplation of characters and events from a distance that *Agantuk*, of all the other films, shares the most. In his other films, irony plays a richer part, albeit subtly staying behind the main statement. Yet *Agantuk* does not quite fit into the *Kanchanjungha* pattern either; it is unique in its own way.

Ray's last three films, all written by himself, suggest a new simplicity and forthrightness about large issues affecting (except *Ganashatru*) the entire civilisation of today. In *Shakha Proshakha* it remained within the mould of say *Jana Aranya*, but in his last film it reached a mature mix of warmth and detachment that may have been brought about by intimations of mortality.

২২
/২/
৮৪

শ্রীমান অনুপনকুমার সহিত ⸺

সপ্রেম নমস্কার।

Dakhhel-Gauger

Science Fiction ও Fantasy

staples ⸺

# Classicism

## I

Ray's closeness to literature was an essential element in his classicism. He was trained to be a painter at Tagore's university at Santiniketan; his knowledge of western music was formidable and he developed a keen understanding of Indian music as well; there is hardly a branch of eastern and western art of which he was not aware and to which he could not respond. He made significant documentaries on painting (*The Inner Eye*, on the paintings of his teacher Binode Bihari Mukhopadhyay), and dancing (*Bala*, on the famous South Indian dancer Balasaraswati). Yet his approach to film-making was firmly based on the narrative and descriptive. His feature films were structured like the novel, and not the modern novel at that. Even his documentaries were never impressionistic; they were structured into a clear narrative and a firmly objective-descriptive attitude. Talking to me about my project of a film on Ananda Coomarawamy (*Dance of Shiva*, 1973), Ray said: "What you think is unimportant; you must show what *he* thought, did". Consistently, he opposed whatever in my ideas sought to give an impression instead of a description. "He was a writer", Ray asked. "Where is the shot of him writing?"

Except where the stories were his own, Ray's films were based on well-known literary originals, mostly classics. Bibhutibhushan' novels of Apu, the wonder child, have a delightfully rambling flow, often getting lost on the way in odes to nature. With the partial exception of *Aparajito*, Ray disciplines his structure and concentrates his feelings into a tightly-knit pattern. Partly, this is born of necessity; partly, I suspect, of preference. It is far removed from the Renoir that Andre Bazin celebrates, who so often stops on the way, forgets where he was going, distracted by something that captures the attention of his ever youthful self, a little like Bibhutibhushan himself. The depth of feeling which Ray creates in the trilogy, all his fragile and ineffable evocations of beauty and mortality, are contained firmly within the story framework and expressed with the utmost economy. There is hardly any room, in the majority of Ray films, for rambling.

Ray's own stories are even more tightly constructed, sometimes to the point of being over-structured. *Kanchanjungha's* action takes the same time as the running time of the film itself and takes place in a very small section of the hill town of Darjeeling. Unity of time, place and action could not be more tightly organised. To this, *Nayak's* one-night train ride, although punctuated by seven flashbacks and two dream sequences, comes a close second. Predictably, such accent on the unities can impose a certain schematism on the unfolding of a film, the strain of which is visible in the second. The stories for children are much more spontaneous and have a depth of charm not always apparent to those who dismiss them as lightweight.

There is no doubt that it is in transforming literature into cinema that he is in his element. It is astonishing how deeply he absorbs the work of Bibhutibhushan and Tagore, digesting them much the same way as the young man in *Parash Pathar*—the philosopher's stone disappears into his system with his high metabolism. In his early years, he dealt exclusively with classic literature with a perfection of its own, lifting it to an even higher order of creativity. The transformation of literature into the vivid palpability of cinema is always a more taxing task in terms of credibility. In literature internal, deductive logic counts for rather more than the inductive: the spectator in the cinema, who is not conjuring up visions in his mind but is seeing them before him, is quick to return to his own concept, or experience, of reality and check it against the director's. Both in the trilogy, and in *Charulata*, Ray made major departures from the text, but because they become intensely credible, neither audience nor critic (except for a very few) found fault with them. Bibhutibhushan's Apu is a kind of divine wonder-child who not only leaves his son, at the end of the novel, to wander off to indeterminate, distant lands; in a sort of sequel, called *Debajan*, he actually becomes an angel—not exactly the stuff of realist cinema. In Tagore's story, Charulata's husband refuses to live with a wife who is constantly going to think of another man, and escapes to a job in South India. In Ray, the helpless woman wipes her tears, invites her husband to come in as he hesitates on the threshold. She knows she is entering a life of suspended animation (the hands freeze before they touch), thereby making a more practical and credible ending.

In his later films, he had often picked contemporary fiction by younger writers, and lifted stories such as *Aranyer Din Ratri, Pratidwandi, Seemabaddha* and *Jana Aranya* to creative levels that their authors had never dreamed of. Changes were made more freely, sometimes making the final outcome well-nigh unrecognisable. Yet he needed to borrow from them a set of characters and situations with which their authors were more familiar than himself, and which already had a basic organisation on which the film could be built.

II

In a letter to the Sri Lankan director, Lester Peries (quoted in Marie Seton's *Portrait of A Director: Satyajit Ray*), Ray lamented that:

> The exterior of a film is beginning to count for more than before. People don't seem to bother about what you say as long as you say it in a sufficiently oblique and unconventional manner—and the normal-*looking* film is at a discount—I don't imply that all the new European film makers are without talent, but I do seriously doubt if they could continue to make a living without the very liberal exploitation of sex that their code seems to permit.*

At home, he never saw any of the freshness that others praised in Mrinal Sen's *Bhuvan Shome*—except in the personality of Suhasini Mulay. Similarly he expressed disapproval of young Indian directors who attempt unconventional modes of expression. Discussing Mani Kaul and Kumar Sahani in *Our Films, Their Films,* his collection of essays, he talked about the lack of economic viability of their films without as much as mentioning any talent they might have. In other words, to him, there is only one kind of valid film-making—the classical.

The use of the moods of nature to reinforce human emotions is one of the oldest devices ("the pathetic fallacy") in literature—one that modern novelists are as anxious to avoid or to make oblique as classical writers were to make obvious. It is a favourite device of Ray's and he uses it in classical style—direct and forceful.

Nowhere is this more repeatedly, more stunningly employed, or more successfully, than in *Charulata*. Amal arrives in a bold striped shirt, flying hair and raised umbrella in the middle of the first storm, just when the surface calm of the couple's daily routine has been established, but we have evidence of the wife's inner restlessness. It is literary cliche, so worn

---

\*    Here he was obviously less than fair; for instance there was no exploitation of sex in the French *Nouvelle vague,* in the work of Truffaut or Godard, Demy or Renais or Chabrol. What motivated such a sweeping remark is difficult to say.

out that even in transposing it to the cinema (where it burdens our memories rather less), Ray clothes it in the disguise of Amal's comical cry—"*Haray Muraray, Madhukaitabhray*" (O Krishna, the slayer of the demons, Madhu and Kaitabh)! That cry has a self-consciousness which reflects the director's own, in using the age-old device. It just comes off, Ray saving himself from the banal by the skin of his teeth, as he quickly moves on to the next scene—before we begin to hear the creaks at the joints of the theatrical prop.

The storm next comes in handy (it is the Bengali summer, when "Nor'westers" are frequent), after the last garden scene, where Charu has found that Amal's interest in her is not of his own making, but inspired by her husband. Thunder rumbles, Amal comes looking for her, too dumb in the vanity of his own literary prowess, male superiority and general irresponsibility, to know what it is that has hurt her so. Near the door he finds Manda (who has sexually interested him from the time he first saw her), is told she is on the terrace, and wanders off uncertainly in the direction of her room. The wind howls. Enter Charu with a bundle of clothes under her arm, caustically putting Manda (whom she has recognised as her rival) in her place, for Manda should have brought them down, seeing that the storm was coming. Again, the storm is a metaphor of the storm brewing in Charu's mind, in classic literary style, safe in the cinema where it can go unrecognised. Perhaps it is also more apt in a period film. Ray would probably not use it so freely, or directly, in treating a contemporary subject.

But nowhere is the device more brilliantly brought off than in the scene of Charu's breakdown into violent sobbing towards the end of the film. The couple have just come back from the seaside, reconciled to their respective losses: Bhupati's open one of the loss of money and trust in human nature, in his manager (Charu's brother)'s betrayal, Charu's secret one of the loss of Amal, who, realising that he was about to betray another trust, has disappeared.

Amal's letter has come, has been read by Bhupati, and Charu knows now that he has decided to get married and go off to England. Bhupati has just left the room to go out for a while. Charu has the letter in her hand, and the memory of her happiness with Amal swells up in her as the storm rises. The wind howls, thunder rumbles, and in what is surely one of the finest moments of acting by any woman in the Indian cinema, Madhabi Mukherjee is trying desperately to control herself. A window bangs, the glass splinters with a tense tinkle, and Madhabi falls on the bed, breaking into uncontrollable sobs speaking out her secret loudly for the first time, just in time for her husband to come back for his umbrella and to overhear. The timing of that tinkle is exactly calculated, and completely successful in its intent. It is not just the poetry of *Fort Apache*'s flying kick to the tin can and its faint tinkle as it falls in the gorge below (*Our Films, Their Films*); the musical quality would count for nothing in Ray's *Charulata* if it did not serve his literary-dramatic intent.

## III

Ray's classicism, like so much else in his outlook, is derived from Tagore. It was in Tagore that the restless reformism of the "Bengal Renaissance", casting about for the right blend of East and West, had found its equilibrium. It was Tagore's concept of India, traditional and yet modern, aglow with a new hope, its doors and windows flung open to the world, that provided the base of the Nehruvian dream; Nehru stood somewhere between Gandhi and Tagore, and the truth of the Tagore value-world never quite lost its appeal in Nehru's India. In fact, it found new expression in the ideals, if not all the realities, of the Nehru era.

The idealism of that period often underplayed unpleasant truths of character and the contradictory urges inevitable in human beings. Biographers of this period, for instance, never bring out the man in his total psychology; they select the more noble, publicly displayable, traits. Tagore himself never revealed his personal life in the ways Gandhi did. Gandhi's outlook was not contained within the framework of the rise of the middle class in India; Tagore's was. At its best, the Tagore trend resulted in the emergence of noble images of character; at its worst, it was hypocritical, a little puritan, a little afraid of Freud. It was never suited to the depiction of life in the raw. In his early work (till *Charulata*), Ray portrayed the past evolution of the middle class as reflected in the long period dominated by Tagore. It is something that had gone into the making of himself and his generation; something he knew and understood. In a broad way, it formed the background of his experience. The experience did not need to be directly personal; the people, the customs, the attitudes reflected in the literature of the Tagore era became, through repetition and constant explication, part of the fabric of personal experience. Ray's early characters were contained, in a powerfully consolidated form, within the broad outlines of the typology of the period. They are more or less all of a piece, and inner contradictions are rather rare.

## IV

It is when he steps out of this framework that Ray is ill at ease. The capitalist of *Jalsaghar* is an awkward cut-out; the taxi driver of *Abhijan* never fails to reveal his middle class mind (by comparison, Ritwik Ghatak's played by Kali Banerjee in *Ajantrik*, is more convincing), the tea-planter of *Kapurush* tried hard not to be a cut-out but does not quite succeed; the star of *Nayak*, rather untypically, rejects the advances of would-be heroines (although he is otherwise typical to the point of boredom), perhaps in deference to Ray's puritan ethic; in *Pratidwandi*, when the nurse takes off her bra, the image goes into negative.

What is more, in many of the later films, the characters of the post-Tagore era are observed from a Tagorean moral viewpoints. In *Jana Aranya*, the focal point of the moral judgement is in the retired father with a memory of the uprightness of his times. The brief love affair is observed from the outside; the mass of suffering humanity in *Pratidwandi* is seen from way above. This is not to say that the films are without sympathy or understanding, but that they point to clues that separate them from the director's intense involvement with the characters in, say, the trilogy or the trio of films on the awakening woman (*Mahanagar, Charulata, Kapurush*). Ray is no longer kneeling in the dust; he is an observer, trying to understand a somewhat unfamiliar milieu charged with values foreign to his nature. Not that he condemns this younger generation. It is just that he is unable to station himself at a point from which the direction in which the positive forces are moving towards fresh awareness; hope and humanity becomes visible. More convincing, as far as this goes, is an early work of this group—*Aranyer Din Ratri*, which concerns itself more with purely moral values, unrelated to the political forces which assumed a frightening identity in the years of *Pratidwandi* and *Jana Aranya* (political murders were a daily occurrence at the time of one and the rigours of the Emergency had arrived during the other).

In characterisation, there is also a marked preference for a clear orientation in one direction; Ray is not naturally drawn towards contradictions in mental make-up. The one example that comes to mind is of Priyagopal, the old father in *Mahanagar*. His opposition to Arati's taking a job is not sufficiently clear in the motivation; it is a set attitude, more typical than individual. Its juxtaposition with Priyagopal's resentment of his students' success and his penchant for collecting money from them, is somewhat unrelated, although the latter is a distinctly individual rather than typical characteristic. Here is a character from modern fiction who lies rather outside the typology of the earlier era, and is probably for that reason not as fully understood as most others in the Ray menagerie. Apurba of the trilogy, Bishwambhar Roy of *Jalsaghar*, Umaprasad in *Devi*, Amulya in *Samapti*, Bhupati or Amal in *Charulata*, to name some of the older films, for that matter the heroes of *Aranyer Din Ratri* or *Seemabaddha, Nayak* or *Pratidwandi*, to take some of the later titles, all have their faces set in a certain distinct direction. The same seems to be true of the women too. A very clearly distinct lack of contradiction within the character from complexity of behaviour. Ray's one-way facing characters are often very complex in their motivations and behavior. Charu's mind is analysed strand by strand, moment by moment, and this is a very rewarding experience. At times she is pulled in different directions, towards her husband; towards her lover, but she does not herself initiate moves in opposite directions. The later films share this characteristic with the early ones.

Throughout the British period and a good part of the period of Independence, progress in India has been brought about by the cultural elite, which in Bengal was largely identified with the rich landed gentry—the zamindar class—created by the "Permanent Settlement" system of British management of land revenue. Tagore was himself a hereditary zamindar or landowner of no mean proportions; like him, many others in Bengal utilised the leisure which their status brought them, and initiated most of the reformist and intellectual movements of the times. Elitism, flowing from that context, does not therefore carry the fashionable opprobrium it has collected in more recent decades.

It is also interesting to consider the looks of his heroes and heroines. A great many of them have the recognised classically handsome features. Of the young men, Soumitra Chatterjee, who looks strikingly like the young Tagore in *Apur Sansar*, is obviously a favourite type for Ray. The looks represent a clear affiliation with the cultural elite; the features and the colouring are Brahmin, *Ravindrik* (Tagorean), what Aparna's mother calls god-like at first glance in *Apur Sansar*. Sympathetic characters portrayed in later films are similar in type, introspective latter-day Apus subtly changed with the times and yet recognisable—Dhritiman Chatterjee in *Pratidwandi*, Pradip Mukherjee in *Jana Aranya*. Among the young women, the two most important are Sharmila Tagore and Madhabi Mukherjee. It is interesting to observe that the other women don't play a really dominant role in any film. It was not for nothing that Sharmila was cast as the goddess in *Devi*; she is distinctly the type described in Bengal as Durga-like. Her similarity to the image of goddess, at the beginning and end of the film, is very marked. Although Madhabi Mukherjee's features are too individual to fall into this category, she nevertheless has a classical beauty of her own, and an introspective aspect which places her among the cultural elite. Babita, the Brahmin wife in *Asani Sanket*, does not share the introspection of Sharmila or Madhabi but has the "upper class" good looks.

There are thus old-fashioned aspects of his work (some of which Robin Wood is constrained to defend in his *The Apu Trilogy*) which can be understood only in relation to the classical framework.

২২/
১/
৮৪

শ্রীমান সন্দীপকুমার মল্লিক —

সতৃম স্নেহাস্পদ,

২।

Doppel-Gänger (

Science Fiction বা Fantasy

staples —

# Creative Approaches

The script of a Satyajit Ray film was never duplicated, bound and distributed. Ray held it close to his chest when he read it out to the performers to initiate them into his concept. It contained much more than dialogue and notation of action and location. It had sketches, notes, musical ideas, elaborate descriptions that would evoke his original concepts, and relationships, faces, places, throughout the time of shooting and editing. A note in the script of *Aparajito* asks: "Where does Sarbajaya keep her money?"

Increasingly over the years, Ray had extended his hand directly into the many departments of film-making. He had, of course, always written his own scripts; at times, his own stories as well. He could not dream of making a film of someone else's script. Even in the days of *Pather Panchali*, I would see him towering behind the editor working at the moviola, chewing his handkercheif to shreds as he watched the image, and shouting "Cut!" so sharply as to startle people in the next room. His editor made occasional creative suggestions, some of which he would accept with a childlike thrill, and reject others with a glum face. But there was no question, as so often in the West, of leaving the cutting to the editor, to approve it later on and to make a few broad changes based on other people's reactions. Every little step in film-making was, for Ray, an intimate act of great importance which only he could handle. Very unlike Hollywood, which many suppose to have been his mentor, partly by himself as well.

Contrast with this the Sidney Lumet approach: "In spite of his box office prominence, Lumet has sometimes failed to garner critical acclaim; his talent, some claimed, was "interpretative" rather than personal. He was not, these critics accused, an *auteur*. Lumet, his eyes glittering behind dark-framed glasses, sneers at them: "Film for me is a performing, communal, art form, and not the work of a single individual". He acknowledges his dependence on the cast and crew no less than on unpredictable factors—even the weather. "I think the magic is in the *communality* of it." Indeed in a photograph of a script conference of Lumet's *Prince of the City*, I counted 22 heads gathered round a square table.

That also has a lot to do with cost, a kind of cost no honest Third World film-maker can flaunt. It was often said that a Ray masterpiece could be made for a fraction of the transport budget of a Hindi or Tamil mainstream film. Told that Attenborough's *Gandhi* had cost 20 million dollars, Ray observed that he could have brought in the same film in under five million Indian rupees (at that time equivalent to less than four hundred thousand US dollars).

Direction of acting is something most film-makers go into in detail, perhaps greater detail, than Ray. He would not rehearse dialogue in advance of shooting as some do; dialogue plays a part in his films so different from theatre and it is so integrally a part of the milieu that to rehearse it inside a room might render it meaningless. On the other hand, especially with non-professionals, he would dictate every angle of the head, every minute gesture and make sure to inform the gestures, with human significance. With children he would go down on his knees and whisper conspiratorially, but try to get as exact a conformity as possible, leaving only the remainder (still a lot) to the child's spontaneity. With professionals, much was left to a silent understanding, but positions, movements, stances were often dictated clearly. Very early in his career, just after *Aparajito*, Ray was directing Chhabi Biswas in *Jalsaghar*. The famous actor was dreaded by most other directors, whom in fact he often directed. On Ray's set he overwhelmed everyone by coming in fully costumed and asking: "Mr Ray, where shall I stand?" Ray told him, showed him when to pat his bulging stomach, and to look at the mirror.

The natural character of an actor was important to Ray not only in the case of the non-professional but in that of the professional as well. He must, in real life, reflect some of the basic qualities sought in the character to be portrayed. Acting against the grain of the actor's nature was unacceptable in Ray's scheme of things. In *Abhijan*, for once, he put a beard on Soumitra Chatterjee and made him play a man of an altogether different social class from the actor's own; yet the contemplative base of his nature was not changed. The deviation he accepted was unusual in

Ray's work, and put too much of a middle-class complexion on a working-class character to be a complete success. In Bengal's miniscule film industry, the number of capable actors and actresses available is so small that the insistence on a natural casting imposes a severe limitation. Not for nothing did Ray often express his envy of Bergman, who could call upon an actress of the calibre of Liv Ullmann to play *Scenes from a Marriage* from out of his stock company. Ray's actors and actresses exude more or less the same impression of themselves in real life as they do on screen. Soumitra Chatterjee, Dhritiman Chatterjee (of *Pratidwandi)* or Pradip Mukherjee (of *Jana Aranya*) all have the unmistakable imprint on them of an intellectual bent of mind, and a contemplative nature. The characters they play on the screen are very like themselves. This reduces the gap between professional and non-professional, except for a certain fluency and insight into effects which the former develop through experience. Ray himself noted that in Bengali, it is easy to personally act out the scenes to guide the actors; this he could not do in *Shatranj ke Khilari* because it was in Urdu—hence he had to rely on professionals of recognised talent.

A great deal of acting today is concerned with hyping and emotionalising—a sort of digging deeper and deeper into the present moment. Much of what is called professionalism in acting consists of this extraction of the last ounce of emotion out of any situation, as though the more a character tears his/her guts out in public, the greater the acting is. The more this happens, the farther and farther away it gets from the space and time surrounding an event and the parallels with other events which make it unique. It brings about a tremendous emphasis on the present moment, as though it will last for ever. It is the sense of permanence rather than the impermanence of life that it creates in the audience. It is precisely this kind of acting that Ray carefully avoided. He was much more concerned with his characters reflecting upon their actions even as they acted them out; hence the contemplative feeling about the acting style he adopted.

As far as camera placements, choice of angle and lens were concerned, the decisions were always entirely his. Often Ray would admonish the cameraman and ask him to reduce the light at a certain point because it was too bright, sometimes against the wishes of the cameraman. The impossible became possible so often at his insistence that the cameraman learnt to do as he was told. With Subrata Mitra, he developed a style of bounced lighting to simulate daylight in interior scenes, which makes for naturalness; and speed in taking shots, as it eliminates basic changes in lighting with every change of camera set-up. It also serves to give a simple but effective continuity to the quality of light, and a soft, shadowless modelling to the faces. From after *Charulata*, he began more and more to operate the camera himself; he had to be sure of what was happening before the lens by looking through it during the take. Sometimes this would result in a slight fault of operation which would have to be compensated in the editing, or even allowed to stand if the main effect was right. However, one has to admit that photographically his films never quite acquired the quality that Subrata Mitra had given him in most of his films upto *Nayak*. (1966).

Ray's favourite lens was the 40 mm, which corresponds best to normal human vision. He tended to avoid the extreme close shot and the extreme wide angle, both of which to him were a sort of hyping, one invading privacy and the other falsifying perspective.

In set design, as much as in the camera work, the collaboration between him and the designer (Bansilal Chandra Gupta in most of the films) was extremely detailed and the understanding had to be complete in every respect. All title designs of his films were his own, and the majority featured his own calligraphy. Technical contributions had to be completely subordinated to his, not overall, but detailed and specific concept.

With his lifelong passion for music (mostly Western in the earlier days), it became increasingly difficult for him to accept what famous musicians did for him—Ravi Shankar, Ali Akbar Khan, Vilayat Khan—even after detailed discussion and tiresome attempts to impose his will on theirs. Seeing *Pather Panchali* again today, one is struck by the rightness of folk melody and the variations on it in the instrumentation, but must find some of the classical set pieces—sounding like excerpts from stage recitals—equally jarring. Also disturbing is the over-use of music where none is needed, even in as perfect a work as *Apur Sansar*. Some of Vilayat Khan's crescendoes in *Jalsaghar* are strident and unimaginative—a falling back on film-music cliches which must have jarred on Ray's sensitive ears. One is forced to sympathise with Ray, as Vanraj Bhatia, for long the only western-trained classical music composer working in the cinema in India did, about his impatience with musicians writing music for his films.

*Charulata* showed the rightness of his decision in taking up the composing himself not only in the singular aptness and memorability of the compositions, but in the austerity of their use. Too often, music composers impose not only their interpretation of concepts, but the mode and extent of application of music, on the film director; and too often, film directors are content to accept them, not being as acutely aware of music as Ray. Besides, a film like *Charulata, Aranyer din Ratri, Jana Aranya* or *Shatranj Ke Khilari* is conceived in terms of the exactness of flow of western classical music. To transmit such conceptions to another person without loss must be a difficult task.

For *Hirak Rajar Deshe*, a fantasy sequel to *Goopi Gyne Bagha Byne*, Ray made bound volumes of his costume designs, complete with material clippings, selected by himself, pinned to the pages next to each illustration. To Ray, creativity was indivisible; he was as completely the *auteur* of his work as anyone could be.

## II

The key to this almost obsessive onemanship imposed on a medium well-known for collaborative functioning may be found in an episode during the shooting of *Pathar Panchali*, which he described in an essay in *Our Films, Their Films*:

> One of the shots I had to take on that first day was of the girl Durga observing her brother Apu—who is unaware of her presence—from behind a cluster of tall, swaying reeds. I had planned on a medium close-up with a normal lens, showing her from waist upwards. We had with us that day a friend who was a professional cameraman, while I stood behind the reeds explaining to Durga what she had to do in the shot, I had a fleeting glimpse of our friend fiddling with the lenses. What he had done was take out the normal lens from the camera and substitute one with a long focal length. "Just take a look at her with this one," he told me as I came to look through the view finder. I had done a lot of still photography before, but in my unswerving allegiance to Cartier-Bresson, I had never worked with a long lens. What the finder now revealed was an enormous close-up of Durga's face, backlit by the sun and framed by the swaying, shimmering reeds she had parted with her hands. It was irresistible. I thanked my friend for his timely advice and took the shot. A few days later, in the cutting room, I was horrified to discover that the scene simply did not call for such an emphatic close-up. For all its beauty, or perhaps because of it, the shot stood out in blatant isolation from its companions and thereby spoilt the scene. This taught me, at one stroke, two fundamental lessons of film making: (a) a shot is beautiful only if it is right in its context, and this rightness has little to do with what appears beautiful to the eye; and (b) never listen to advice on details from someone who does not have the whole film in his head as clearly as you do.

This early episode put Satyajit on his guard against creative ideas suggested by others who did not carry in their minds the extremely detailed visualisation of the film he had made, often complete even with music, long before a foot was shot.

Is it really necessary to be so singular in film-making in order to be creative? The extent of it in Ray may appear somewhat egocentric. Many directors have been known to leave the various departments of film-making largely to the experts, develop their ideas through various stages of production and exercise only a general control over them, yet leaving a personal stamp upon the end product. A case I have personally observed is of James Ivory directing *The Guru*. Ivory presided uncertainly over a collection of outstanding talent, guided as much by them as guiding them himself. This was true to the extent that to be on the set of *The Guru* was to think that the cameraman, Subrata Mitra, was the director, judging by the way he was controlling the groupings and action, not to speak of camera set-ups. Ivory's mark on his films was, at that time solely in terms of certain broad creative choices exercised mainly before and after the shooting and preliminary editing rather than through an intense personal involvement in the processes in between. Many European directors, Renais for instance, barely look through the lens; they are content to outline their broad requirements to the director of photography. Even Jean Renoir did not go into every detail of every shot or costume himself to the extent that Ray would do. Perhaps Ray's method resulted from the rare combination in one person that he happened to represent. Perhaps the particular kind of film he made required this single-minded direction—an exquisite film like *Charulata*, for instance, in which every movement is so fragile, so delicately poised and conceived with the exactness of music, that the minutest deviation would shatter the entire illusion. If the same attention to detail appears to be wasted on a film like, say, *Mahapurush*, it is because the unitary style of working had become a part of Ray's nature.

### III

A remarkable feature of Ray's method, especially in the earlier films, is his constant awareness of the flow of life outside the tight circle of the business at hand. Harihar is dying; Apu is going to fetch the holy water from the river at dawn. The athletes exercising at the riverside have no direct bearing upon the scene except to remind us of the inexorable flow of life, indifferent to individual joys and sorrows. The stars reflected in the still waters of the tank on the eve of Sarbajaya's death carry resonances of cosmic cycles, turning in disregard of the woman pining for her son in a village on planet earth.

This is closely related to the slow rhythm of Ray's films, again especially the early ones, which some audiences abroad find hard to bear. His films do not meet the rhythm of their lives, not even ours, in much of urban India. They impose their own rhythm on the audience. Like many literary classics, they are never in a hurry. One is lifted out of the pace of middle-class city life and placed in the heart of Indian reality, surrendering to the rhythm of life as it is lived by the majority of the people, and has been, for hundreds of years. Identification with this rhythm of the life of the people is important; in most of Ray films, especially those placed in rural or period settings, is expressed a deeper sense of Indian reality than the one we are used to in our islands of modernity in India. It is very different from the slow tempo of the Italian film-maker Antonioni, who demands a response not natural to the western way of life today, and thereby creates an inner tension. Antonioni seeks, as it were, the identification of his audience with the particular rhythm of the life an individual alienated from that of the society around him. The majority is lured into an understanding of a minority. Ray's is exactly the opposite; it is inducing the small minority of city-bred individuals to find time to listen to the slower heart-beat of the way of life of rural people or people held within a long tradition of unhurried movement.

The characters in Ray's films are borne on the flow of a river, as it were, in which a large force carries them towards their destiny, and their own manoeuvres do not count for a great deal. Charu is drawn, by an invisible force which she does not know, into a sort of rhythmic flow. Think of the gentle rocking movements in the last swing scene where the camera tracks along the ground, showing the crumpled pieces of paper, her rejected efforts at writing lying among the dead leaves, and climbs up her arm to her face, as the super-impositions come one after the other, the highlights in the eyes looking like the burning sun; the boat slowly swings down the frame, the *Charak* dancers rock forward and back in counterpoint to the lateral movement of her face as she rocks gently on the swing. The design of the movement not only maintains the continuity of her swinging throughout the visions that are pressing through her mind, but parallels the rhythm of the process through which she arrives at a sure idea of what she wants to write. It is in a scene like this that we see Ray's mastery of rhythm, arising exactly from the action and revealing its exact meaning without the help of words. It is interesting to remember here that Ray himself, in a letter to me, compared his films with the paintings of Pierre Bonnard, "Where the human figure has not much more importance than the table, the fruit, the flowers, the landscape, the door."

In films like *Pratidwandi* or *Jana Aranya*, the pace is much more brisk; the sense of a flow is less evident, but underlies the action nevertheless. The rhythm, even when not slow, is never interrupted. It holds all the characters and the action within it in a musical exactness. All his films, with the possible exception of *Shatranj ke Khilari*, have a perfection of structure built brick by brick, which sometimes rescues even a banal content, as in *Nayak*, and gives it a compelling interest. The beginning of *Jana Aranya* keeps piling detail upon detail without apparent reason; but from the moment Somnath slips on that banana peel, it begins to move—

the introduction is over—and as it moves towards its tight drama, all the earlier detail come into play, holding up the structure of the action in the foreground. The slow rhythm is also an outcome of Ray's "silent observer" point of view. He wants us to see the events take place before us and to draw our own conclusions. Of course, this is a device, and we are being manipulated; but it also communicates a mood of silence. Since words do not play a large part, what is happening in a character's mind must be expressed through his actions. This communication of events of the mind is the most difficult thing in the cinema since the camera records only the surfaces of reality; it is here that Ray is the undisputed master.

Necessarily, the process of a character's thought takes time to communicate itself silently. Apu stands before the mirror after Aparna's death and stares at his unshaven image in the mirror with distaste; the familiar sound of the train acquires a new ominous overtone and prepares us for the cut to the railway track and the impending attempt at suicide. There are innumerable instances of this nature in Ray's work, where the avoidance of overt comment expands the time element and gives every movement or sound an exact psychological meaning, and invests the whole sequence with the transparency of glass. Slow movement becomes inevitable to such detail-rich and complex textures. If anything, in his best films, the pace is not slow enough for us to take in everything; every repeat viewing brings its own reward, for new aspects come to light every time. But in the earlier films, almost all characters move slowly, sometimes in a mannered way. Amulya picks up the letter from his bed in *Samapti*—a very casual action—at an impossibly slow pace, as if he was going to touch dynamite. It is as though there is a fixed metronomic measure of movement for all characters. A jerky movement would have been more natural, but the actor has not been wound up that way. In contrast, a film like *Aranyer Din Ratri* has each character moving to a rhythm of his own. The elite, the thinking ones—represented by Soumitra Chatterjee and Subhendu Chatterjee—move slowly; the man of action, played by Shamit Bhanja, moves to a brisk measure of his own; the comical hanger-on, acted by Robi Ghosh, moves restlessly, perhaps to hide his diffidence. The film itself moves in a confident, unhurried manner, secure in the inevitability of the path described. Parts of *Jana Aranya* move very fast indeed, complete with hand-held shots and tracking down narrow lanes in shaky cars. But Somnath, with his introspection, always moves more slowly than the other characters. Again the rhythm of the film as a whole remains even, unruffled, sure of where it is going. Even when the rhythm speeds up, it does so imperceptibly. Ray's films are not overly long, and often much seems to happen in them; yet there is never a sense of hurry, because of this fine structural rhythm.

An interesting aspect of this structural quality is Ray's concern with the obvious, sometimes, indeed the overstressing of it. Since he builds brick by brick from the ground, he is careful not to ignore what might seem obvious to some sections of his audience. In *Kanchanjungha*, the Rai Bahadur's admiration of the British is not implied; it is made plentifully clear, almost more than necessary. In *Parash Pathar*, considerable time is spent on establishing the conditions of the life of the clerk before he finds the stone, in *Mahanagar* in piling on the details of the work that Arati does, in *Aranyer Din Ratri* in the exact way in which the friends come to occupy, and to stay on in, the government bungalow for which they have no reservation. In *Seemabaddha* and in *Shatranj ke Khilari*, documentary methods are used to establish the facts. In Ritwik Ghatak's brilliant film *Ajaantrik*, the tribals suddenly and rather disconcertingly break upon the screen in the second half of the film. Ray would never have countenanced such a thing; he would have painstakingly introduced them somewhere towards the beginning so that we would easily pick up the thread when they came later.

At times, this concern with the obvious results in awkward exaggeration and symbolism. In *Jalsaghar*, Mahim, the ugly capitalist, takes snuff and makes eyes in an almost silent-film-style exaggeration. The symbolism of the upturned model boat on a shelf, the insect struggling in the wine glass before news comes of the death of the zamindar's wife and son in a boat disaster are equally silent-film-like, and somewhat unnecessarily heavy. On the other hand, the chandelier reflected in the wine is exquisite; it is not merely a symbol—it is an expression of visual delight in a deeply relevant image. In *Aranyer Din Ratri*, as Sharmila refers to the slowness of time, she has to let a handful of sand filter through her fingers, suggesting the loneliness. But nowhere is Ray's fondness for the obvious more apparent than in the dream sequences of *Nayak*. They are "given" dreams, celebrated in the myths of millions of filmgoers. Indeed, they are not the dreams of the individual who is the film-star, they are the dreams that the public thinks he should dream.

At its worst, this penchant for the obvious makes him slip into the banal; at its best, it gives his structures a singular clarity and strength, making most of his denouements extraordinarily credible.

Perhaps because there is always a sense of the flow of characters and events carried along time by forces greater than themselves, flashbacks are not a part of Ray's standard technique. Where they occur, they are seldom altogether happy—witness them in *Kapurush*, *Nayak* or *Pratidwandi*; Ray prefers the direct chronological order, with interrelated characters and events flowing along a time sequence.

Perhaps also when a time sequence is clear, and all questions arising from it have been resolved in the script, the motivations have been analysed, the shooting has come to be so clearly visualised that there is no need for options to be left open for later decision. Many famous film directors all over the world shoot whole sequences which they do not use in the final cut. Ray did that once—in *Pather Panchali*. Sarbajaya finds, during her hard days in the absence of Harihar, a piece from a chandelier which someone describes as a diamond. She does not believe, but later takes it to a jeweller in secret, only to be told that it was indeed glass. Part of the sequence was shot, but it could not be completed for lack of money. In Bengali film-making, the financial constraints are such that few people can keep their options open on whole sequences; in the case of Ray, this applies to some extent even to shots, not only for financial reasons, but by reason of the detailed visualisation. His script books—bound and preserved—contain numerous sketches of camera set-ups, and notes on every aspect of a situation.

For *Kanchanjungha*, Ray prepared maps of areas to be shot in misty, sunny and cloudy weather; for *Sonar Kella*, he had a chart of travel and movements in colour, all done by himself. He could usually predict what he was going to do three months and six days hence. There was indeed room for improvisation, never because the ideas for a certain part of the film were not clear to him but because the local circumstances required on-the-spot changes. He had been known to say that it was not enough to visualise the highlights of a film, because all parts of a film were equally important, and must be clearly visualised. He often noted musical ideas alongside dialogues or notes of action, or sketches of camera set-ups, not to speak of sound effects (which he, more often than not, recorded himself).

## IV

Ray seldom used dialogue simply to convey information. The only instance before his last phase—*Ganashatru* and *Shakha Proshaka* in particular—I can think of is the opening of *Abhijan*, where the device was too transparent. In spite of the visual gimmick of the character making his long opening remarks addressed to the image of Narsingh reflected in the mirror, the trick is a bore. In most of his films dialogue expresses as a part of the total ambience; it might be half a sentence, with the rest implied by a gesture or an action. It might supply information while establishing or enhancing a relationship. Sometimes the information was of no importance for story development but is used only to illuminate a relationship; for instance in *Apur Sansar*, Aparna's letter berated Apu for having written only seven letters instead of eight, in eight days. Ray saw dialogue in the cinema as completely different from that in the theatre or in the novel, and rarely failed to break it up to make it part of the texture and feeling of a scene, giving a lot of weightage to what is left unsaid. In *Jana Aranya*, when Somnath comes home and says, with averted eyes, that he has got the contract, it is defined by the large shadow of himself that enters before him, dark with his sense of guilt and self-denigration.

The grace of Ray's films often came from the way he tangentially approached confrontations, averted actions, decisions, events. Where he tried to be direct, the result was often ineffective or jarring. The impact of Durga's death comes in the recollection of it on Harihar's return; Indir Thakrun's death is discovered by the children. Sarbajaya's occurs when Apu is away, and is silently communicated by the still figure of the old uncle standing in the shadows. Aparna dies while she is far away from Apu, and his reaction to the news is direct but not altogether convincing. Harihar's death agony we actually observe; but it is lifted to a philosophical plane by the cuts to the clouds over Benares, the muscleman exercising at dawn, the symphony of light and music and chanting in the *arati* at the Vishwanath temple, the sudden flight of the pigeons, the sense of Benares' timelessness. When Apu returns to Mansapota on hearing of his mother's illness, he sees the Orion reflected in the water tank; when the landlord comes to demand rent from Apu, he asks: "Apurba Babu, what day of the month is it?" He does want his rent, but he also avoids insulting this personable young Brahmin who studies so hard and cooks his own. Apu turns down Pulu's urgings, but, later comes along to marry Aparna; when Pulu asks him to look after his son, he refuses, but we see him turn up at the house later on.

In *Devi*, the formality of the composition and the distance from which Umaprasad speaks to his father tempers the violence of the confrontation. In *Jalsaghar*, the confrontation between feudal lord and capitalist takes place in terms of musical soirees. Bishwambhar Roy's wife dies off-screen; the son's body is brought rather suddenly, and the directness is awkward in the context. *Mahanagar's* spurt of events and coincidences at the end is similarly a little jarring. In *Charulata*, intensity of love is expressed without the lovers even holding hands; there is one impulsive embrace camouflaged by apparent familial affection, but it contributes only a minor note in the tension created between the two. The captivating memory game in *Aranyer Din Ratri*, taken together with the walks, the interplay and repetition of themes, creates a musical statement in which the seduction scenes are only the fortissimos, not raucous even where there is a touch of violence. Because of the gentle nature of story and character development in which "everyone has his reason", sudden forays into the very direct, as in the introduction of the man with the half-burnt face in *Asani Sanket*, become jarring. Even in *Jana Aranya*'s traumatic experience, we are in sympathy with Somnath; it is as if we say to ourselves: what else can he do, this is the world we live in. Somnath and his "public relations" man look for a girl for the client, but never cast a glance at her for themselves. His business associates are all affectionate towards him, and want to help him. In their degeneration, they are not without humanity.

Ray's acceptance of the narrative illusion as the basis of his films dictated much of his technique. One important aim was that the illusion should not be interrupted by any sudden change or intrusion that might make the audience conscious that it was seeing a film. This is evident in his use of similes. In *Aparajito*, Harihar's death is compared to the flight of a bird—a familiar simile in India and elsewhere—but it is cut in such a way that it should not stand out as an intellectual statement as in the silent cinema of, say, Eisenstein. In *Potemkin*, for instance, the three sculpted lions, lying, sitting and standing, are used suddenly to illustrate the literary idea of the royal power waking up to retaliate against the mutineers. Ray carefully establishes the pigeons in advance, the particular place where they gather and fly, so that when he cuts quickly to their flutter and then gently to their flight into the distance, there is no suddenness to wake us up to the intellectual-literary nature of the statement. It becomes a part of our experience of the event as we would see it in real life with the relevant intermingled with the irrelevant; but it leaves a certain complex resonance in the mind. The philosophical and the emotional are fused together into the experience from which they arise. In *Jana Aranya* the song, "shadows are gathering over the forest," makes a comment, through a simile comparing the city to the jungle and the corruption and evil descending over it to the gathering shadows, but care is taken to see that it merges into the narrative flow and does not call attention to itself.

*Shatranj Ke Khilari* is perhaps the only Ray film which broke loose from the narrative format and blended the documentary and the fictional and directly called upon the intellectual faculty. Although there is "documentary" exposition in *Seemabaddha*, it is still a part of the narrative in a way quite different from the conscious transitions from fact to fiction in *Shatranj*.

V

Ray's use of music had a lot to do with the naturalistic surface of his films. Again, the effort is to make the music as spare and imperceptible by itself as possible, especially in the films scored by himself. In *Charulata*, the memorability of the melodies (especially the main theme, which appears with the titles), and the need for not making the audience conscious of the music, come together most successfully. Like Antonioni, Ray appears to reduce music to a minimum and to make it, at least in the first use, come from a recognisable source in reality as far as possible. The use of music in his earlier films is far more plentiful and marked than in the later ones. Even in the earlier films scored by others, Ray's hand is visible in the singing of the folk melody by Indira Thakrun and the later instrumentation and variations on it in *Pather Panchali*. In *Charulata* the song *Aami chini go chini tomaray, ogo bideshini* (I know you, O woman from foreign land) is sung by Amal and later its instrumental variations are used in the background. The other important theme is based on a Tagore song extremely well-known to the Bengali audience: *Mamo chittay niti nrityay/ Ke je baaje, ta-ta thoi-thoi*. Although it is not sung, the Bengali audience knows the words behind the instrumental rendering and can readily see their connection with Charu's restlessness.

Tagore melodies are used in instrumental music elsewhere, such as the melody of the song *Sakhi bohay galo bela, shudhu hasi khela eki aar bhalo lagay* (the day is drawing to a close, empty laughter pleases me no more) used repeatedly in *Devi*. Similarly in *Postmaster*, the melody of the song *Aamaar mon maanay na* (my mind cannot contain itself any more) provides much of the instrumental music. The melodies have a life of their own, and echo feelings which, for Bengali audiences, cannot be totally divorced from the meaning of the words associated with them.

He repeatedly spoke of western music as a source for the nature of form in his films:

> Cinema is a medium which is closer to western music than to Indian music because in Indian tradition, the concept of inflexible time does not exist—There are no "compositions"—the duration is flexible and depends on the mood of the musician.
>
> But cinema is a composition bound by time. That is why I feel that my knowledge of western forms is an advantage. For one thing, the form of the sonata is a dramatic form with a development, a recapitulation and a coda.—Musical forms like the symphony or the sonata have much influenced the structure of my films. For *Charulata*, I thought endlessly of Mozart.

But no matter what the source of the melody, even where it is well-known or has some autonomy, the effort is to make it merge into the narrative. It is worth repeating that in almost all of Ray's films, the narrative illusion predominates, and its smooth, uninterrupted flow is the primary concern in the use of technique. It is important to see that this concern with the narrative, indeed Ray's entire creative approach, arises from a concern for the human being, in a very Indian manifestation. There is an acceptance of the conditions of religious art—art that must fulfil a given spiritual task. Personal expression must be subordinated to the expression of the content dictated by the awareness of social conditions. Yet Ray's cinema is not bound by any social or political ideology; it is the work of a man of conscience.

VI

Satyajit Ray had a close, lifelong friendship with Bansi Chandragupta, the Art Director of all his films from *Pather Panchali* to *Pratidwandi* Thereafter he went away to Bombay, the capital of the film industry in order to earn a better livelihood, in which he was of course quite successful. Ray recalled him for his ambitious period film *Shatranj Ke Khilari* in 1977. The two had such a warm relationship and identity of views that they were able to work together as one, as it were. Both had clear ideas on what they wanted to achieve and did not have any difficulty in combining their talents.

Chandragupta had given up his college studies in Srinagar, Kashmir, during the 1942 agitation. Around this time he met Shubho Tagore the artist and collector who urged him to become a painter. Off went Chandragupta to Calcutta, then devastated by the man-made 1943 famine (the subject of Ray's *Asani Sanket*) and bombed by the Japanese. He found work as assistant to an art director and acted in the film as well. Ray happened to see the film sometime later and liked Bansi's work in it. The two met and became friends in no time. They saw together *Battleship Potemkin* which the Calcutta Film Society, founded in 1947, had imported, and were equally impressed. It was around this time that Jean Renoir came to Calcutta to survey locations for his *The River*. A reception given to him by the Calcutta Film Society brought Renoir together with Ray, Chandragupta, and Subrata Mitra who was later to become Ray's cameraman for many years. Chandragupta became Assistant to Eugene Lourie, Renoir's Art Director. The next landmark of his life was to be the Art Director of *Pather Panchali*, Ray's first film (in which he did an outstanding job), and to continue to work with Ray in that capacity for decades.

In an article on his work, Chandragupta mentions how, during the apprenticeship in the pre-Ray period, he had already come to understand the inter-relations of the art director's function with the other aspects of film-making. Of his work with Renoir, he remarks that the only materials in use then in the Bengali film industry were paper, board and canvas. It astonished him to discover the use of bricks and cement in *The River*. But his main discovery, he goes on to say, was plaster of Paris and its astonishing plasticity and virtuosity as a material which he put to generous use, for the first time, in *Jalsaghar*. It came in handy in achieving his objective of (in his own words) "maintaining the rhythm of the exteriors of the actual palace in designing its interiors", and here the use of plaster of Paris which he had learnt from Eugene Lourie came in very handy.

Among other discoveries he made at this time was "the importance of providing complete flexibility for the camera. The set should be so designed that the director and the cameraman have complete freedom in placing the camera. In other words the elements of the set should not be separately created and then joined together with nuts and bolts or whatever (as was generally done in those days in Calcutta) because then the joints and divides are likely to show up and make camera placements very difficult to devise. The set should be one seamless whole". This was the principle he applied in *Jalsaghar*. A very important factor in doing so was the weathering of all elements to show the graduality of the effect of aging upon various surfaces. He would often use devices like burning a surface, sandpapering, bleaching with caustic soda, roughening with brushes of different sizes and hardness, etc. Most of the time during the making of period films, or scenes of poor homes, Chandragupta would be seen finishing a surface for hours with his own hands, throwing sand from varying distances on a surface before putting plaster of Paris on it so as to obtain a weathered texture. Altogether, the absence of sophisticated gadgetry (such as spider's web machine) caused for constant improvisational skill which Chandragupta was able to provide in plenty. Remarking on his work, Satyajit Ray said "He was a perfectionist. He would go on and on trying to get the effect right until he was satisfied. The way he worked had to be seen to be believed. Research was one of his main preoccupations." There were times during the shooting when Chandragupta often had to be pulled away from a set because the director and the cameraman thought it was already very good and the shooting should get along.

> A set exists only in relation to the script—a set which is an end in itself is a bad set. The Art Director creates the physical surroundings of the dramatic action, so that the characters merge with the surroundings.
> My first chance to prove this came in *Bhor Hoye Elo* (The Dawn is Coming, Satyen Bose 1952) and I think I successfully created the depressing reality and drab claustrophobic surroundings that the lower middle class lives in. It was a breakthrough and the film-makers as well as the public became conscious that reality could be so forcefully created on the screen. *Pather Panchali* had different problems. Merging artificially created settings with already existing ones in

natural surroundings is a problem which required meticulous care and judgement. This sort of set was something new to me.

*Jalsaghar* was a challenge of a different sort and required a lot of technical know-how to achieve the effect. Sets in films must look convincing; they should seem to belong to the characters but this does not necessarily mean realism. Sets must be done in such a way that camera mobility is not hampered and that characters fit in.

I was attached to Bengal National Studio for about one year. I learnt quite a lot about art direction from Eugene Lourie when he came to India with Jean Renoir. This opportunity came because Renoir was looking for local technicians and I with others was chosen. Renoir was very much satisfied with our work.

I believe art directors must know a good deal of architecture, painting and social history and must above all have enough imagination to touch the heart of the subject. In *Aparajito* the house was a set inside the studio. The interiors in *Apur Sansar* were also built in the studio (something that many people did not realise; the general impression was that the neo-realist Ray was always at that stage shooting real interiors). Generally speaking the art direction in our country is primitive. The prevalent system of set construction is antiquated and hampers the movement of equipment. Although we have a fine lot of construction workers in Calcutta studios, some basic minimum mechanical aids are absolutely necessary to aid human skill, save labour and time. The working conditions in our studios are miserable.

## VII

Ray's usual tendency was to stick to the normal human vision which led him to the predominant use of the 40mm lens—the lens that draws the least attention to itself. For the same reason, he tended to avoid, as far as possible, the big close-up, the extreme wide angle as also the extreme low angle and the direct top shot. He did not shun any of these with any absolutism; but an examination of his work shows a clear preference for the shot without flourish, the shot that provides the greatest transparence between the subject and the spectator, leaving the illusion as uninterrupted as possible by any awareness of the camera. To an extent this is true of all narrative cinema, especially of Hollywood; but American cinema admits considerable hype within, the parameters of the audience unawareness doctrine, respecting only the frontiers beyond which the continuity of illusion would be completely broken. In Ray's approach, the camera showed progressively greater humility as his experience of film-making grew and his sensibility ripened.

*Jalsaghar* provides, along with *Devi* an outstanding exception to these principles. Here there is abundant use of low and top angles, the close shot and the wide angle shot but with camera movements kept to the barest minimum. Obviously, the object was to emphasise the formal dignity of the subject with stasis, and to suggest the larger-than-life element that Bishwambhar Roy's mantle of aristocracy imposed upon him. The camera is shrewdly used to imply the landlord's exalted sense of his own image.

Like Bansi Chandragupta with art direction, Subrata Mitra, Ray's cinematographer, had a great sense of identity with the director's approach and purpose from the very beginning of their association. He had begun life as a still photographer. It is said that when he first used a 35 mm movie camera to shoot Ray's first film, *Pather Panchali*, he had to be shown which button to press in order get the camera rolling. Like Chandragupta, he too associated with the Calcutta Film Society and encountered Renoir during the work on *The River*. He became a regular observer of the shooting and learnt a great deal from it.

Perhaps Mitra's most important contribution to Ray's films was the lighting of the interiors. For instance, there was much improvisional skill in the way he photographed the chandelier in *Jalsaghar*, using almost imperceptible movement forward, raising all the lights to the cat's walk, and subduing the major lighting scheme to the clarity of the candles. Bansi Chandragupta would repeatedly look through the lens and treat the body of the lamps to make sure the candles were showing up. Co-ordination between the camera and the art direction was close and complete.

In Ray's *Aparajito*'s interiors in the ancient city of Varanasi, Mitra had already developed his famous technique of shadowless reflected light typical of ancient rooms and enclosed courtyards untouched by direct sunlight. Like Chandragupta, he too strove to achieve a unity between exteriors and interiors and succeeded eminently, by avoiding hard, contrast lights in either.

Much of this inventiveness is worth exploring today because it was so conspicuous in its absence in the Bengali cinema of the time. The difference between outdoors and indoors would be sharp and obvious. Drama was sought in strong direct lighting and the deployment of shadows in Hollywood style but without striving for depth of field. A certain flatness predominated and the monotony of the eye-level shot made things worse. Faced with this tradition, Ray, Mitra and Chandragupta had to devise their departure from the norms of the Bengali film by constantly watching foreign films, Hollywood films in the cinema theatres and European films at the film society, and formulating their own techniques. Besides, they had had their experience of the shooting of *The River*. Film society viewings were enormously enlarged by India's

First International Film Festival in 1952. Ray himself had had a much wider exposure particularly to Italian neo-realism during a few month's stay in London in 1950. From these, the trio evolved their ways of film-making with meagre resources.

Mitra explains the nature of his collaboration with Ray in these words:

As we have been working together for a quite a long time (since 1952), we hardly need any lighting conferences beforehand as such. Unless Manikda (Ray) wants something special, I decide the lighting set-ups on the set. The usual thing is to go to the set on the evening prior to the shooting, when one can be sure of getting at least the bare walls even if the set is unfinished. I find it convenient to discuss things with him as it is usually much easier to visualise the lighting set up after discussing the main camera set-ups, the camera movements or the movements of the actors. If it is an interior day scene, the source of light is usually governed by the position of the doors and windows—through which the set will be mainly illuminated—unless it is a darkish day scene perhaps with all the windows closed. If it is a night scene, the source of light is first determined. It could be the usual room lights hanging from the above, or it may be a table lamp by the bedside which would be the only source of light.

As we basically believe in naturalistic lighting—these decisions about the source of light in the set more or less determine the basic pattern of lighting and also the mood, to a great extent. When he wants even that single table lamp to be off—it obviously means something regarding the mood of the lighting....We practised bounced lighting (first developed in *Aparajito's* Benares interiors by bouncing light off a false sky) in all our films while shooting interior scenes, as this light resembles the kind of light which is available in the interiors in day time in real life. Besides its realistic character, bounced light has a delicate artistic quality as an additional advantage. It is this particular quality, and not only its realistic character which is often demanded in a film, that motivated still photographers like Irving Penn and Richard Avedon to practise bounced lighting. To me, to shoot with nothing but direct lights inside the studios is something like photographing the exterior only in sunlight, sacrificing all the subtle tints of a rainy day or an overcast sky or dawn and dusk. It is like someone refusing to shoot in the mist or not caring for the poetry present in a cloudy sky.

শ্রীমান সন্দীপরঞ্জন মজুমদার —

২২/
৭/
৬৪

সুধীর কল্যাণ,

তোমার পোস্টাল অর্ডার সমেত চিঠি পেয়ে
মনে চিরকাল, এই সব মনে রাখি যে।

তোমরা বোধহয় অনেক এমন কিছু
পাঠায়েছিলে। আমার কাছে বোধ হয় তবে মারাত্মক
এত বা দিতে পারতে, সেই এই কিছু এমন মনে পারিনা,
এ সব বেশ খারাপই তবে আগারি। কিন্তু বিশেষ—
বিলোকী হয়ে এই বছর এত কেন পড়িনি
বেনিয়ম আমরা বড়িয়ে অর্থ পাই। কিন্তু
কথার বাড়িয়ে, এই ঝামেলা বেনের পারি
আমতন — এ ধরেই আমরা এমন কিছু বনেন
বিরে কেই মনে বড় ওইখেন পরিছে বরদ মুল
মরিছি- দিন বেনারাই ঝুমুর এই কারিছে নকন
মুক্ষ আবার মুগুলাই। এবং মেমারী মুলবিরিছে
বিদুর মারিনা।

২।

সবরকমই সমান মুগুলে মুকিন বিমন বুমন বেলগার
মানির এই মার দিয়ে মুর্শিদাবাদ মুনালাগরে। এমার
বেরলর সানকয় মীমগি বিবিকলেই (বিবিবিদ
মানির) মবনমিত মারিতই। Dokhel-Gauguer
বরিমন্ত মানির এই।) দিয়ে সমন সার কবিগা
সমান মরিন।

মুম- মৃগুমিম সময় মারিগে সে সকল আইম আমার
মুন এই সমরাম মুগুমে মুলম মনম মেগানে বেল ও বন
লিগালি। নবে দিখত সময়াল মুগুরা আমার বিগামের,
এই সময় বোম নমা মামায় মুবিত মরন-বরন মবে
মুমগী মবলে এই সমরত সার কুমে তে। মাম মুবুলা
আগম মুমন বিবাগা আম আমল মিবাবত, এমন
মনে মুবিল।

একটা অফিসে আমায় মন মনা বিষ্টি ছিল নিয়ে।
আমু ও বিগুলা মুক্তরা বমিন্দ, মবিক মামনি মিনা বিগাবি
Science Fiction র Fantasy মিমন মেমন মুন্তিত ঘুমনে র
staples - ব মমন মুমন নমন ভবিগ মা, মেমবিই,
মুমর, মবিত মিন দিন্দা মরা। মেমুন বামমতা।নমে
মেন। মবিগানে দমামগী মামুমা মানিমি মিমন

# Modernism and Mythicality

## I

The modernist enterprise in Ray's films is easily discernible. The trilogy takes the young Apu from a traditional village to a liberal modern education in the humanities; *Devi, Ganashatru* expose the dangers of blind faith; *Mahapurush* and *Joi Baba Felunath* satirise India's godmen; *Sadgati* directs a cold anger at the country's age-old caste hierarchy—the list is long and its modernism unmistakable. The nineteenth century Bengal Renaissance makes itself evident at every step in his long career. Its rationalism, and its propaganda for the cultivation of the 'scientific temper' is obvious in his writings; his detective stories, his stories for children, the children's magazine, are clearly all many coloured essays on a rationalist positivism he inherited from his father and grandfather. Despite his unique ability to treat children as equals, which invests the children in his films with a living character and an authenticity rare in Indian cinema, his urge to teach them to grow up as rational, secular and democratic human beings is instantly detectable. On the face of it, therefore, the mythopoeic seems to be far from his concerns. But is it really so?

The relationship of what an artist says about his work and what the work says about him, has always been an intriguing one. To define the contours of what is consciously formulated and what rises from within the depths of the psyche has ever proved a contentious area not only in itself but particularly between the artist's view and the critic's. Even where a film director selects a certain option overtly imposed by the exigencies of the situation in an art which manipulates reality to the extent of the cinema, the selection is often traced to psychological predisposition's hotly denied by the director himself.

Satyajit Ray considered himself an eminently conscious artist, well aware of what he was doing and why. He was given to a great degree of meticulous planning and subdued the improvisatory elements to the minimum. Thus when the present writer once stated that Ray's *Mahanagar, Charulata* and *Kapurush* formed a continuous line of thought on the condition of woman in today's India, Ray instantly countered that he had thought of the second film long before the first and therefore the formulation of such a sequence would not be valid. The idea that the chronology of the thought was less important than the sequence that actually emerged did not endear itself to him at all.

In his writings, interviews and pronouncements, Ray frequently endorsed the modernist element in his mental make-up, he repeatedly emphasised his agnostic indifference to religion. What is more, he acknowledged his debt to Hollywood and to western classical music with its fully pre-composed dramatic structure as opposed to the improvisatory linearity of its Indian counterpart. In a letter to me (27 September 1989) he said:

> I don't think Indian art traditions have had anything at all to do with my development as film maker...I am firmly of the opinion that cinema is a product of the west—where the concept of an art form existing in time has been prevalent for several centuries. Indian culture shows no awareness of such a concept. If I have succeeded as a film maker, it is due to my familiarity with western artistic, literary and musical traditions. Add to that my observation of Indian life and you have my prescription.

But whether he liked it or was aware of it or not, Ray inherited, from his grandfather, his father and Rabindranath Tagore as well as his school at Santiniketan where Ray studied art for two and a half years, their modernist-social reformist tradition on the one hand and a religious-philosophical Indianness on the other. Both became distinctly discernible in his films.

The dominant religious orientation in his ambience was derived from a modernised and selective version of the Upanishadic and Buddhist wisdom of the late second to the middle of the first millennia BC, the first imbued with a sense of an intelligence permeating the universe and the second with non-violence and compassion. Both ingrained in him a feeling for India's spiritual tradition—something he hardly ever talked about. Besides, he acquired from his cultural heritage a sense of the unity of the country in the midst of its diversity which Tagore enunciated with much influence on the country's leadership. As we shall see later, these strands manifest themselves in Ray's work in counterpoint to the western form of the construction of his films. Of Santiniketan itself he says, after bemoaning the absences he felt in his city-bred self and the lack of films to see :

> It was a world of vast open spaces, vaulted over with a dustless sky, that on a clear night showed the constellations as no city sky could ever do. The same sky, on a clear day, could summon up in moments, an awesome invasion of billowing darkness (during the monsoon) that seemed to engulf the entire universe. And there was the *Khoai* (soil-eroded edges of downgoing land) with its serried ranks of *taal* (palm) trees, and the *Kopai* (a river), snaking its way through its rough-hewn undulations. If Santiniketan did nothing else, it induced contemplation, and a sense of wonder in the most prosaic and earthbound of minds.
>
> In the two and a half years, I had time to think, and time to realise that, almost without being aware of it, the place had opened windows for me. More than anything else, it had brought to me an awareness of our tradition, which I knew would serve as a foundation for any branch of art that I wished to pursue. ....Santiniketan taught me two things—to look at paintings and to look at nature.

The contradiction between the western form of cinema he consciously pursued and thought of as his own, and the invisibles that took over their background is discernible from more of his Santiniketan experience recounted by himself:

> It was Santiniketan which opened my eyes to the fact that the kind of painting that I used to admire that provoked the reaction: 'How lifelike', should be a preoccupation that lasted only 400 years. It started with the first awareness of perspective in the fifteenth century, and ended with the invention of photography in the 19th. The first representations of nature by man are believed to be the stone age cave paintings of 20,000 years ago. What is 400 years in a span of 200 centuries?
>
> Neither Egyptian nor Chinese, Japanese or Indian art ever concerned itself with factual representation. Here the primary aim was to get at the essence of things; a probing beneath the surface. Nature was the point of departure for the artist to arrive at a personal vision.
>
> Two trips to the great art centres of India—Ajanta, Ellora, Elephanta, Konarak and others—consolidated the idea of Indian tradition in my mind. At last I was begining to find myself, and find my roots.

Obviously, what we have here is markedly different from what he asserts in the excerpt from his letter to me quoted earlier. The letter almost claims the status of a foreigner (Lord Macaulay's "Brown Englishman") making films in India. What his thoughts on Santiniketan speak of is a quintessential Indian who borrowed the medium of cinema from the west along with its grammar if not all of its idiomatic structure.

It is not only in association with Bibhutibhushan Bandyopadhyaya that Ray's most Indian traits can be discerned in his films. We see them even in *Devi*, ostensibly a film of protest against superstition. In the "Postmaster" segment of *Teen Kanya* the heartlessness of the postmaster's casual departure, unaware of the feelings of the little maidservant who has grown so fond of him, interpreting his casual gestures of kindness and interest in her welfare as signs of a close personal bond, is as much a part of the forces of nature and the inexorability of change as the father-in-law in *Devi* who victimises his son's young wife without any knowledge of the forces acting within him. In *Aranyer Din Raatri* one cannot but feel the sense of the young men and women caught at a given point of time and place in the inevitabilities of courage and cowardice, mindlessness and lust. Tomorrow everything will change, but today they exist, and somehow, must behave as they do. Ray is miraculously able to always make us conscious of this at the back of our minds. Even in the dance sequence in *Shatranj Ke Khilari* while the king's minister waits for the exquisite dance to be over before informing his Lord of the British usurpation of his throne, there is the same sense of the inexorability of what has to happen. The delicate, fugitive beauty of the dance emphasises the evanescence of the moment, a critical moment in the history of the land. The same sense emanates from the very character of Nikhilesh in *Ghare-Baire*. At the back of our minds, the thought impinges on us that all these characters could have been at some other time and place, caught in entirely different situations, but are at this moment where they are, not by choice but by the play of forces beyond their control. This contemplation of time and fate is forced on us even as we think of the foolishness of the two princes who are obsessively playing chess while their world is collapsing around them without their knowledge (curiously, it is the women in this film, one trying to get her husband to make love and the other trying to conceal her lover from her husband, who seem to be more in control of their actions and to will them).

Ray's creation of a contemplative space for his audience is one of his prime characteristics and a very Indian one at that, running counter to his claim of not being influenced by Indian art traditions. The proposition he presents us in his writings is the somewhat questionable one that as a person he is completely Indian, firmly rooted in his own soil, but his films are western in form, structurally based on western classical music. Apparently he belongs to one culture but produces the art of another. The questions: is it possible for the form to be that independent of the culture within which its content exists? A revealing sidelight on this problem comes through in Stanley Kaufman's comment on the release of *Aparajito* on its faulty sense of timing:

> There is still a bit of difficulty with Ray's sense of timing; a few scenes are brushed off too quickly, a few dwelled on too long. But ideals of timing vary from culture to culture and whether Ray is adhering to the standards of his country or has not mastered timing as practiced by the western artists from whom he has learned so much else, it is difficult to say. The Brahmin looking for a wife, Apu's visit to the temple of the privileged monkeys—are novelistic material, discursive in a film.

Obviously Kaufman does not see that such apparently irrelevant details produce a sense of flow of life going on regardless of the events, the ups and downs, in the life of individuals. The musclemen on the ghats of Benares, the widows in white listening to the reading of religious scriptures or discourses upon them are, he could have added, equally irrelevant. Yet it is these surrounding non-events that give the central event of the growth of Apu's mind and of his father's impending death their uniquely non-western quality. At Harihar's death, a flock of pigeons fly away all of a sudden: the allusion is obviously to the traditional thought of the soul leaving the body like a bird. In *Aparajito*, the tank by the side of which Sarbajaya would sit in the evenings under a tree, reflects the Orion, bringing in a suggestion of infinite time and space within which human life is lived out. In *Apur Sansar*, Apu playing the flute by the riverside evokes the mythological image of the young God Krishna on the banks of Yamuna; when Aparna (Apu's bride-to-be)'s mother sees him, she remarks that she had seen that face before, in folk paintings of the gods; when after Aparna's death, Apu grows a full beard and goes away into the wilderness, throwing away the pages of the manuscript of his much-beloved novel, any Hindu will think of the god Shiva who, in mythology, put his dead wife's body on his shoulder and roamed the mountains of the Himalayas. Ray's work is thus replete with the evocation of ancient myths.

By contrast, Ray's treatment in *Devi* has a much more western, tight and well shaped, structure than the trilogy's relaxed and meandering, discursive form close to the style of Indian classical music in its linearity. In *Devi*, the sense of the premeditated bears strongly upon the viewer. Russian silent cinema techniques with broad spaces and static compositions predominate, helping to establish the period, the formality of relationships, without establishing the geography of the village or any attempt to recreate the period details in the exterior in any depth. The shot of the meandering line of the sick coming to the Goddess to be healed recalls Ivan standing with his staff looking at the vast plain across which his subjects are coming. The howl of jackals suggests the darkness not only of the night but of the age, an age of darkness when human sacrifice to the Goddess was not uncommon. The sound of the wooden clogs on the father-in-law's feet create a sense of menace and doom. Grand formal gestures like this predominate in the style. There are no subplots; the concentration on the grim central tale is absolute.

In the trilogy, he took pains to retain the sense of spontaneous flow of the original; in *Devi* he deals with a much inferior literary work on whose spiritual and artistic qualities he feels obliged to improve in order to bring it upto his own level. For the feel of the film he does not have to rely on the author. In this he succeeds to a degree obvious in the extreme to those who know the rather simplistic original in Bengali. He imposed on it a sense of formality, design and distance to emphasise the universality of the mindset in Hindu society, its propensity towards rationally insupportable beliefs, and the lack of sufficient self-awareness to detect self-deceit and avoid the promotion of that self-deceit to religiosity.

It is essential for Ray here to project an innocent unawareness of the self in order to contrast it to the more modern consciousness represented by the young husband and to prevent the wife's transition into a more modern mindset. Ray feels motivated to propel this change forward through his medium. The enterprise was in no way unique to him; modern Bengali literature has been doing so well into this century. It was only given a further lease of life by the Marxist movement which gained ground in the immediate pre-and post-independence periods, and has been marginalised only recently with the collapse of international socialist power structures and the rise of a cynical consumerism. Of course the modernist project was not confined to Bengal; Ray's two Hindi films, *Sadgati* and *Shatranj Ke Khilari* were both based on Premchand's short stories and took him out of the geography of the Bengal renaissance.

### III

There is another, rather curious route to the discovery of the strand of mythicality in Ray's films and its connection with Indian art tradition; it is through the costuming of his women.

Since the story of *Pather Panchali* is obviously placed somewhere in the late 19th or early 20th century, the natural dress for Sarbajaya would have been a simple cotton sari, an unstitched stretch of bordered cloth wrapped round her frame without a petticoat or a blouse. The petticoat, being worn under the sari would have made little visual difference but the blouse does, as it was introduced to the Bengali woman by Gnanadanandini Devi, wife of Satyendranath Tagore, Rabindranath's eldest brother and the first Indian to join the Indian Civil Service under the Government of British India, in the 1890s. She was the first Bengali woman to come out in public, much to the horror of the orthodox, and accompanied her husband to official parties. She was obliged to develop a suitable style of clothing for the modern Bengali woman and did so by adapting the way of wearing the sari introduced by the Parsi community in Bombay which consisted of a petticoat underneath to make the sari opaque to the view and a blouse to cover the torso fully, particularly the back and the upper arms which the sari did not adequately hide especially when the body was in movement. It was nicknamed in Bengal the "Brahmika sari" after the name of the reformist Hindu community to which the Tagores and later Satyajit Ray himself belonged. By the early decades of the twentieth century, the style had begun to spread among the urban middle class but took much longer to reach the village where older women still dress the traditional way.

It should also be noted that there was in fact a socio-religious injunction among the Hindus against the wearing of stitched clothes to which an exception had been made for men who served the government in any way or were in business or belonged to the zamindar (large landowning) class. The probable reason for this prohibition could be the fact that according to tradition (and the majority of historians) the "Aryans" wore unstitched silk clothes (to this day Hindus are enjoined to wear unstitched silk clothing at all religious ceremonies). Cotton, although traditionally associated with the "non-Aryan", was allowed for daily use perhaps because silk was too expensive. Especially among Brahmins, stitched clothing was rarely worn. As a Brahmin wife, it would have been improper for Sarbajaya to be in anything other than a sari, and a wrapper for the torso for going out of the house, if she could afford it. Stitched clothing on a woman would in those days indicate a Muslim or a Christian.

It is interesting to ask why Ray, who was quite meticulous about the accuracy of such period detail, chose to dress Sarbajaya in clothing that belonged to a later period (except in a few scenes of *Aparajito*—to supply an oedipal undertone to the relationship between mother and son?). Indeed the problem arises not only in the case of Sarbajaya but that of all Ray's women in his period films. It is also interesting to note that he allowed the bare arms and back in the case of very young girls such as Durga in *Pather Panchali*, Ratan in *Postmaster*, Mrinmoyee in *Samapti*, but not in Sarbajaya in *Pather Panchali*, Aparna in *Aparajito*, Doyamoyee in *Devi*. The only exception in a woman in any period film is Ananga in *Asani Sanket* which in fact belongs to a late period, that of World War II, by which time stitched clothes had become somewhat more acceptable in rural Bengal. Even Charulata in the film of the same name is a doubtful case as it is placed in 1879.

The only possible explanation appears to lie in Ray's sense of how much sexuality to allow in the presence of a woman in a particular situation. By and large, his tendency was to cover them, regardless of the period. Only in Ananga in *Asani Sanket* do we see a slight departure. It is in this film that the women, who form an almost secret group in their camaraderie shielded from the menfolk, have a degree of sexuality in them, apart from the two Muslim noblemens' wives in *Shatranj Ke Khilari* whose bodies are of course fully covered, in very period-correct stitched clothing designed by Shama Zaidi (in Ray's other period films there are no dress designers as such). The exposure of a woman's body appears thus to have weighed heavily in Ray's consideration of how to clothe them.

In *Pather Panchali* and the early part of *Aparajito*, Sarbajaya is still a young woman, but in his anxiety to depict her as only the Mother, Ray denies her the sexuality natural to her age and circumstance as a married woman. She does her wifely duties towards Harihar but there is never the faintest suggestion that the two have a marital life in physical terms.

Similarly in *Apur Sansar*, Aparna must be seen as the innocent young girl. The warmth of her sexual life we are allowed to deduce, but to show her arms and back bare would bring out her sexuality too stridently for Ray's taste. She is to him an embodiment of the mythical Aparna, God Shiva's wife whose death would later find her forlorn husband wandering in the forest like Shiva himself. She is an *idea* manifested in a temporal and spatial context. Stressing her flesh and blood presence would take away from her mythicality, her embodiment as the traditional wife with whom her husband would fall in love after marriage. It would make her too much of an individual, appropriate her excessively into a particular time and space and destroy her status as an ideal being, a type embodying the entire history of the ideal feminine in the context of a race and a civilisation. "The mythic in the ordinary" consists of a powerful compression of a historical image, even an action like that of a woman sweeping a floor into a living, believable figure or the repetition of an age-old action in a freshly individuated manner.

It is interesting here to recall what the painter Nandalal Bose, Satyajit's teacher at the art school in Santiniketan, says in an essay on Indian art, "The Image of the Buddha is not the image of a man; it is an image of the idea of meditation, the image of dancing Shiva of the idea of universal rhythm."

Coming to *Devi*, Doyamoyee, also played by Sharmila Tagore with the shadow of Aparna hovering over her, is the embodiment of mythic innocence about to turn into The Goddess. Although she is just married and we have seen a peck of a kiss between husband and wife half hidden by the mosquito curtain, Ray cannot afford to invest her with sexuality because that would obviously in his eyes come in the way of her elevation to Divinity.

The twin motivations that emerge to incline Ray away from women's sexual expression through their bodily presence to the extent of ignoring the essential period detail, are thus interlocked. One may well be his Brahmo puritanical self disinclined to entertain the suggested presence of the flesh implied in the correct period clothing (rather the brevity of clothing); but more importantly, it is his treatment of woman as an embodiment of certain virtues, differently emphasised in different films, in a mythic way which can often be traced to actual mythical figures such as Shiva and Parvati (in her various aspects, including that of Kali) in Hindu mythology. No wonder Pauline Kael, with the habitual keenness of her intuition, found in his work a way of seeing, and showing, "the mythic in the ordinary".

What would have been the consequences if Ray had allowed the innate sexuality natural to Sarbajaya or Daya in their less crisis-ridden moments to emerge? Obviously Ray's task in establishing their characteristics in the situations in which they are placed would be more complicated and make the characters themselves more full of natural contradictions which he would have had to allow for. The relationship of contradictory stands in a character would have had to be explored deeply and made credible. In other words, he would have had to fill in more of their naturalistic detail on the lines of a somewhat western-modern realism. In terms of painting, his evasion of that type of detail, shot with contradictions and yet forming a whole would have been to dim the simplicity and strength of outline which goes back two thousand years to Ajanta Bagh cave paintings enclosing a flat space within well-defined lines (and dependant on linear expressiveness like Indian Classical music; though Ray repeatedly refers to western music, yet his treatment is unique in its linear flow), or say Bankura or Kalighat (Calcutta) folk painting of the 19th century or perhaps more properly to a *folk*-derived style such as Jamini Roy's The Mother, The Wife, The Worker, and similar portraits of typicality enshrining traditional, uni-linear and uncomplicated views which nonetheless compress age-old visions and invest them with a somewhat nostalgic gentleness and charm, a touch of the utopian, in which there is no place for evil. Even the Kalighat style of semi-western shading and modelling of the body is absent in Jamini Roy who at once refines and simplifies his subjects into two-dimensional ideas. Bibhutibhusan's own vision was markedly similar to this; indeed it may have launched Ray in the same direction, a vision that lasted till *Charulata* and then went on adapting itself to the assessment of contemporary reality through the eyes of a changing, modernising, despairing and beleaguered Apu, the Apu of *Apur Sansar* caught in a vicious latterday world. Underlying this simplified vision, there is simple musicality, a detached observation and an absence of the complex interplays of contradiction which create the western type of drama of conflict and resolution in which there is less of a place for compassion and more of involvement in the events moment by moment. In a sense, Ray's world is timeless, even though the films chronicle change; Ray does not throw himself into the welter of things, passionately taking sides. He remains the distant observer who sees the whole being of his characters in a flattered perspective without tonality, volume or mass.

In comparison there is more agony in the work of Ray's contemporaries such as Mrinal Sen or Ritwik Ghatak. Ghatak is particularly relevant here because, despite his more conscious involvement with myths, they choose to encounter the characters at a moment of the loss of the mythic in their lives. They cry out, as it were, for what they are about to lose or know they have lost. Because the moment claims them, the reality wrenches them out of the mythic and throws them headlong into the present. *Subarnarekha* (Ghatak, 1962)'s protagonists are bereaved souls at grips with stark reality where goodness has already given way to cynical, survival-only situations.

Ray is far more concerned with the transition of society and his characters from one state of being to another. In *Devi* he does represent blind faith, unrelieved by rationality whose lack he does emphasise; but what is surprising is that he does not in the process either oversimplify the superstition nor lose sympathy for the characters caught in a predicament whose origins and reasons are apparent to their creator but not to them. The father-in-law who deifies his son's young and beautiful wife and thus takes her away from his son is gloriously unaware of the fact. There is not a trace of malice in him. In fact he is as much a victim of circumstances—history, tradition, beliefs handed down from ancestors, given beliefs in a given place and time in which he was born and which were not of his choice. Ray's keen awareness of this aspect is enshrined in his treatment of the song for instance which the old grandfather sings sitting on the steps of the temple of the goddess with his dying grandson on his lap. It is set in a traditional tune and there are numerous extant songs by the author Ramprasad in the eighteenth century of the same intent from which Ray could have chosen one. But he chose to write the song himself in the style of Ramprasad. The only motivation one can see in this is that he wanted to enter deeply into the spirit of the song and of the faith with which it was sung and was careful not to trivialise it. Composing the words of the song was a way of orienting himself into it as it were. The *mise-en-scène* bears this out; the attitude of the forlorn old man, the way he sits, the way in which he sings and is portrayed on the screen, are all entirely sympathetic; they reflect fully the state of *his* mind, not the director's. There is here no insolent attempt to dismiss the old man's simple faith with modernist disdain. Similarly when the father-in-law prostrates himself before the young woman as the Goddess, it is with full faith which is no way marginalised or made ever so faintly ridiculous. His son studies in Calcutta at a time and place where rationalist ideas are being inducted into him. That too is a fact of life, not an ideal state prescribed for society. It is the tragedy of the outcome that is emphasised, not the rightness or wrongness of action. Doya is caught between the old and the new and her identity is destroyed by the tension; the truth, the indivisible process through which it happens is what most concerns the director. Ray is in fact here much more detached than say in *Jalsaghar* where he displays a shade of wicked delight in the old landlord's disdain for her young upstart capitalist. At the end of *Devi*, Ray makes one of the many significant changes in the literary original he employs to adapt it to his ways of thinking. One of the most beautiful, most Indian, is the last shot of Doyamoyee running, disappearing, into a misty field of flowers; going back, as it were to her mother earth, making it faintly reminiscent of Sita in the Indian epic of the Ramayana for whom the earth had opened up at the moment of her ultimate humiliation. In Prabhat Mukhopadhyay's short story, she commits suicide by hanging herself by her sari from a girder on the roof.

However, from a formal point of view, the most important non-western feature in Ray is the slowness of the tempo and what has been called the contemplative space his cutting always provides despite its basically western style. Another is his use of the camera, in which there is a preference for the natural human vision (the 40mm lens) and the general avoidance, with some exceptions, of the big close-up which, he once told me, gave him the sense of the head falling off the screen, something that seemed hyped and false to him. How very different this is not only from the Hollywood style in general and even of say Bergman, possibly the greatest votary of the close-up in the cinema. As Liv Ullmann says;

> I love close-ups. To me they are a challenge. The closer a camera comes, the more eager I am to show a completely naked face, show what is behind the skin, the eyes; inside the head. Show the thoughts that are forming. ....Closer to the audience than in any other medium.....the human being is shown on the screen. The audience, at the time of the identification, meets a person, not a role, not an actress.

Here there is a celebration of the individual, not the type, not even the type slowly becoming an individual for the purpose of the audience. It is not content with the broad contours of folk art, the flat surfaces, the two-dimensionality of virtually all Indian art, classical or folk, even including sculpture in the round which is best seen from one point of view. Western photographers who have tried to photograph overhead figures in Indian temples by getting up to their height only to discover how this distorts the image actually meant to be seen from below. What Liv Ullman is saying of Bergman's close-ups is also utterly different; unlike Indian art, it is all perspective, completely western, showing all details, all tonality within the human being, the whole human being and not just one aspect of him, the particular person, going even beyond the actor's identity into the person that he is. Sarbajaya in *Pather Panchali* is first a type, a mother, a timeless myth, before she is a person. There are aspects of her personality that are carefully hidden from us, as in the case of her sexuality which we know must be present somewhere in her but which, if shown, would reveal her in not the outline stressing one aspect of her character but the entire complexity of her being, full of shading, perspective and tonality. It would divest her of her timelessness, her mythicality and fix her into a particular time and place and a single personality. Perhaps this is also the reason why Ray depended so little on rehearsals and so much more on spontaneous expressions of the natural self of the actor.

Leaving Bergman alone as a unique phenomenon, we find in the Hollywood product of any quality, a liberal use of the big close up in order either to emphasise glamour or to dramatise details of the acting, or both. The Hollywood style of acting more often than not demands the spilling of the guts of a performer in order to create drama. It calls for big close-ups because emotion has to be wrung out of the juices in the actor's system in order to bathe the audience in them, as it were. Hollywood gives its actors the hyped rhythm of the audience's own world; Ray like Bergman or Antonioni, imposed his own rhythm on the audience. He would himself emphasise the rhythm as a product of the subject itself; but behind this justifying philosophy, would lie the rhythm sought by Ray's own feeling which he was anxious not to bring to the fore.

Altogether, much of the impact, the interiority and the sense of timeless mythicality is achieved in Ray's style by a process of holding back the emotional expression in what he once named, talking about Asian cinema (and, in a way, identifying himself with it), as "Calm Without: Fire Within".

# Filmography

### 1955     Pather Panchali (Song of the Road)

Producer: Government of West Bengal. Screenplay: Satyajit Ray, from the novel *Pather Panchali* by Bibhutibhushan Bandopadhyay. Photography: Subrata Mitra. Editor: Dulal Dutta. Art Director: Bansi Chandragupta. Music: Ravi Shankar. Sound: Bhupen Ghosh. 115 mins.

    Cast: Kanu Banerjee *(Harihar)*, Karuna Banerjee *(Sarbajaya)*, Subir Banerjee *(Apu)*, Uma Das Gupta *(Durga)*, Chunibala Devi *(Indira Thakrun)*, Aparna Devi *(Nilomoni's wife)*, Tulsi Chakravarti *(Prasanna, School-teacher)*, Binoy Mukherjee *(Baidynath Majumdar)*, Haren Banerjee *(Chinibash, Sweet-seller)*, Harimohan Nag *(Doctor)*, Haridhan Nag *(Chakravarti)*, Nibhanoni Devi *(Dasi)*, Ksirodh Roy *(Priest)*, Roma Ganguli *(Roma)*.

### 1956     Aparajito (The Unvanquished)

Producer: Epic Films (Satyajit Ray). Screenplay: Satyajit Ray, from the novel *Aparajito* by Bibhutibhushan Bandopadhyay. Photography: Subrata Mitra. Editor: Dulal Dutta. Art Director: Bansi Chandragupta. Music: Ravi Shankar. Sound: Durgadas Mitra. 113 mins.

    Cast: Kanu Banerjee *(Harihar)*, Karuna Banerjee *(Sarbajaya)*, Pinaki Sen Gupta *(Boy Apu)*, Smaran Ghosal *(Adolescent Apu)*, Santi Gupta *(Lahiri's wife)*, Ramani Sen Gupta *(Bhabataran)*, Ranibala *(Telt)*, Sudipta Roy *(Nirupama)*, Ajay Mitra *(Anil)*, Charuprakash Ghosh *(Nanda)*, Subodh Ganguli *(Headmaster)*, Moni Srimani *(Inspector)*, Hemanta Chatterjee *(Professor)*, Kali Banerjee *(Kathak)*, Kalicharan Roy *(Akhil, press proprietor)*, Kamala Adhikari *(Moksada)*, Lalchand Banerjee *(Lahiri)*, KS Pandey *(Pandey)*, Meenaksi Devi *(Pandey's wife)*, Anil Mukherjee *(Abinash)*, Harendrakumar Chakravarti *(Doctor)*, Bhaganu Palwan *(Palwan)*.

### 1958     Parash Pathar (The Philosopher's Stone)

Producer: Promod Lahiri. Screenplay: Satyajit Ray, from the short story

*Parash Pathar* by Parasuram. Photography: Subrata Mitra. Editor: Dulal Dutta. Art Director: Bansi Chandragupta. Music: Ravi Shankar. Sound: Durgadas Mitra. 111 mins.

Cast: Tulsi Chakravarti (*Paresh Chandra Dutta*), Ranibala (*His wife*), Kali Banerjee (*Priyatosh Henry Biswas*), Gangapada Bose (*Kachalu*), Haridhan (*Inspector Chatterjee*), Jahar Roy (*Bhajahari*), Bireswar Sen (*Police officer*), Moni Srimani (*Dr Nandi*), Chhabi Biswas, Jahar Ganguli, Pahari Sanyal, Kamal Mitra, Nitish Mukherjee, Subodh Ganguli, Tulsi Lahiri, Amar Mullick (*Male guests at cocktail party*), Chandrabati Devi, Renuka Roy, Bharati Devi (*Female guests at cocktail party*).

### 1958 Jalsaghar (The Music Room)

Producer: Satyajit Ray Productions. Screenplay: Satyajit Ray, from the short story *Jalsaghar* by Tarasankar Banerjee. Photography: Subrata Mitra. Editor: Dulal Dutta. Art Director: Bansi Chandragupta. Music: Vilayat Khan. Music and dance performed by Begum Akhtar, Roshan Kumari, Waheed Khan, Bismillah Khan and company (on screen), and Daksinamohan Thakar, Asish Kumar, Robin Majumdar and Imrat Khan (off screen). Sound: Durgadas Mitra. 100 mins.

Cast: Chhabi Biswas (*Biswambhar Roy*), Padma Devi (*Mahamaya, his wife*), Pinaki Sen Gupta (*Bireswar, his son*), Gangapada Bose (*Mahim Ganguli*), Tulis Lahiri (*Taraprasanna, bearer*), Kali Sarkar (*Ananta, cook*), Waheed Khan, (*Ustad Ujir Khan*), Roshan Kumari (*Krishna Bai*)

### 1959 Apur Sansar (The World of Apu)

Producer: Satyajit Ray Productions. Screenplay: Satyajit Ray, from the novel *Aparajito* by Bibhutibhushan Bandopadhyay. Photography: Subrata Mitra. Editor: Dulal Dutta. Art Director: Bansi Chandragupta. Music: Ravi Shankar. Sound: Durgadas Mitra. 106 mins.

Cast: Soumitra Chatterjee (*Apu*), Sarmila Tagore (*Aparna*), Alok Chakravarti (*Koyal*), Swapan Mukherjee (*Pulu*), Dhiresh Majumdar (*Sasinarayan*), Sefalika Devi (*Sasinarayan's wife*), Dhiren Ghosh (*Landlord*).

### 1960 Devi (The Goddess)

Producer: Satyajit Ray Productions. Screenplay: Satyajit Ray, from the short story *Devi* by Prabhat Kumar Mukherjee, on a theme by Rabindranath Tagore. Photography: Subrata Mitra. Editor: Dulal Dutta. Art Director: Bansi Chandragupta. Music: Ali Akbar Khan. Sound: Durgadas Mitra. 93 mins.

Cast: Chbabi Biswas (*Kalikinkar Roy*), Soumitra Chatterjee (*Umaprasad, younger son*), Sharmila Tagore (*Doyamoyee*), Purnendu Mukherjee (*Taraprasad, elder son*), Karuna Banerjee (*Harasundari, his wife*), Arpan Chowdhury (*Khoka, child*), Anil Chatterjee (*Bhudeb*), Kali Sarkar (*Professor Sarkar*), Nagendranath Kabyabyakarantirtha (*Priest*), Santa Devi (*Sarala*).

### 1961 Teen Kanya (Three Daughters)

Producer: Satyajit Ray Productions. Screenplay: Satyajit Ray, from three stories by Rabindranath Tagore. Photography: Soumendu Roy. Editor: Dulal Dutta. Art Director: Bansi Chandragupta. Music: Satyajit Ray. Sound: Durgadas Mitra. **The Postmaster**, 50 mins. **Monihara**, 61 mins. **Samapti**, 56 mins.

  Cast: **The Postmaster:** Anil Chatterjee (*Nandalal*), Chandana Banerjee (*Ratan*), Nripati Chatterjee (*Bisay*), Khagen Pathak (*Khagen*), Gopal Roy (*Bilash*). **Monihara (The Lost Jewels):** Kali Banerjee (*Phanibhusan Saha*), Kanika Majumdar (*Manimalika*), Kumar Roy (*Madhusudhan*), Gobinda Chakravarti (*Schoolmaster and narrator*). **Samapti (The Conclusion):** Sita Mukherjee (*Jogmaya*), Gita Dey (*Nistarini*), Santosh Dutta (*Kisori*), Mihir Chakravarti (*Rakhal*), Devi Neogy (*Haripada*).

**1961**  **Rabindranath Tagore**

  Producer: Films Division, Government of India. Script and Commentary: Satyajit Ray. Photography: Soumendu Roy. Editor: Dulal Dutta. Art Director: Bansi Chandragupta. Music: Jyotirindra Moitra. Songs and dances performed by Asesh Banerjee (*esraj*) and Gitabitan (both offscreen). 54 mins.

  Cast: Raya Chatterjee, Sovanlal Ganguli, Smaran Ghosal, Purnendu Mukherjee, Kallol Bose, Subir Bose, Phani Nan, Norman Ellis.

**1962**  **Kanchanjungha**

  Producer: NCA Productions. Original Screenplay: Satyajit Ray. Photography: Subrata Mitra. Editor: Dulal Dutta. Art Director: Bansi Chandragupta. Music: Satyajit Ray. Sound: Durgadas Mitra. 120 mins.

  Cast: Chhabi Biswas (*Indranath Roy*), Anil Chatterjee (*Anil*), Karuna Banerjee (*Labanya*), Anubha Gupta (*Anima*), Subrata Sen (*Sankar*), Sibani Singh (*Tuklu*), Alaknanda Roy (*Manisa*), Arun Mukherjee (*Asok*), N Viswanathan (*Mr Banerjee*), Pahari Sanyal (*Jogadish*), Nilima Chatterjee, Vidya Sinha (*Girlfriends of Anil*).

**1962**  **Abhijan (The Expedition)**

  Producer: Abhijatrik. Screenplay: Satyajit Ray, from the novel *Abhijan* by Tarasankar Banerjee. Photography: Soumendu Roy. Editor: Dulal Dutta. Art Director: Bansi Chandragupta. Music: Satyajit Ray. Sound: Durgadas Mitra, Nripen Paul, Sujit Sarkar. 150 mins.

  Cast: Soumitra Chatterjee (*Narsingh*), Waheeda Rehman (*Gulabi*), Ruma Guha Thakurta (*Neeli*), Ganesh Mukherjee (*Joseph*), Charuprakash Ghosh (*Sukhanram*), Robi Ghosh (*Rama*), Arun Roy (*Naskar*), Sekhar Chatterjee (*Rameswar*), Ajit Banerjee (*Banerjee*), Reba Devi (*Joseph's mother*), Abani Mukherjee (*Lawyer*)

**1963**  **Mahanagar (The Big City)**

  Producer: RDB and Co. (RD Bansal). Screeplay: Satyajit Ray, from the short story *Abataranika* by Narendranath Mitra. Photography: Subrata Mitra. Editor: Dulal Dutta. Art Director: Bansi Chandragupta. Music: Satyajit Ray. Sound: Debesh Ghosh, Atul Chatterjee, Sujit Sarkar. 131 mins.

Cast: Anil Chatterjee (*Subrata Mazumdar*), Madhabi Mukherjee (*Arati Mazumdar*), Jaya Bhaduri (*Bani*), Haren Chatterjee (*Priyagopal, Subrata's father*), Sefalika Devi (*Sarojini, Subrata's mother*), Prasonjit Sarkar (*Pintu*), Haradhan Banerjee (*Himangsu Mukherjee*), Vicky Redwood (*Edith*).

1964    **Charulata (The Lonely Wife)**

Producer: RDB and Co. (RD Bansal). Screenplay: Satyajit Ray, from the novel *Nastanirh* by Rabindranath Tagore. Photography: Subrata Mitra. Editor: Dulal Dutta. Art Director: Bansi Chandragupta. Music: Satyajit Ray. Sound: Nripen Paul, Atul Chattterjee, Sujit Sarkar, 117 mins.

Cast: Soumitra Chatterjee (*Amal*), Madhabi Mukherjee (*Charu*), Sailen Mukherjee (*Bhupati*), Syamal Ghosal (*Umapada*), Gitali Roy (*Mandakini*), Bholanath Koyal (*Braja*), Suku Mukherjee (*Nisikanta*), Dilip Bose (*Sasanka*), Subrata Sen Sharma (*Motilal*), Joydeb (*Nilatpal Dey*), Bankin Ghosh (*Jaganath*).

1964    **Two**

Producer: Esso World Theater. Original Screenplay: Satyajit Ray. Photography: Soumendu Roy. Editor: Dulal Dutta. Art Director: Bansi Chandragupta. Music: Satyajit Ray. Sound: Sujit Sarkar. 15 mins.

Cast: Ravi Kiran.

1965    **Kapurush-O-Mahapurush (The Coward and the Holy Man)**

Producer: RDB and Co. (RD Bansal). Screenplay: Satyajit Ray, from the short story *Janaiko Kapuruser Kahini* by Premendra Mitra and *Birinchi Baba* by Parasuram. Photography: Soumendu Roy. Editor: Dulal Dutta. Art Director: Bansi Chandragupta. Music: Satyajit Ray. Sound: Nripen Paul, Atul Chatterjee, Sujit Sarkar. **Kapurush,** 74 mins. **Mahapurush,** 65 mins.

Cast: **Kapurush:** Soumitra Chatterjee (*Amitava Roy*), Madhabi Mukherjee (*Karuna Gupta*), Haradhan Banerjee (*Bimal Gupta*). **Mahapurush:** Charuprakash Ghosh (*Birinchi Baba*), Robi Ghosh (*His assistant*), Prasad Mukherjee (*Gurupada Mitter*), Gitali Roy (*Buchki*), Satindra Bhattacharya (*Satya*), Somen Bose (*Nibaran*), Santosh Dutta (*Professor Nani*), Renuka Roy (*Nani's wife*).

1966    **Nayak (The Hero)**

Producer: RDB and Co. (RD Bansal). Original Screenplay: Satyajit Ray. Photography: Subrata Mitra. Editor: Dulal Dutta. Art Director: Bansi Chandragupta. Music: Satyajit Ray. Sound: Nripen Paul, Atul Chatterjee, Sujit Sarkar. 120 mins.

Cast: Uttam Kumar (*Arindam Mukherjee*), Sharmila Tagore (*Aditi Sen Gupta*), Bireswar Sen (*Mukunda Lahiri*), Somen Bose (*Sankar*), Nirmal Ghosh (*Jyoti*), Premangsu Bose (*Biresh*), Sumita Sanyal (*Promila*), Ranjit Sen (*Mr Bose*), Bharati Devi (*Manorama, his wife*), Lali Chowdhury (*Bulbul, his daughter*), Kamu Mukherjee (*Pritish Sarkar*), Susmita Mukherjee (*Molly, his wife*), Subrata Sen Sharma (*Ajoy*), Jamuna Sinha (*Sefalika, his wife*), Hiralal

(*Kamal Misra*), Jogesh Chatterjee (*Aghore, elderly journalist*), Satya Banerjee (*Swamiji*), Gopal Dey (*Conductor*).

## 1967     Chidiakhana (The Zoo)

Producer: Star Production (Harendranath Bhattacharya). Screenplay: Satyajit Ray, from the novel *Chidiakhana* by Saradindu Banerjee. Photography: Soumendu Roy. Editor: Dulal Dutta. Art Director: Bansi Chandragupta. Music: Satyajit Ray. Sound: Nripen Paul, Atul Chatterjee, Sujit Sarkar. 125 mins. approx.

Cast: Uttam Kumar (*Byomkesh Baksi*), Sailen Mukherjee (*Ajit*), Susil Majumdar (*Nisanath Sen*), Kanika Majumdar (*Damyanti, his wife*), Subhendu Chatterjee (*Bijoy*), Syamal Ghosal (*Dr Bhujangadhar Das*), Prasad Mukherjee (*Nepal Gupta*), Subira Roy (*Mukul, his daughter*), Nripati Chatterjee (*Muskil Mia*), Subrata Chatterjee (*Nasarbibi, his wife*), Gitali Roy (*Banalakshmi*), Kalipada Chakravarti (*Rasiklal*), Chinmoy Roy (*Ranagopal*), Raman Mullick (*Jahar Ganguli*), Chinmoy Roy (*Panagopal*), Nilatpal Dey (*Inspector*).

## 1968     Goopy Gyne Bagha Byne (The Adventures of Goopy and Bagha)

Producer: Purnima Pictures (Nepal Dutta, Asim Dutta). Screenplay: Satyajit Ray, from the story by Upendrakisore Ray. Photography: Soumendu Roy. Editor: Dulal Dutta. Art Director: Bansi Chandragupta. Music: Satyajit Ray. Goopy's songs sung by Anup Kumar Ghosal. Dance Director: Sambhunath Bhattacharya. Sound: Nripen Paul, Atul Chatterjee, Sujit Sarkar, 132 mins.

Cast: Tapen Chatterjee (*Goopy*), Robi Ghosh (*Bagha*), Santosh Dutta (*King of Shundi/King of Halla*), Jahar Roy (*Prime Minister of Halla*), Santi Chatterjee (*Commander-in-chief of Halla*), Harindranath Chatterjee (*Barfi, magician*), Chinmoy Roy (*Spy of Halla*), Durgadas Banerjee (*King of Amloki*), Gobind Chakravarti (*Goopy's father*), Prasad Mukherjee (*King of Ghosts*), Haridhan Mukherjee, Abani Chatterjee, Khagen Pathak, Binoy Bose, Prasad Mukherjee (*Village elders*), Joykrishna Sanya, Tarun Mitra, Ratan Banerjee, Kartik Chatterjee (*Singers of the court of Shundi*), Gopal Dey (*Executioner*), Ajoy Banerjee, Sailen Ganguli, Moni Srimani, Binoy Bose, Kartik Chatterjee (*Visitors to Halla*).

## 1969     Aranyer Din Ratri (Days and Nights In the Forest)

Producer: Priya Films (Nepal Dutta, Asim Dutta). Screenplay: Satyajit Ray, from the novel *Aranyer Din Ratri* by Sunil Ganguli. Photography: Soumendu Roy, Purnendu Bose. Editor: Dulal Dutta. Art Director: Bansi Chandragupta. Music: Satyajit Ray. Sound: Sujit Sarkar. 115 mins.

Cast: Soumitra Chatterjee (*Asim*), Subhendu Chatterjee (*Sanjoy*), Samit Bhanja (*Harinath*), Robi Ghosh (*Sekhar*), Pahari Sanyal (*Sadasiv Tripathi*), Sharmila Tagore (*Aparna*), Kaveri Bose (*Jaya*); Simi Garewal (*Duli*), Aparna Sen (*Atasi*).

## 1970     Pratidwandi (The Adversary)

Producer: Priya Films (Nepal Dutta, Asim Dutta). Screenplay: Satyajit Ray, from the novel *Pratidwandi* by Sunil Ganguli. Photography: Soumendu Roy, Purnendu Bose. Editor: Dulal Dutta. Art Direction: Bansi Chandragupta. Music: Satyajit Ray. Sound: JD Irani, Durgadas Mitra. 110 mins.

Cast: Dhritiman Chatterjee (*Siddhartha Chowdhury*), Indira Devi (*Sarojini*), Debraj Roy (*Tunu*), Krishna Bose (*Sutapa*), Kalyan Chowdhury (*Siben*), Joysree Roy (*Keya*), Sefali (*Lotika*), Soven Lahiri (*Sanyal*), Pisu Majumdar (*Keya's father*), Dhara Roy (*Keya's aunt*), Mamata Chatterjee (*Sanyal's wife*).

### 1971 Seemabaddha (Company Limited)

Producer: Chitranjali (Bharat Shamsher Jung Bahadur Rana). Screenplay: Satyajit Ray, from the novel *Seemabaddha* by Sankar. Photography: Soumendu Roy. Editor: Dulal Dutta. Art director: Asok Bose. Music: Satyajit Ray. Sound: JD Irani, Durgadas Mitra. 112 mins.

Cast: Barun Chanda (*Syamal Chatterjee*), Sharmila Tagore (*Sudarsana known as Tutul*), Paromita Chowdhury (*Syamal's wife*), Harindranath Chatterjee (*Sir Baren Roy*), Haradhan Banerjee (*Talukdar*), Indira Roy (*Syamal's mother*), Promod (*Syamal's father*).

### 1971 Sikkim

Producer: the Chogyal of Sikkim. Script and Commentary: Satyajit Ray. Photography: Soumendu Roy. Editor: Dulal Dutta. Music: Satyajit Ray. Sound: Satyajit Ray.

### 1972 The Inner eye

Producer: Films Division, Government of India. Script and Commentary: Satyajit Ray. Photography: Soumendu Roy. Editor: Dulal Dutta. Music: Satyajit Ray. Sound: Satyajit Ray.

### 1973 Asani Sanket (Distant Thunder)

Producer: Balaka Movies (Sarbani Bhattacharya). Screenplay: Satyajit Ray, from the novel *Asani Sanket* by Bibhutibhushan Bandopadhyay. Photography: Soumendu Roy. Editor: Dulal Dutta. Art Director: Asok Bose. Music: Satyajit Ray. Sound: JD Irani, Durgadas Mitra. 101 mins.

Cast: Soumitra Chatterjee (*Gangacharan Chakravarti*), Babita (*Ananga, his wife*), Ramesh Mukherjee (*Biswas*), Chitra Banerjee (*Moti*), Gobind Chakravarti (*Dinabandhu*), Sandhya Roy (*Chutki*), Noni Ganguli (*'Scarface' Jadu*), Seli Pal (*Moksada*), Suchita Roy (*Khenti*), Anil Ganguli (*Nibaran*), Debatosh Ghosh (*Adhar*).

### 1974 Sonar Kella (The Golden Fortress)

Producer: Government of West Bengal. Screenplay: Satyajit Ray, based on his own novel *Sonar Kella*. Photography: Soumendu Roy. Editor: Dulal Dutta. Art Director: Asok Bose, Music: Satyajit Ray. Sound: JD Irani, Anil Talukdar. 120 mins.

Cast: Soumitra Chatterjee (*Pradosh Mitter known as Felu*), Santosh Dutta (*Lalmohan Ganguli known as Jotayu*), Siddhartha Chatterjee (*Tapesh Mitter known as Topse*), Kusal Chakravarti (*Mukul Dhar*), Sailen Mukherjee (*Dr*

*Hemanga Hajra*), Ajoy Banerjee (*Amiyanath Burman*), Kamu Mukherjee (*Mandar Bose*), Santanu Bagchi (*Mukul 2*), Harindranath Chatterjee (*Uncle Sidhu*), Sunil Sarkar (*Mukul's father*), Siuli Mukherjee (*Mukul's mother*), Haradhan Banerjee (*Tapesh's father*), Rekha Chatterjee (*Tapesh's mother*), Asok Mukherjee (*Journalist*), Bimal Chatterjee (*Advocate*).

**1975    Jana Aranya (The Middle Man)**

Producer: Indus Films (Subir Guha). Screenplay: Satyajit Ray, from the novel *Jana Aranya* by Sankar. Photography: Soumendu Roy. Editor: Dulal Dutta. Art Director: Asok Bose. Music: Satyajit Ray. Sound: JD Irani, Anil Talukdar, Adinath Nag, Sujit Ghosh. 131 mins.

  Cast: Pradip Mukherjee (*Somnath Banerjee*), Satya Banerjee (*Somnath's father*), Dipankar Dey (*Bhombol*), Lily Chakravarti (*Kamala, his wife*), Aparna Sen (*Somnath's girl-friend*), Gautam Chakravarti (*Sukumar*), Sudesna Das (*Karuna known as Juthika*), Utpal Dutt (*Bisu*), Robi Ghosh (*Mr Mitter*), Bimal Chatterjee (*Adok*), Arati Bhattacharya (*Mrs Ganguli*), Padma Devi (*Mrs Biswas*, Soven Lahiri (*Goenka*), Santosh Dutta (*Hiralal*), Bimal Deb (*Jagabandhu, MLA/MP*), Ajeya Mukherjee (*Pimp*), Kalyan Sen (*Mr Baksi*), Alokendu Dey (*Fakirchand, office bearer*).

**1976    Bala**

Producer: National Centre for the Performing Arts, Bombay and Government of Tamil Nadu. Script and Commentary: Satyajit Ray. Photography: Soumendu Roy. Editor: Dulal Dutta. Music: Satyajit Ray. Sound: SP Ramanathan, Sujit Sarkar, David. 33 mins.

**1977    Shatranj Ke Khilari (The Chess Players)**

Producer: Devki Chitra Productions (Suresh Jindal). Screenplay: Satyajit Ray, from the short story *Shatranj Ke Khilari* by Prem Chand. Dialogue: Satyajit Ray, Shama Zaidi, Javed Siddiqi, Editor: Dulal Dutta. Art Director: Bansi Chandragupta. Associate Art Director: Asok Bose. Costumes: Shama Zaidi. Music: Satyajit Ray. Songs sung by Reba Muhuri, Birju Maharaj, Calcutta Youth Choir. Dance Director: Birju Maharaj. Dances peformed by Saswati Sen, Gitanjali, Kathak Ballet Troupe. Sound: Narinder Singh, Samir Majumdar. 113 mins.

  Cast: Sanjeev Kumar (*Mirza Sajjad Ali*), Saeed Jaffrey (*Mir Roshan Ali*), Amjad Khan (*Wajid Ali Shah*), Richard Attenborough (*General Outram*), Shabana Azmi (*Khurshid*), Farida Jalal (*Nafeesa*), Veena (*Aulea Begum, Queen Mother*), David Abraham (*Munshi Nandlal*), Victor Banerjee (*Ali Naqi Khan, Prime Minister*), Farooq Shaikh (*Aqil*), Tom Alter (*Captain Weston*), Leela Mishra (*Hiria*), Barry John (*Dr Joseph Fayrer*), Samarth Narain (*Kalloo*), Budho Advani (*Imtiaz Hussain*), Kamu Mukherjee (*Bookie*).

**1978    Joi Baba Felunath (The Elephant God)**

Producer: RDB and Co. (RD Bansal). Screenplay: Satyajit Ray, from his own novel *Joi Baba Felunath*. Photography: Soumendu Roy. Editor: Dulal Dutta.

Art Director: Asok Bose. Music: Satyajit Ray. Sound: Robin Sen Gupta. 112 mins.

Cast: Soumitra Chatterjee (*Pradosh Mitter known as Felu*), Santosh Dutta (*Lalmohan Ganguli known as Jotayu*), Siddhartha Chatterjee (*Tapesh Mitter known as Topse*), Utpal Dutt (*Maganlal Meghraj*), Jit Bose (*Ruku Ghosal*), Haradhan Banerjee (*Umanath Ghosal*), Bimal Chatterjee (*Ambika Ghosal*), Biplab Chatterjee (*Bikash Sinha*), Satya Banerjee (*Nibaran Chakravarti*), Moloy Roy (*Gunomoy Bagchi*), Santosh Sinha (*Sasi Pal*), Manu Mukherjee (*Machli Baba*), Indubhusan Gujral (*Inspector Tewari*), Kamu Mukherjee (*Arjun*).

### 1980 Hirak Rajar Deshe (The Kingdom of Diamonds)

Producer: Government of West Bengal. Original Screenplay: Satyajit Ray. Photography: Soumendu Roy. Editor: Dulal Dutta. Art Director: Asok Bose. Music: Satyajit Ray. Goopy's songs sung by Anup Kumar Ghosal. Sound: Robin Sen Gupta, Durgadas Mitra. 118 mins.

Cast: Soumitra Chatterjee (*Udayan, the school-teacher*), Utpal Dutt (*King Hirak*), Tapen Chatterjee (*Goopy*), Robi Ghosh (*Bagha*), Santosh Dutta (*King of Shundi/Gabesak inventor*), Promod Ganguli (*Udayan's father*), Alpana Gupta (*Udayan's mother*), Rabin Majumdar (*Charandas*), Sunil Sarkar (*Fazl Mia*), Nani Ganguli (*Balaram*), Ajoy Banerjee (*Bidusak*), Kartik Chatterjee (*Court Poet*), Haridhan Mukherjee (*Court Astrologer*), Bimal Deb, Tarun Mitra, Gopal Dey, Sailen Ganguli, Samir Mukherjee (*Ministers.*)

### 1980 Pikoo

Producer: Henri Fraise. Screenplay: Satyajit Ray, from his own short story *Pikur Diary*. Photography: Soumendu Roy. Editor: Dulal Dutta. Art Director: Asok Bose. Music: Satyajit Ray. Sound: Robin Sen Gupta, Sujit Sarkar, 26 mins.

Cast: Arjun Guha Thakurta (*Pikoo*), Aparna Sen (*Seema, his mother*), Soven Lahiri (*Ranjan*), Promod Ganguli (*Grandfather Loknath*), Victor Banerjee (*Uncle Hitesh*).

### 1981 Sadgati (Deliverance)

Producer: Doordarshan, Government of India. Screenplay: Satyajit Ray, from the short sory *Sadgati* by Prem Chand. Dialogue: Satyajit Ray and Amrit Rai. Photography: Soumendu Roy. Editor: Dulal Dutta. Art Director. Asok Bose. Music: Satyajit Ray. Sound. Amulya Das. 52 mins.

Cast: Om Puri (*Dukhi Chamar*), Smita Patil (*Jhuria, Dukhi's wife*), Richa Mishra (*Dhania, Dukhi's daughter*), Mohan Agashe (*Ghasiram*), Gita Siddhartha (*Lakshmi, Ghashiram's wife*), Bhaiala Hedao (*The Gond*).

### 1984 Ghare Baire (The Home and the World)

Producer: National Film Development Corporation of India. Screenplay: Satyajit Ray, from the novel *Ghare Baire* by Rabindranath Tagore. Photography: Soumendu Roy. Editor: Dulal Dutta. Art Director: Asok Bose. Music: Satyajit Ray. Sound: Robin Sen Gupta, Jyoti Chatterjee, Anup Mukherjee. 140 mins.

Cast: Soumitra Chatterjee (*Sandip*), Victor Banerjee (*Nikhilesh*), Swatile-kha Chatterjee (*Bimala*), Gopa Aich (*Nikhilesh's sister-in-law*), Jennifer Ka-poor (Kendal) (*Miss Gilby, English governess*), Manoj Mitra (*Headmaster*), Indrapramit Roy (*Amulya*), Bimal Chatterjee (*Kulada*).

**1987**    **Sukumar Ray**

Producer: Government of West Bengal. Script: Satyajit Ray. Commentary: Soumitra Chatterjee. Photography: Barun Baba. Editor: Dulal Dutta. Music: Satyajit Ray. Sound: Sujit Sarkar. 30 mins.
Cast: Soumitra Chatterjee, Utpal Dutt, Santosh Dutt, Tapen Chatterji.

**1989**    **Ganashatru (An Enemy of the People)**

Producer: National Film Development Corporation of India. Screenplay: Satyajit Ray, from the play *An Enemy of the People* by Henrik Ibsen. Photography: Barun Raha. Editor: Dulal Dutta. Art Director: Asok Bose. Music: Satyajit Ray. Sound: Sujit Sarkar. 100 mins.
Cast: Soumitra Chatterjee (*Dr Asok Gupta*), Ruma Guha Thakurta (*Maya, his wife*), Mamata Shankar (*Indrani, his daughter*), Dhritiman Chat-terjee (*Nisith*), Dipankar Dey (*Haridas Bagchi*), Subhendu Chatterjee (*Biresh*), Manoj Mitra (*Adhir*) Viswa Guha Thakurta (*Ranen Haldar*), Rajaram Yagnik (*Bhargava*), Satya Banerjee (*Manmotha*), Gobind Mukherjee (*Chandan*).

**1990**    **Shakha Proshakha (Branches of a Tree)**

Producer: Satyajit Ray Productions (India), Gerard Depardieu and Daniel Toscan Du Planter (Paris). Screenplay: Satyajit Ray. Photography: Barun Raha. Editor: Dulal Dutta. Art Director: Asok Bose, Music: Satyajit Ray. Sound: Sujit Sarkar. 121 mins
Cast: Promod Ganguli, Ajit Banerje, Soumitra Chatterjee, Haradhan Banerjee, Dipankar Dey, Ranjit Mullick, Mamata Shankar, Lily Chakra-varti.

**1991**    **Agantuk (The Stranger)**

Producer: National Film Development Corporation of India. Original Screen-play: Satyajit Ray. Photography: Barun Raha. Editor: Dulal Dutta. Art Director: Asok Bose. Music: Satyajit Ray. Sound: Sujit Sarkar. 100 mins.
Cast: Utpal Dutt, Dipankar Dey, Mamata Shanker, Dhritiman Chatterjee.

## Biographical Outline

1921    Born on May 22.

1923    Father dies. The publishing business is severely in debt.

1926    Ray and his mother move to an uncle's house in Calcutta. He joins a school nearby without showing much flair for studies. But by the age of ten he begins to get attracted to western classical music.

1927    The family's famous publishing house, U.Roy & Sons goes into liquidation.

1935    Admitted to Presidency College, Calcutta, Bengal's foremost institution of its kind.

1940    Graduates with honours in Economics. In the same year he goes to Santiniketan to study at Rabindranath Tagore's University, about 145 kilometres from Calcutta, at the art school there, at the poet's suggestion.

1941    Goes on a study tour with a group to visit major sites of classical Indian art within the country.

1942    In December, Ray gives up the art school and returns to Calcutta.

1943    Joins D.J. Keymer & Co., a British-owned advertising agency in Calcutta on a salary of Rs 85 per month (about 6 US$ at the time). Around this time, Ray writes a script for a film on "Prisoner of Zenda".

1947    Founds, along with Chidananda Das Gupta and others, the Calcutta Film Society, the first such institution in Calcutta.

1948    Ray and mother move to an independent flat in Calcutta. Meets Jean Renoir who had come for his reconnaissance trip to Calcutta in preparation of his film *The River*. Renoir and his wife Dido come to a meeting with members of the Calcutta Film Society where he counsels would-be film makers to forget Hollywood and look at their own reality in order to lay the foundations of a national cinema.

1948    Signs a contract for a script of Tagore's novel "The Home and the World" at the instance of Harisadhan Das Gupta, a graduate of the University of California's Film School, Los Angeles (UCLA) who had recently returned home and joined the Calcutta Film Society.

Illustrates a children's version of the Bibhutibhusan Bandhyopadhyay classic "Pather Panchali" and conceives the idea of one day making a film of it.

The contract for the script for "The Home and the World" is cancelled because of Ray's refusal to amend his screenplay in accordance with the producer's anxiety to conform to the standards of the current commercial cinema.

Jean Renoir comes to Calcutta to survey locations for the Hollywood film *The River*. Ray and the Calcutta Film Soceity come into immediate contact with him through Harisadhan Das Gupta who had been to guest lectures by Renoir at the film school in Los Angeles.

1949    Gets married to Bijoya, a first cousin with whom he had been attached for about nine years, in contravention of the Hindu socio-religious injunction against the marriage of closely related cousins. Renoir comes back to Calcutta and the shooting of *The River* takes place. Ray often goes to watch the shooting.

Writes an article on "Renoir in Calcutta" for the magazine "Sequence" published by Gavin Lambert in Cambridge at the suggestion of Lindsay Anderson.

1950    Becomes the Art Director of D.J. Keymer & Co. and is sent to England to work at the London office for a few months, during which he sees about a hundred films including major works of Italian neo-realism.

1952    India holds its first International Film Festival in Delhi with International Film Weeks in Calcutta, Bombay and Madras. Ray sees 22 films in one week. Preliminary work on *Pather Panchali* (The Song of the Road) begins with Ray's own funds.

1953    Ray's son Sandip, his only child, is born.

1955    *Pather Panchali* is shown at the Museum of Modern Art in New York to an appreciative audience. The film is premiered at the Ordnance Club on the annual day of the Advertising Club of Calcutta to a somewhat inattentive audience. Subsequently, the film is released in Calcutta in a 4-week contract and is a furious success by the third week but is taken off at the end of the fourth week according to contract.

1956    *Pather Panchali* is awarded the prize for "The Best Human Document" at the Cannes Film Festival.

1956    Makes *Aparajito* (The Unvanquished)

1957    *Aparajito* wins the Golden Lion at the Venice Film Festival as well as the Selznick Award for *Pather Panchali* and *Aparajito* taken together. David O. Selznick writes to Ray making a *carte blanche* offer for making films under his banner in Hollywood; Ray turns it down, pleading inability to make films outside the milieu and language he knows well, namely, Bengal and Bengali.

1958    *Parash Pathar* (The Philosopher's Stone) is made in the first part of the year and *Jalsaghar* (The Music Room) in the second.

   Ray makes his first visit to the United States on the invitation of Frances Flaherty, to speak at the Robert Flaherty seminar of that year.

   *Aparajito* wins the San Francisco awards for Best Film and Best Direction. *Pather Panchali* has by now won five international awards.

1959    *Apur Sansar* (The World of Apu) gets made.

1960    Edward Harrison, Ray's distributor in the United States, shows the trilogy at one continuous show with much success.

   The first American retrospective of Ray's work is held at the University of California, Berkeley.

1961    In the birth centenary year of Rabindranath Tagore, Ray makes a long documentary on him and films a triptych of his short stories in *Teen Kanya* (Three Daughters) consisting of: *Monihara* (The Lost Jewel), *The Postmaster* and *Samapti* (The Conclusion). The film was exported as *Two Daughters*, omitting *Monihara*. It is the first film in which Ray composes his own music. From here on he continues to do so till the end.

1962    Makes *Kanchanjungha*. His first from an original script by himself and his first film in colour.

   *Abhijan* (The Expedition) is the second film to be made this year.

1963    *Mahanagar* (The Big City) is made and wins the Best Direction award at the Berlin Film Festival.

1964    *Charulata* (The Lonely Wife), based on a story by Rabindranath Tagore, one of Ray's most admired films is made and wins the Best Direction award at the Berlin Film Festival.
   Ray makes a 15-minute film for Esso World Theatre.

1965    *Kapurush-O-Mahapurush* (The Coward and the Holy Man), consisting of two separate stories is made.

1966    *Nayak* (The Hero) is made from Ray's original screenplay and shown at the Berlin film Festival where Ray receives an award for the totality of his work.

1967    *Chidiakhana* (The Zoo), Ray's first detective film.

1968    *Goopy Gyne Bagha Byne* (The Adventures of Goopy and Bagha) is Ray's first film for children, and is based on a story by his grandfather. The film is marked by an animated dance sequence the only one of its kind in Ray's oeuvre. The film and its songs are both a great success with children in Bengal.

1969    *Aranyer Din Ratri* (Days and Nights in the Forest), is Ray's first film with multiple lead characters (Four men and four women).

1970    *Pratidwandi* (The Adversary), first of a series of three films set in contemporary Calcutta.

1971    *Seemabaddha* (Company Limited), second of the contemporary Calcutta films.

Makes a documentary on the independent state of Sikkim for its ruler (The Chogyal). Later Sikkim joins the Republic of India and the film is not released in India. It is however included in a retrospective of his work in New York the same year by The Museum of Modern Art and The Asia Society.

1972    *The Inner Eye*, a documentary on one of Ray's erstwhile art teachers in Santiniketan, the prominent painter Binode Behari Mukherjee, who continued to paint even after he gradually lost his vision and went completely blind.

1973    *Asani Sanket* (Distant Thunder) a film on the impending famine in a year of rich harvest caused by British block-buying of grain to feed the army during World War II is made with the heroine coming from Bangladesh (Babita)

1974    *Sonar Kella* (The Golden Fortress), a children's film shot largely in the desert town of Jaisalmer in the state of Rajasthan from whose yellow marble the name of the film is derived.

1975    *Jana Aranya* (The Middle Man) the third of the films on contemporary Calcutta.

1976    *Bala*, a documentary on the famous dancer Bala Saraswati.

1977    *Shatranj Ke Khilari* (The Chess Players), Ray's first feature film in a language other than Bengali (Hindi, more correctly Hindustani), set in 19th century, Lucknow.

1978    *Joi Baba Felunath* (The Elephant God), Ray's third film for children, based on a story in a famous detective series written by himself.

1980    *Hirak Rajar Deshe* (The Kingdom of Diamonds) another children's film this time with dialogue set to rhyme, as a sequel to *Goopy Gyne Bagha Byne*.

   -*Pikoo*, a 26-minute television film made for French producer Henri Fraise. Ray's first film to be commissioned by France and the second to be commissioned by a producer abroad.

1981    *Sadgati* (Deliverance) a 52-minute film, Ray's second in Hindi, made for television.

1982-83    Ray is prevented from making films by a persistent heart ailment.

1984    *Ghare Baire* (The Home and the World) is made based on a novel by Rabindranath Tagore.

   -Ray has by-pass surgery in Houston, USA.

   On return to India he has to undergo further surgery.

1987    *Sukumar Roy*, a documentary on his father.

1989    *Ganashatru* (An Enemy of the People) Ray's first film based on a foreign original, in this case Ibsen's play of the same name. The film is shot in the presence of doctors and an intensive care unit standing by. This procedure is followed in both films made after this as well.

1990    *Shakha Proshakha* (Branches of A Tree) based on his own original screenplay.

   For the first time, the major part of the music is western classical, including a Gregorian Chant.

   The President of France, Francois Mitterand, comes to Calcutta and Confers the *Legion d'Honneur* on Ray.

   The President of India awards Ray India's highest honour, the *Bharatratna* (Jewel of India)

1991    *Agantuk* (The Stranger) Ray's last film, based again on an original screenplay. On what proved to be his deathbed, Ray is conferred the Hollywood Oscar for his lifetime achievement.

1992    Ray dies on 23 April.

**Top** Ray (extreme left) shooting *Pather Panchali*: third from left, cameraman Subrata Mitra.
**Bottom** *Pather Panchali*: Durga Shares stolen fruits with the old woman (Chunibala Devi).

**Top** *Pather Panchali:* Apu and Durga in the field of flax where they have gone to see a railway train for the first time in their lives.

**Bottom** *Pather Panchali:* Times are hard, and Sarbajoya, mother of Apu and Durga is getting impatient with the old woman's presence in their midst.

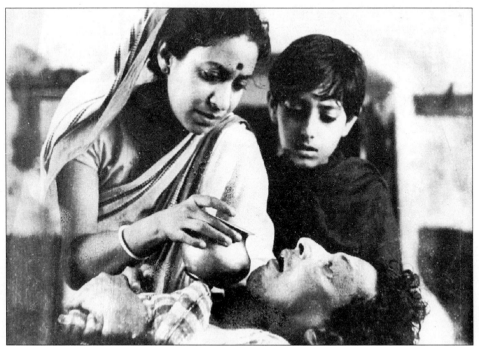

**Top** *Aparajito:* Women, mainly widows, gather on the steps of the Ganga in Benaras, where Harihar, Apu's father, now lives on the bank of the river.

**Bottom** *Aparajito:* Sarbajoya (Karuna Banerjee) pours holy water in her husband Harihar's (Kanu Banerjee) mouth in his dying moments, while Apu (Subir Banerjee) looks on.

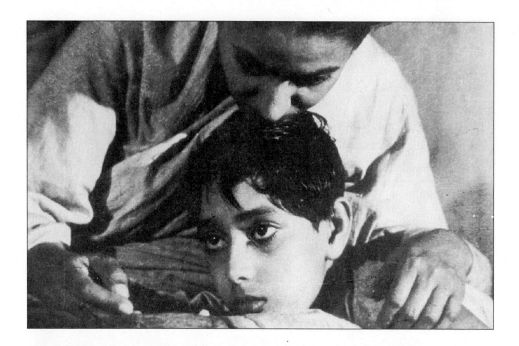

**Top** *Aparajito:* Sarbajoya and Apu after his father's death.
**Bottom** *Aparajito:* Apu is trying to learn his father's trade, priesthood.

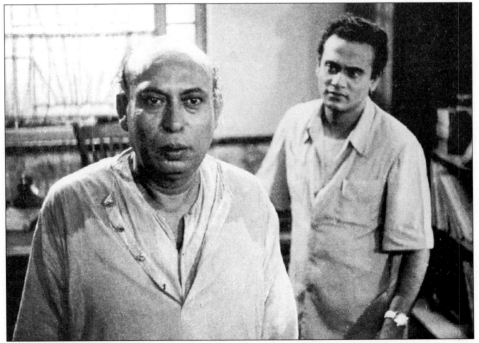

**Top** *Parash Pathar:* The poor clerk (Tulsi Chakravarty) is astonished when a touch of the philosopher's stone turns any metal into gold.
**Bottom** *Parash Pathar:* The clerk, who has become rich after finding the philosopher's stone, with his secretary (Kali Banerjee).

**Top** *Jalsaghar:* Biswambhar Roy (Chhabi Biswas) looks at the last symbol of his past glory—his elephant.
**Bottom** *Jalsaghar:* Biswambhar Roy, the decaying landlord (smoking) at his last musical soiree, with the *nouveau riche* capitalist (Gangapada Basu) sitting next to him.

**Top** *Apur Sansar:* Aparna (Sharmila Tagore) just after his arrival at Apu's house following her marriage with him by an odd turn of events.
**Bottom** *Apur Sansar:* Love after marriage. Apu (Soumitra Chatterjee, right) and Aparna.

**Top** *Apur Sansar:* After Aparna's death, a distraught Apu wanders around alone for a long time before he comes to reclaim his son.
**Bottom** *Apur Sansar:* After prolonged suspicion of him, Kajal (Alok Chakravarti) finally accepts his father and goes away with him.

**Top** *Devi:* The rich old landlord Kalikinkar (Chhabi Biswas), devotee of Goddess Kali.
**Bottom** *Devi:* Kalikinkar looking at his beautiful daughter-in-law (Sharmila Tagore) who, he believes, is an incarnation of Goddess Kali.

**Top** *Rabindranath Tagore:* Young Rabindranath studying under a teacher.
**Bottom** *Teen Kanya:* The elegant Zamindar (Kali Banerjee) and his jewel-crazy wife (Kanika Majumdar) in *Monihara*.

**Top** *Teen Kanya:* The servant girl Ratan (Chandana Banerjee) working in the kitchen in *Postmaster*.
**Bottom** *Teen Kanya:* Mrinmoyee (Aparna Sen), the tomboy who at first refuses to get married in *Samapti*.

**Top** *Kanchenjungha:* The colonial titled brown sahib's elder daughter (Anubha Gupta), who married for money and prestige, cannot bear life with her husband (Subrata Sen).
**Bottom** *Abhijan:* Narsingh (Soumitra Chatterjee), trying to set up a taxi business in a new town, faces resistance.

**Top** *Abhijan:* After more ambitious overtures, Narsingh settles for Gulabi (Waheeda Rehman), the humble woman who has loved him for a long time.
**Bottom** *Mahanagar:* Husband (Anil Chatterjee) spots an advertisement for wife Arati (Madhabi Mukherjee) while their sister (Jaya Bhaduri) looks on.

**Top** *Mahanagar:* Arati, unsure of herself in an alien environment.
**Bottom** *Mahanagar:* Arati goes to a restaurant with an acquaintance and is watched from a distance by her husband.

**Top** *Mahanagar:* Arati, appointment letter in hand.
**Bottom** *Charulata:* The lonely wife Charu (Madhabi Mukherjee) has been provided a teacher-companion her husband's cousin—Amal (Soumitra Chatterjee).

**Top** *Charulata:* Charu realises that she is beginning to fall in love with her husband's cousin.
**Bottom** *Charulata:* Charu and Bhupati (Sailen Mukherjee) after Amal has gone away.

**Top** *Kapurush-O-Mahapurush:* The lovers (in *Kapurush*) as they used to be (Madhabi Mukherjee and Soumitra Chatterjee).
**Bottom** *Kapurush-O-Mahapurush:* The lovers meet again (in *Kapurush*) by coincidence, years after she married someone else when he failed to claim her.

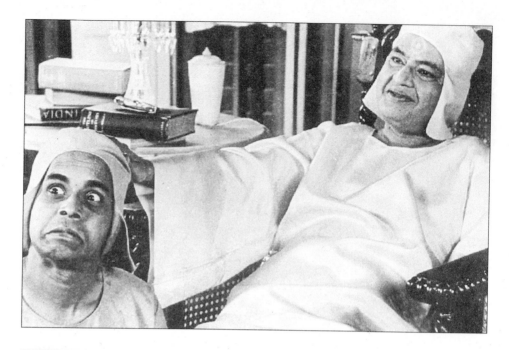

**Top** *Kapurush-O-Mahapurush:* The godman (Charu Prakash Ghosh) with his assistant (Rabi Ghosh) in *Mahapurush.*
**Bottom** *Kapurush-O-Mahapurush:* The godman with a devotee and a relative.

**Top** *Nayak:* Aditi (Sharmila Tagore) presents the magazine she works for to Arindam (Uttam Kumar).
**Bottom** *Nayak:* At first disdainful of him, Aditi finds herself occupied with thoughts of Arindam whom she has been urged to interview by her travelling companion.

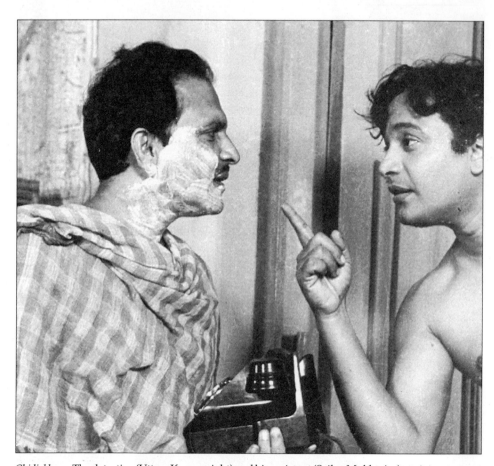

*Chidiakhana:* The detective (Uttam Kumar, right) and his assistant (Sailen Mukherjee).

*Chidiakhana:* The detective finds a clue in a song.

**Top** *Goopy Gyne Bagha Byne:* Goopy (Tapan Chatterjee) and Bagha (Rabi Ghosh) trapped in the kingdom of the bad king.
**Bottom** *Goopy Gyne Bagha Byne:* Goopy and Bagha with the good king (Santosh Dutta).

**Top** *Goopy Gyne Bagha Byne:* Goopy and Bagha make people sing and dance.
**Bottom** *Aranyer Din Ratri:* Three of the friends, Harinath, Sekhar and Asim (Samit Bhanja, Rabi Ghosh and Soumitra Chatterjee respectively) on a holiday, and the tribal maidservant (Simi Garewal) at the forest bungalow.

*Aranyer Din Ratri:* Asim is attracted to Aparna (Sharmila Tagore).

**Top** *Pratidwandi:* Siddhartha (Dhritiman Chatterjee) moralises at his sister (Krishna Bose) who is not averse to being friends with her boss in order to make headway in her job.
**Bottom** *Pratidwandi:* Siddhartha and a close friend (Kalyan Chatterjee) who is very unlike him.

**Top** *Pratidwandi:* His friend takes Siddhartha to meet a nurse (Shefali) who dispenses sexual favours but Siddhartha is unable to take advantage.

**Bottom** *Pratidwandi:* Siddhartha with the girl (Joysree Roy) he be-friends but cannot marry because he has no job.

**Top** *Seemabaddha:* Ray directing Sharmila Tagore and Barun Chanda.
**Bottom** *Seemabaddha:* Shyamalendu (Barun Chanda) would like to win the esteem of his sister-in-law (Sharmila Tagore), but she is not happy with his life style. Shyamalendu's wife (Paramita Chowdhury) who belongs to his society, looks on.

*Seemabaddha:* The two sisters.

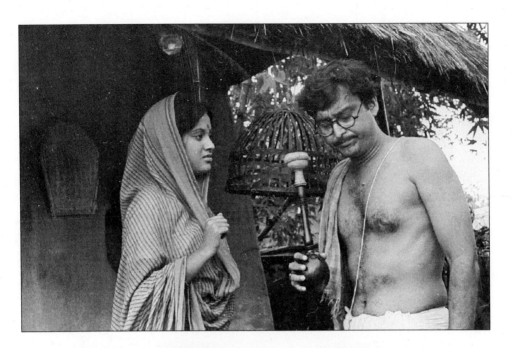

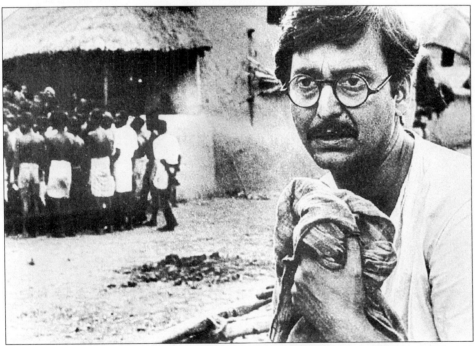

**Top** *Asani Sanket:* Food shortage is plaguing the village. The Brahmin priest (Soumitra Chatterjee) and his beautiful wife (Babita), used to a comfortable existence, are facing difficult times.
**Bottom** *Asani Sanket:* The famine is approaching: no one has a thought for the Brahmin anymore.

**Top** *Asani Sanket:* The neighbour's wife (Sandhya Roy) gives herself to a man for some rice.
**Bottom** *Asani Sanket:* The priest's wife has been raped but no one will ever know about it or about the revenge the women take.

*The Inner Eye:* Ray's documentary on one of his teachers at Kala Bhavan, Visva-Bharati, Binode Behari Mukhopadhyay, who went on painting even after he was blind.

**Top** *Sonar Kella:* Detective (Soumitra Chatterjee) and crime writer (Santosh Dutta) at a palace in Rajasthan.
**Bottom** *Sonar Kella:* The detective, the crime writer and the boy who remembers his previous birth set out on their search through the desert.

**Top** *Jana Aranya:* Somnath (Pradip Mukherjee) with his businessman uncle (Utpal Dutt, left) who is showing him the business district and initiating him to its own laws.
**Bottom** *Jana Aranya:* Business experts who will teach Somnath the tricks of the trade.

**Top** *Jana Aranya:* Somnath and his adviser trying to persuade the call girl (Arati Bhattacharya) to oblige their client.
**Bottom** *Jana Aranya:* Somnath with his friend's sister, Karuna (Sudesna Das) just before sending her in to see his client.

**Top** *Bala:* Ray's documentary on the famous dancer.
**Bottom** *Shatranj ke Khilari:* The nobles of Oudh, Mirza (Sanjeev Kumar, left) and Mir (Saeed Jaffrey), for whom little exists outside a game of chess.

**Top** *Shatranj ke Khilari:* Aqil (Farooq Shaikh) with Nafisa (Farida Jalal).
**Bottom** *Shatranj ke Khilari:* Khurshid (Shabana Azmi), Mirza's wife.

**Top** *Shatranj ke Khilari:* The Nawab of Oudh, India's last independent ruler (Amjad Khan), surrenders his crown to General Outram (Richard Attenborough).
**Bottom** *Sikkim:* Documentary on the state made before it joined the Indian Union.

**Top** *Joy Baba Felunath:* The detective Feluda (Soumitra Chatterjee) and his team make their plans.
**Bottom** *Joy Baba Felunath:* The crime writer (Santosh Dutta) stands up to the incredible knife-throwing of the villain's hired knife-thrower (Kanu Mukherjee).

*Hirak Rajar Deshe:* Soumitra Chatterjee and the two heroes of *Goopy Gyne Bagha Byne* whose story is continued here.

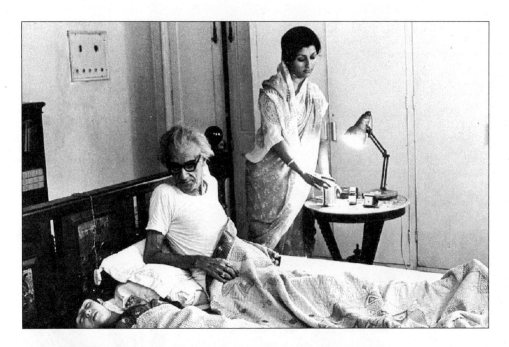

**Top** *Pikoo:* Pikoo (Arjun Guha Thakurta), his grandfather (Pramod Ganguly) and his mother (Aparna Sen).
**Bottom** *Pikoo:* The husband (Soven Lahiri) lets on that he knows his wife (Aparna Sen) has a lover.

**Top** *Sadgati:* Dukhi's wife (Smita Patil) commiserates with her husband (Om Puri) and asks him to take care of himself before he goes off to see the priest.
**Bottom** *Sadgati:* Made to chop wood the whole day, Dukhi is discovered dead by the Brahmin priest (Mohan Agashe) whose services he had come to ask.

**Top** *Sadgati:* Dukhi's wife at the Brahmin's door after her husband's death.
**Bottom** *Ghare Baire:* Nikhilesh (Victor Banerjee) with Miss Gilby (Jennifer Kapoor), the English governess.

**Top** *Ghare Baire:* Introduced to his wife Bimala (Swatilekha), by Nikhilesh, Sandip (Soumitra Chatterjee) proceeds to seduce her.
**Bottom** *Ghare Baire:* Nikhilesh's sister-in-law (Gopa Aich) observes with disapproval Bimala's affair with Sandip.

*Sukumar Ray:* Ray's documentary on his father.

**Top** *Ganashatru:* The scientist (Soumitra Chatterjee) with his daughter (Mamata Shanker) and his wife (Ruma Guha Thakurta).
**Bottom** *Ganashatru:* The mayor of the town (Dhritiman Chatterjee) tries to prevent the editor of the local paper (Dipankar Dey) from printing the scientist's findings about contaminated water.

**Top** Ray directing *Shakha Proshaka*.
**Bottom** *Shakha Proshaka*: The brain-damaged son (Soumitra Chatterjee) in conversation with his father (Ajit Bannerjee).

**Top** *Shakha Proshaka:* Part of the family at the picnic they have when the father is a little better.
**Bottom** *Agantuk:* The guest (Utpal Dutt) is questioned by a friend of the family (Rabi Ghosh) as his niece (Mamata Shanker) and her husband (Dipankar Dey) look on.

*Agantuk:* The guest copes with the insults hurled at him by a friend of his niece's family (Dhritiman Chatterjee).

# Bibliography

*American Cinematographer*, Andrew Robinson, 'Satyajit Ray at Work', Los Angeles, September 1983.

*American Film*, (discussion at the American Film Institute's Center for Advanced Film Studies) Washington DC, July-August 1978 (with Andrew Robinson) October 1985, p. 35.

*Asia*, (interview with Muriel Peters), New York, July-August 1981.

*Atlantic*, Terrence Rafferty, 'Rooms with views', Washington DC, April 1985.

Barnouw, Erik and Krishnaswamy, S. *Indian Film*, (2nd edn.), Oxford University Press, 1980, New York, (extended references).

Bengal Association, 'Satyajit Ray Retrospective', (booklet which includes 'The Prophet Abroad' by Amita Malik, 'Satiyajit Ray-Seeker of Life's Truth' by Subrata Banerjee, 'Looking Back', by Karuna Banerjee), Delhi, April 1981.

Bernard Cohn and Patrick Dujarric: '*Quelques films de Satyajit Ray*', inedits en France, *Positif*, January 1970.

*Cahiers du Cinema* (in English), Georges Sadoul, 'From Film to Film', New York, 1966.

*Cahiers du Cinema*, Paris, January 1969.

Charles Tesson, *Journal de Bord d'un Cineaste*, October 1982.

Chattopadhyay, Amitava, 'Satyajit Ray : A Great Liberal Humanist' in Arun Kumar Ray and Sital Chandra Ghosh (eds), *Twelve Indian Directors*, People's Book Publishers, 1981, Calcutta, pp. 1-24.

*Chitrabhas*, (organ of the North Calcutta Film Society) special issue in English in memory of Bansi Chandragupta, Calcutta, 1981.

*Cine Technique*, Satyajit Ray special issue Calcutta, March 1972.

*Cineaste*, 'The Politics of Humanism', II, 1, New York, 1982.

*Cinema 75*, Henri Micciollo, Paris, March 1981.

*Cinematographe*, Paris, October, 1982.

*Cinemaya: The Asian Film Quarterly*, New Delhi
    – Ashis Nandy, "How Indian is Ray', No.20.
    – Madan Gopal Singh, 'Ray and the Realist Conscience,' No.20.
    – Partha Chatterjee, 'Ray's Home, Ray's World: Calcutta,' No.20.

Cowie, Peter, (ed), *International Film Guide*, London, Tantivy Press, 1965.

Das Gupta, Chidananda, (ed.), *'Film India', 'Satyajit Ray'*, (an anthology of statements on Ray and by Ray for the New York celebration of Ray in 1981). Directorate of Film Festival, Delhi, 1981.

Das Gupta, Chidananda: *Talking About Films*, Orient Longman, 1981, Delhi (extended references).

Datta, Alaknanda and Bandopadhyay Samik, (eds.), *Satyajit Ray: A film by Shyam Benegal*, Seagull Books, Calcutta, 1988 (detailed reconstruction of Benegal's film including interview with Ray).

*Deep Focus*, Vol. II, 1996: Ashis Nandy, 'Satyajit Ray's India'; M.K. Raghavendra, 'Satyajit Ray Re-examined', Vinay Lal, 'Sexuality in The Chess Players'.

Derek Malcolm, 'Satyajit Ray, *Sight and Sound*, Spring, 1982.

*Film Comment*, New York, Summer 1968, September-October 1976.

*Film Frame*, Chidananda Das Gupta, 'Ray and his Work', Colombo, December 1969.

*Film Quarterly*, Berkeley, winter 1958.

*Film World*, Lester James Peries, 'Ray and the Critics', Bombay, October-November 1970. Subrata Banerjee, 'Satyajit Ray: Film-maker and Man', Bombay, April-May 1971. Ranjan Banerjee, 'Satyajit Ray: Why One of the World's Greatest?' Bombay, August 1972.

*Film*, Douglas McVay, 'The Ray Trilogy,' London, Federation of Film Societies, March-April 1960.

*Film*, 'The Oriental Master', London, Federation of Film Societies, winter 1970, January 1974.

*Filmaker*, 4-5, Bombay, 1976-7. (discussion at the Delhi Film Festival among Ray, Antonioni, Kazan and Kurosawa).

*Films and Filming*, Alan Stanbrook, 'The World of Ray', London, November 1965.

*Films and Filming*, London, August 1982.

*Film Quarterly*, Chidananda Das Gupta, 'Charulata'.

*Gentleman*, Bombay, December 1984, January and Febraury 1985 (transcript of Shyam Benegal's interview with Ray for his film Satyajit Ray).

*Guardian*, John Rosselli, 'Poet of the Cinema.' London, 13 July 1963.
    – Pritiman Sarkar, 'Third Trilogy', Vol V, 1983
    – Darius Cooper, 'The Ray Women under the panoptican Hindu Male Gaze in Satyajit Ray's Mahanagar', Vol VIII No. 1 1997.

Houston, Penelope: *The Contemporary Cinema*, Penguin, London, 1963.

Hughes, Robert, (ed.): *Film: Book 1*, 'The Audience and the Filmmaker' Grove Press, New York, 1959.

*Image et Son*, Guy Gauthier, Paris, November 1964.

*India Magazine*, Marie Seton, 'The Vision of Satyajit Ray', Delhi, September 1981.

*Journal of South Asian Literature*, Peter J. Bertocci, 'Bengali Cultural Themes in Satyajit Ray's The World of Apu: An Anthropological Perspective', Michigan, winter 1983-4.

Kael, Pauline: *I Lost it at the Movies*, New York, Little Brown, 1965.

Krupanidhi, Uma and Srivastava, Anil, (eds.), *Montage*, Bombay, Anandam Film Society, July 1966 (special issue on Satyajit Ray including reviews; articles on aspects of Ray; interviews with Ray, Bansi Chandragupta, Subrata Mitra, Ravi Shankar, Ray's actors; the screenplay of Nayak in English; and two pieces by Ray-"Some Aspects of My Craft" and the commentary of B.D. Garga's film about Ray).

*London Magazine*, Andrew Robinson, 'The Inner Eye: Aspects of Satyajit Ray', October 1982.

*Los Angeles Times*, Deborah Caulfield, 'Satyajit Ray Questions E.T. origins', 16 March 1983.

Majumdar, Swapan (ed.), *Satyajit Ray Retrospective Souvenir: The First Decade*, Calcutta, 1975 (booklet).

Manvell, Roger, (ed.) *International Encyclopeida of Film*, London, 1972.

Micciolo, Henri, *Satyajit Ray*, Paris, Editions l'Age D'Homme, 1981.

Michel Ciment, 'Tous les feux du bengale', Paris, June 1979.

Nandy, Ashis *Satyajit Ray's, Secret Guide to Exquisite Murders in the Savage Freud*, Oxford University Press, 1995.

*New York Herald Tribune*, Richard, C. Wald, 'There is no Mystery to Making a Movie', 21 September 1958 (profile).

*New York Review of Books*, Ian Buruma, 'The Last Bengali Renaissance Man', 19 November 1987.

*New York Times*, Howard Thompson, 'Little Road into the Big World,' 7 September 1958.

*Newsweek*, David Ansen, 'The Eyes of Satyajit Ray', 20 July 1981.

*Nouvel Observateur*, Paris, 5 April 1985.

Nyce, Ben: *Satyajit Ray: A Study of his Films*, New York, Praeger, 1988.

*Positif*, Michel Ciment, 'Le monde de Satyajit Ray', Paris, March 1964.

*Positif*, Paris, January 1970, May 1979, June 1979.

Parrain, Philippe, *'Regards sur le Cinema Indien'*, Editions due Cerf, Paris, 1969.

*Quest*, Asish Barman, 'Problems of Identification and the Art of Satyajit Ray', Bombay, July-September 1958.

RaphaelBassan, 'Satyajit Ray : Cineaste des contrastes', May 1982.

*Revue du cinema*, Lausanne, July-August 1971.

Rhode, Eric, *Tower of Babel*, London, Weidenfeld & Nicolson, 1966.

*Rivista del Cinematografo*, Rome, October 1965.

Roy Armes, 'Satyajit Ray : Astride Two Cultures', London, August 1982.

Robinson, Andrew, *Satyajit Ray: The Inner Eye*, Andre Deutsch, London, 1989; pub. in India, Rupa, 1990.

Russell Taylor, John *'Cinema : A Critical Dictionary'*, Richard Roud (ed.), London, Secker & Warburg, 1980, pp. 813-31.

*Sananda*, Aniruddha Dhar, 'Panchali Theke Oscar' (From the Little Road to the Oscar) 1996-97 serialised.

*Satyajit Ray Retrospective Souvenir: The Second Decade*, Swapan Majumdar (ed), Calcutta, 1979, pp. 23-6.

*Screen International*, London, 12 May 1984.

Sen, Mrinal, 'Views on Cinema', Calcutta, Ishan, 1977 (includes Satyajit Ray set the example' and letters exchanged between Ray, Sen and Barman in 1965 concerning Sen's film *Akash Kusum*).

Seton, Marie, *Satyajit Ray: Portrait of a Director*, (extended edn.), London, Dennis Dobson, 1978.

*Sight and Sound*, Eric Rhode, 'Satyajit Ray : A Study', London, Summer 1961.

*Sight and Sound*, Chidananda Dasgupta, 'Ray and Tagore' winter, 1966-67

*Sunday Observer*, Bombay, 14 April 1985.

*Sunday*, R.P. Gupta, 'Three decades of Satyajit Ray's Pather Panchali,' Calcutta, 5-11 January 1986.

*The New Yorker*, Pauline Kael, 'Current Cinema' March 17.

*Tiempo de Cine*, Emir Rodriguez Monegal, 'La Trilogia de Satyajit Ray; un artista integro', Buenos Aires, July-September 1961 (critical assessement).

*Times of India*, Gautam Adhikari, 'The Renaissance Man: The Other Side of Satyajit Ray', Bombay, 2 April 1983 (profile).

Tyler, Parker, *Classics of the Foreign Film*, New York, Citadel Press, 1962.

Wood, Robin, *The Apu Trilogy*, New York, Praeger, 1971.

Wright, Basil, *The Long View: An International History of Cinema*, London, Paladin, 1974.

Laser typeset at Icon Printographics, B-107 Fateh Nagar, New Delhi-110018 and printed at Jay Kay Offset Printers, 17, DSIDC, Rohtak Road, Delhi-110041.